MY BEST SHOT

SELECTED IMAGES
FROM MY CAREER
IN NEW YORK AS A
MUSIC PHOTOGRAPHER

All text and photos by George DuBose

Art direction and design by George DuBose

An imprint of Wonderland Publishing
©2018 George-DuBose.com

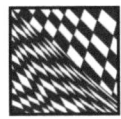

My Best Shots
First Edition
ISBN 978-0-9863-0455-2

Printed in the United States of America
Library of Congress cataloging-in-publication data

All of the images in this book are available
as signed, numbered limited edition fine art prints
for more information contact: boss@george-dubose.com

Other books from Wonderland Publishing

"I Speak Music	- Ramones"	English Edition	ISBN 978-0-9889-2340-9
"Hablo Musica	- Ramones"	Españoles Edición	ISBN 978-0-9889-2341-6
"Eu falo Música	- Ramones"	Português Edição	ISBN 978-0-9889-2345-4
"Parlo Musica	- Ramones"	Edizione Italiana	ISBN 978-0-9889-2347-8
"I Speak Music	- Hip Hop - Old School Volume One"		ISBN 978-0-9889-2342-3
"I Speak Music	- Hip Hop - Old School Volume Two"		ISBN 978-0-9889-2343-0
"I Speak Music	- Hip Hop - Old School Volume Three"		ISBN 978-0-9889-2344-7
"The Big Book of Hip-Hop Photography"	First Edition		ISBN 978-0-9889-2346-1
"Renovate a Sailboat and Cross the Atlantic"	First Edition		ISBN 978-0-9889-2348-5
"Madonna - Raw" - English version	First Edition		ISBN 978-0-9863-0451-4
"Madonna - Raw" - Italian version	First Edition		ISBN 978-0-9863-0452-1
"Madonna - Raw" - German version	First Edition		ISBN 978-0-9863-0453-8
"Madonna - Raw" - Spanish version	First Edition		ISBN 978-0-9863-0454-5

By the time ì got out of the US Navy in 1972, I knew I wanted to be a professional photographer. My original goal was to be a portrait photographer, my inspiration being the work of Yousef Karsh of Ottawa and Phillipe Halsman.

I knew that I had much to learn about the photography business, studio lighting and the technical side of film processing and print-making. I didn't just walk into my first apprenticeship, I washed dishes, found a job in a printing company making offset printing films and learned a lot about graphic design and the prepress side of printing.

Eventually, after many phone calls and knocking on doors, I landed a temporary job as a third assistant to two fashion photographers, Pederson and Erwin. I made myself so useful to these two photographers that they offered me a full-time job with no layoffs when their work slowed down.

The deal they offered me was that after working hours, I could use their film and cameras to begin building my own portfolio. I began shooting test photos with young models, giving them prints in exchange for their time. I met some of the young staff at Andy Warhol's "Interview" magazine and they began to give me little jobs, shooting Andy's promotional t-shirts on the young models.

One day, I got a call from the assistant art director of "Interview" who asked me if I would like to go to the nightclub, "Max's Kansas City", a well-known restaurant and music club. He told me that the band was from Georgia. I was curious about this band having once lived in Atlanta, but I told my pal, I didn't have any money to pay for admission.

"No problem", my friend replied. "I can get you on the guest list."

So I took my bosses' camera to Max's. I had been shooting musicians in concert for several years and was quite comfortable shooting in low light situations. The first act was called "Teenage Jesus and the Jerks" featuring Lydia Lunch. Lydia was into minimalist punk rock which was not my cup of tea. I took some photos of her anyway.

Then before the second act came on, there was a sound coming out of the PA that sounded like buzzing bees. Bees... Then as the band began to come on stage and pickup their instruments, they started playing "The Peter Gunn Theme" by Henry Mancini who wrote the score for a '50s television detective series. That tune happened to be the first thing I could ever play when I got my first guitar at the age of 14. I was blown away. The song morphed into "Planet Claire". The band was the B52s and I was in love.

I met them after their set backstage and offered to photograph them in "my" studio, but they were returning to Athens, Georgia that same night. They would return.

The next time they played NYC, I was able to get them to come to "my" studio, telling them that I would submit the photo to "Interview". When they showed up at the studio, one of the women, Cindy, had already returned to Athens, so I didn't have the full band lineup. As their manager, Maureen, was a woman and nobody actually knew what the band looked like, I asked Maureen if she would stand in for Cindy.

"Interview" | published the photo with Maureen.

The third time the band returned to Manhattan, I was able to entice them to come to the studio by offering piña coladas and banana daiquiris. That, plus the fact that I had gotten the "wrong" photo published got the right lineup to the studio. My original concept was to recreate The Ventures "Walk, Don't Run '64" cover, since The Ventures had woman dressed the way the women in the B52s were and the guitarists in The Ventures played Mosrite electric guitars, the same as Ricky, the guitarist for the B52s.

In the end, the band chose a more simple lineup shot without any instruments. I took that image and designed a 16 x 20" B&W poster using the Japanese headline text from a Japanese magazine that had used the "wrong" photo. I printed 1000 copies at my own expense and would go around the block where Max's was, taping the posters to mailboxes and anything else that didn't move. By the time I went around the block, the first posters were gone! I didn't know about wheat paste.

Eventually, I tried selling the posters at their concerts for 52¢ or two for a dollar.

My first break:

A year or so passed and the B52s were signed to Island Records, their album was to be produced by the owner of the label himself, Chris Blackwell. I got a phone call one day from a Tony Wright, who wanted to see my B52s images. I took my portfolio and collection of photos of the Bs to show him, but it was immediately clear that the band had already decided to use the same image as the poster that I had made.

Tony asked me how much money I wanted to allow the record company to use that photo as a cover for their LP. I had no idea. Tony offered me $750 and as I calculated that to be about five weeks of my assistant's pay, I agreed. Then Tony asked if he could colorized the original B&W photo. No problem for me. I made a sepia toned print and Tony made color overlays to change the color of the band's clothing.

In the end, Tony found the band to be so picky and I don't think he

"got" their sound, that he wrote his own design credit as "Sue Absurd"...so absurd...

The B's debut album eventually went gold and the cover won many accolades. It became one of my and Tony's greatest covers.

Tony began to give me more assignments to shoot covers for Island and funny enough after I shot Kid Creole and the Coconuts "Off the Coast of Me", Tony asked me to shoot the cover for "Queen of Siam" the debut LP of Lydia Lunch. ...whose music I didn't particularly care for when I saw her opening up for the B52s.

When Island Records wanted to start an in-house art department for their New York office, Tony asked me if I would run it. Thinking that it would be good to have a steady income, I agreed and bought the necessary equipment and assembled a staff. Unfortunately, there just wasn't that much to do, so when Glenn O'Brien got me a job as art director for the startup of SPIN magazine, I jumped ship.

At SPIN, I quickly had to face the reality that I had no formal design training and counting words in articles wasn't my cup of tea, so I demoted myself to the job of photo editor. I really enjoyed meeting potential contributing photographers, viewing their portfolios and then, being a photographer myself, I would frequently give a young photographer an assignment that would force him or her to work outside their comfort zone. Personally, I didn't do many photoshootings for SPIN, preferring to give the work to other photographers. On one occasion when the publisher asked me who should we send to Montreal, Canada to shoot ZZ Top, I had to volunteer myself, having been a fan of ZZ Top since the day their first LP was released and seeing them as a support for Black Oak Arkansas back in 1971. On other occasions, I would let SPIN use my pre-existing images.

After two years at SPIN, trying to survive on the meager salary, I left and returned to my job at Island. By now, I was beginning to pickup a lot of freelance work as a photographer and art director. I made it part of my agreement with Island that after six pm I was allowed to work on my freelance projects.

Island gave me the assignment to shoot Alphonso Ribiero aka The Tap Dance Kid for his album cover. A few weeks after I did that shooting, I got a phone call from a small label that had originally signed Alphonso. This small recording company was called Prism Records. when I met with Lenny Fichtelberg, the label head, he told me that he had a rapper named Biz Markie who needed a photo for a 12" single cover. I set up a shooting for Biz and he was wearing black shorts and a black and white striped shirt making him look like a referee. Biz was the "human beatbox" and could make all kinds of percussion sounds with his mouth. I found him quite entertaining.

When I delivered the Biz shoot to Prism, I met with Dee Garner who acted as a product manager and was overseeing the production of Biz's record. She like the shots and when I asked her who was doing the design graphics, she said she had no idea. I told her that I could design the single cover as well.

Biz had worn a hat with a modified Gothic font, Fraktur, that read "Biz Markie". I asked Biz where he got the lettering and he told me a shop in Times Square. A visit to Times Square led me to find several shops that would iron letters on t-shirts or anything else one wanted. I bought the letters that would spell out "Make the Music with your Mouth, Biz" and his name and used this lettering to design the single cover. While Fraktur was popular amongst the gangs in the Bronx, I think I was the first to design a record sleeve with that font.

A month later, I got a call from Lenny who wanted to see me in his office. When I met him, he asked me what kind of camera did one use to make album covers. I saw where this conversation was going. I told him that I used a Hasselblad middle format camera as it took square photos and LPs were square. He asked me how much a Hasselblad cost and I told him "thousands".

That was the beginning of my relationship with Prism who became Cold Chillin', one of the seminal rap labels. When Warner Bros. got into the Hip-Hop game they started distributing Cold Chillin' product and the budgets for packaging increased 10 fold.

I worked with Cold Chillin' until they folded..

Due to this work I was doing for Cold Chillin', Island decided that I would be the "black artist packaging" expert and for my remaining time at Island, now owned by Polygram, I worked almost exclusively with their black artists.

In 1997, I met a beautiful German doctor, fell in love and in 1998, I moved to Germany, abandoning my career In NYC. That was twenty years ago and in the meantime I raised two boys, basically retiring from photography.

In the following pages, I have chosen a single favorite photo from the artists that I worked with throughout my time in New York with some German artists thrown in. This is an overview of my career. In other books I have produced, I go into detail of my working relationships with groups such as the Ramones and many of the Hip-Hop artists that I worked with and show many of the photos we produced. In this volume, I am only showing single images.

...my best shot.

The B52s

As a teenager, I was enthralled with The Ventures, a California surf rock band. When I saw that Ricky played the same Mosrite guitar and the girls dressed the way the women on the Ventures cover did, I tried to recreate the cover of "Walk - Don't Run '64". Unfortunately, the band chose a more boring lineup for the cover of their debut album.

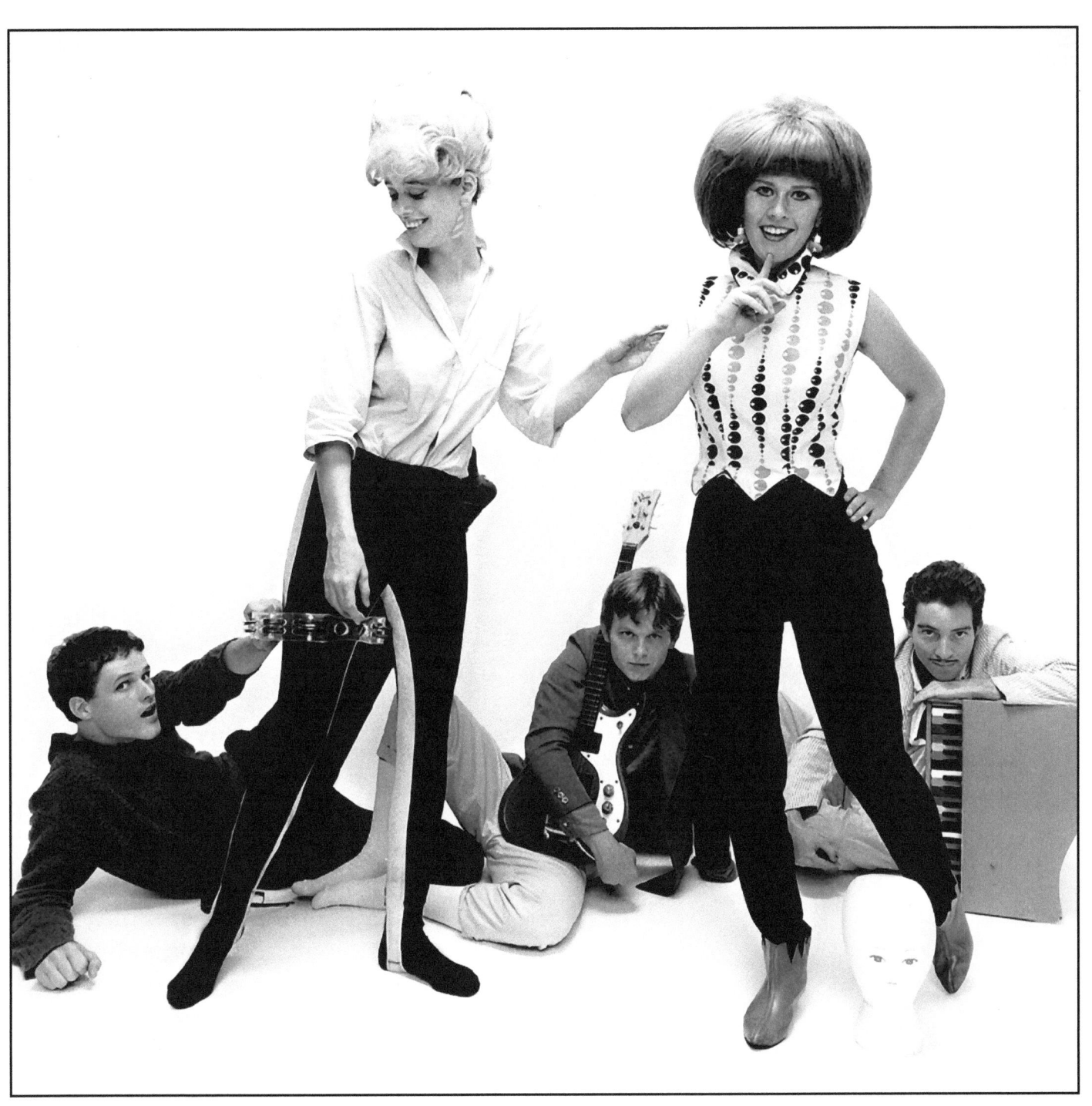

Bonaparte

I first saw Bonaparte at
PopKomm in Berlin when they
were a three piece group and
the drummer was playing
cardboard boxes.
The next time I saw Bonaparte
was in Cologne, Germany where
they packed a small club and
nearly caused a riot.

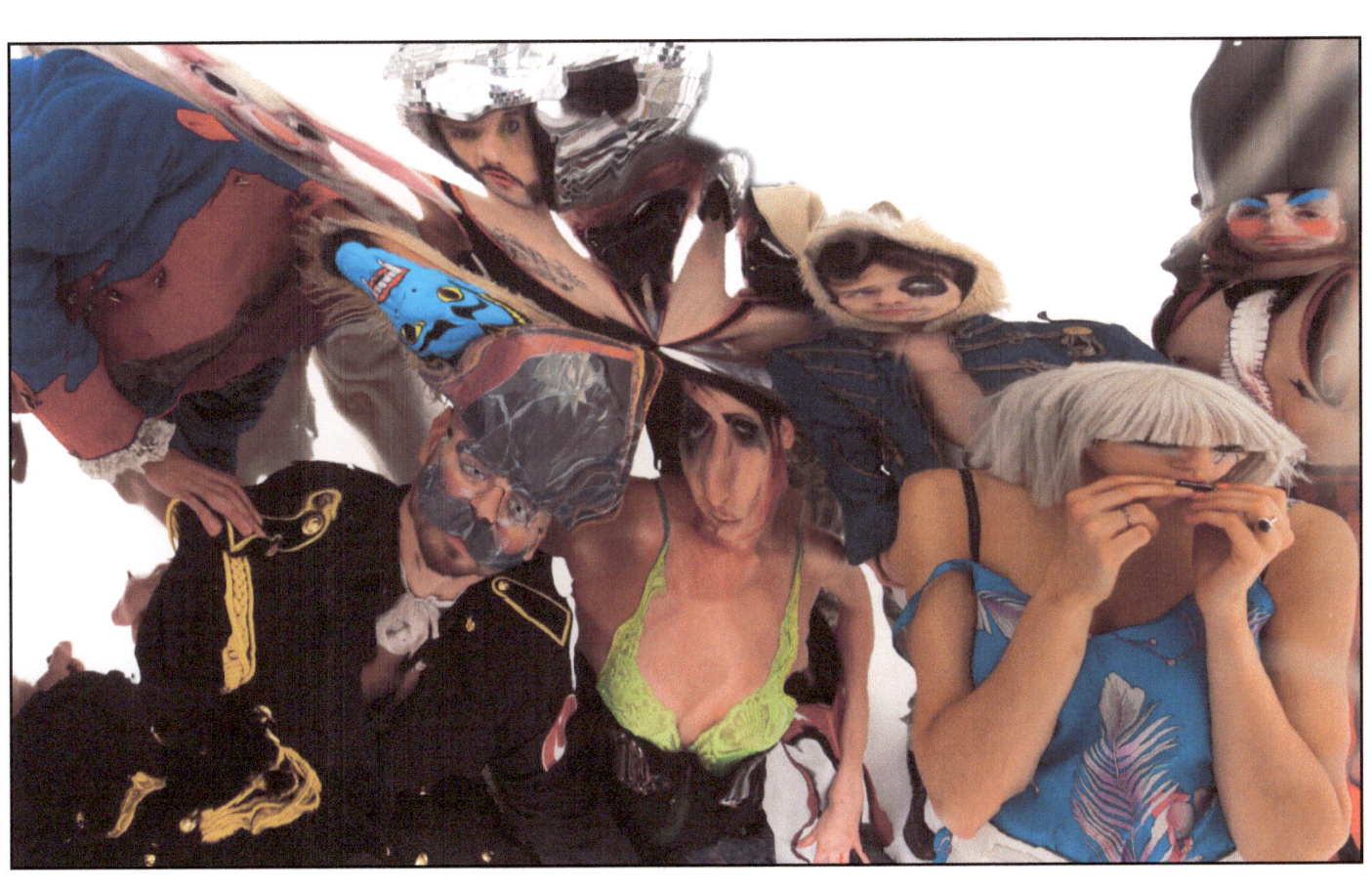

Boy Sets Fire

This was a shot I did in a bar in
Cologne for Slam magazine.
I don't know if they wanted
to play mumblypeg or spin
the bottle.

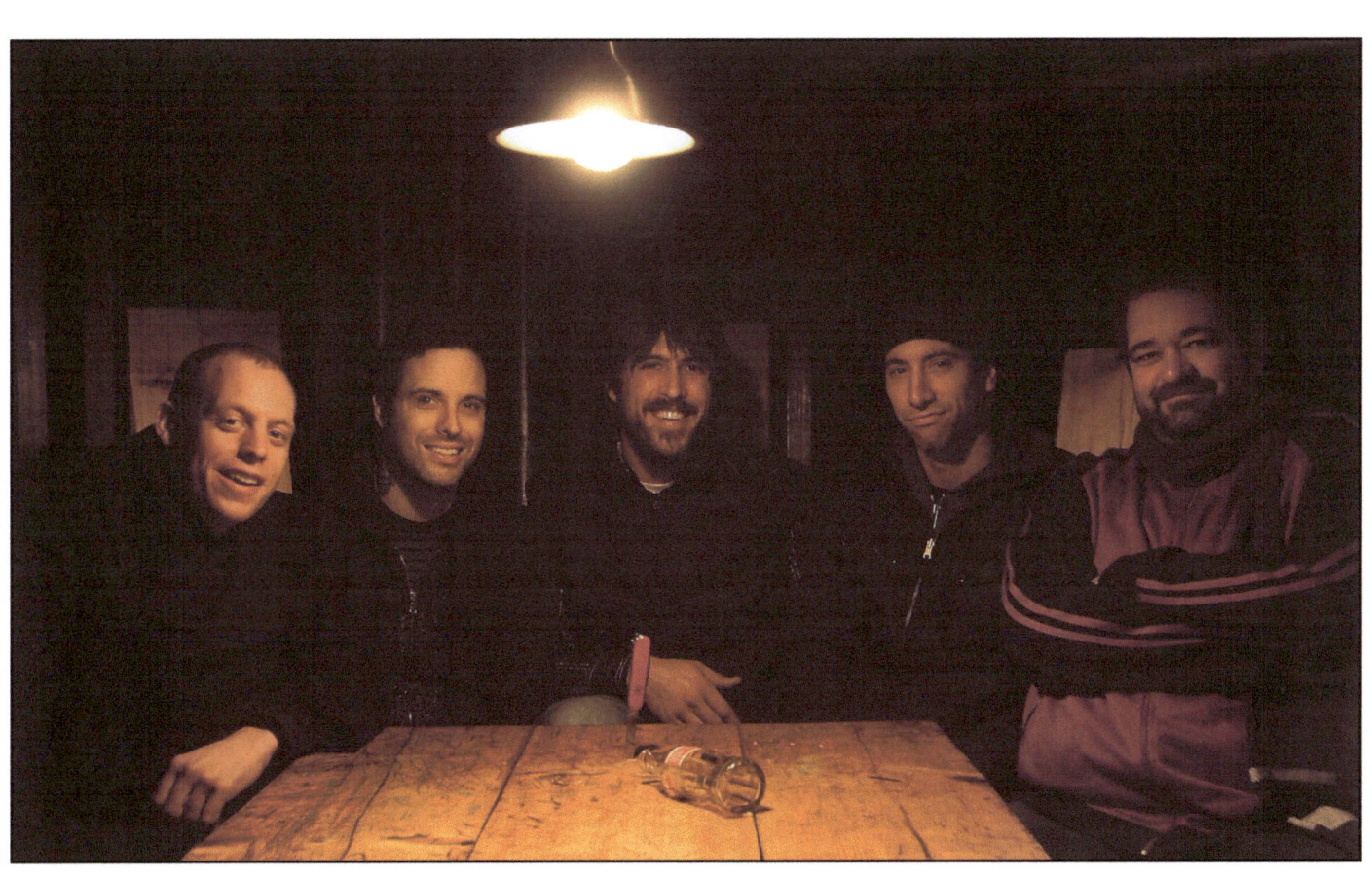

The Breakfast Club

actually had Madonna as their drummer for a while. Not in this configuration however.

THE BREAKFAST CLUB

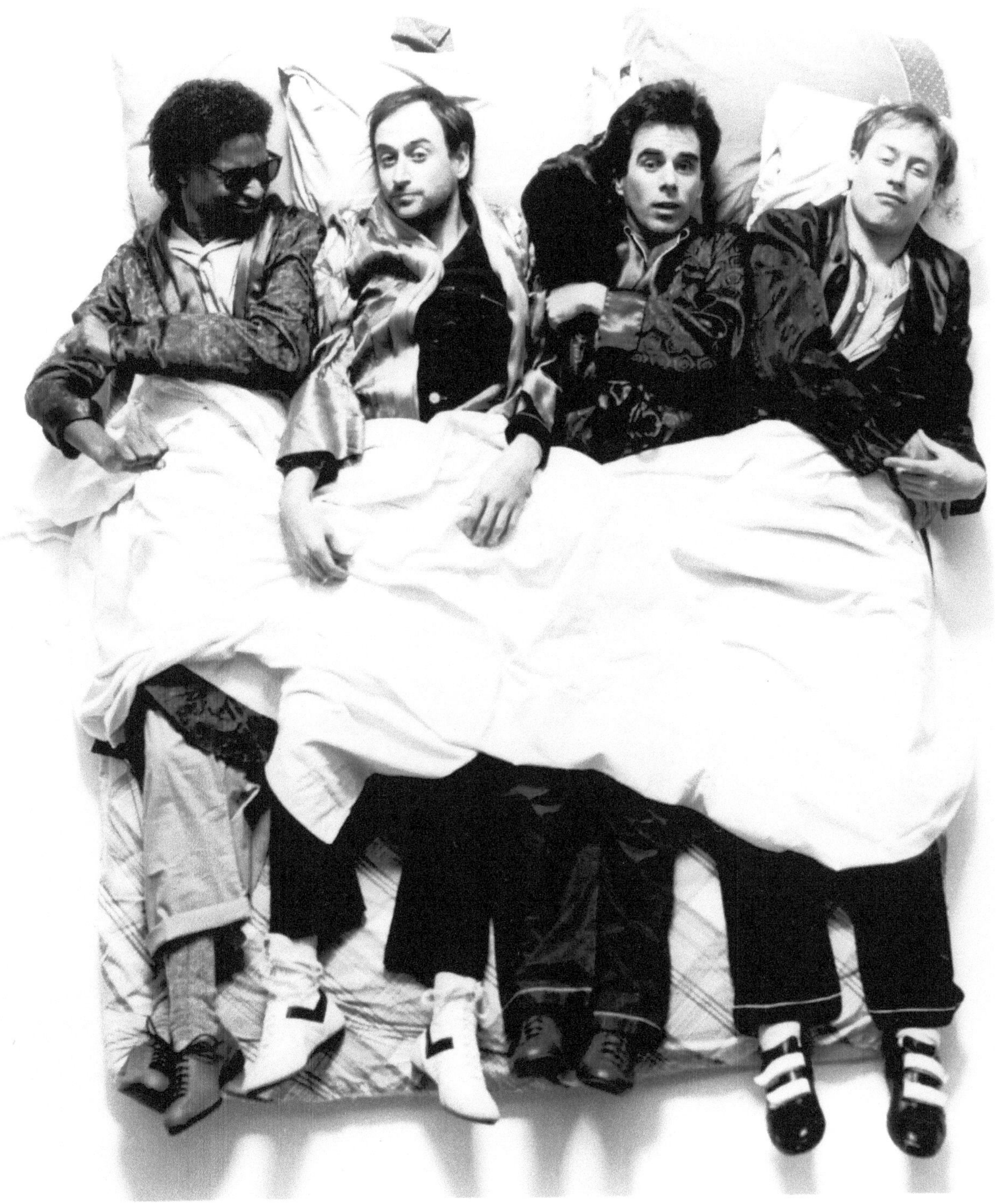

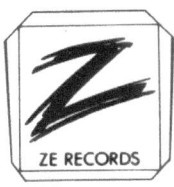

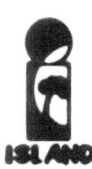

Photo Credit: George DuBose

15

Bryan Adams

I shot Bryan during his first promotional tour for his disco hit single "Let Me Take You Dancin". As he was a rocker, I think he was embarrassed about the remix of his song. After the day's shoot, my gal pals from Andy Warhol's "Interview" magazine and I took him to Studio 54 and got his single played.

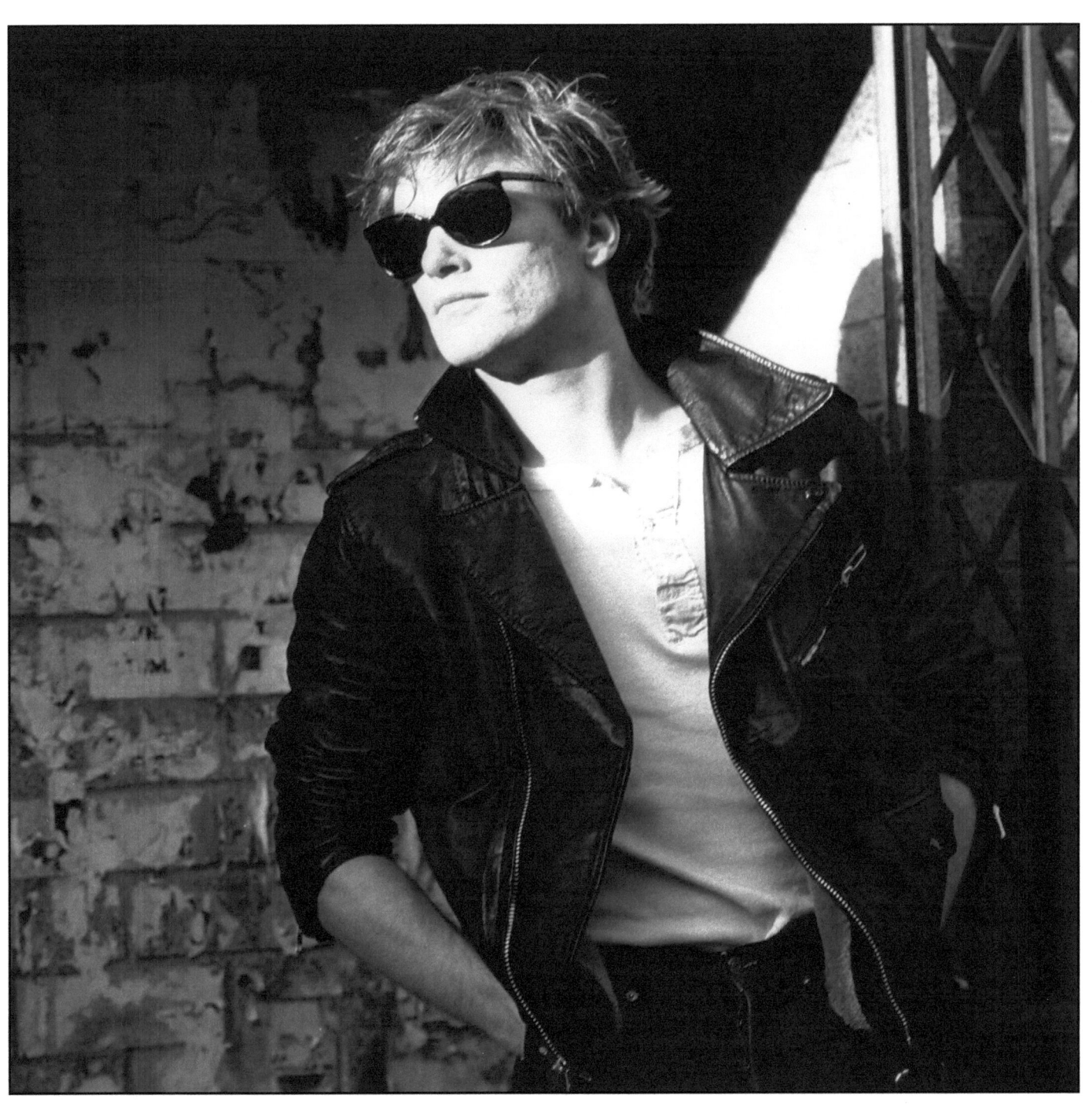

The Cramps

You know this rockabilly horror
band. I shot them for IRS
Records, but didn't particularly
care for their music and they
thought I was gay.
It was a wash.

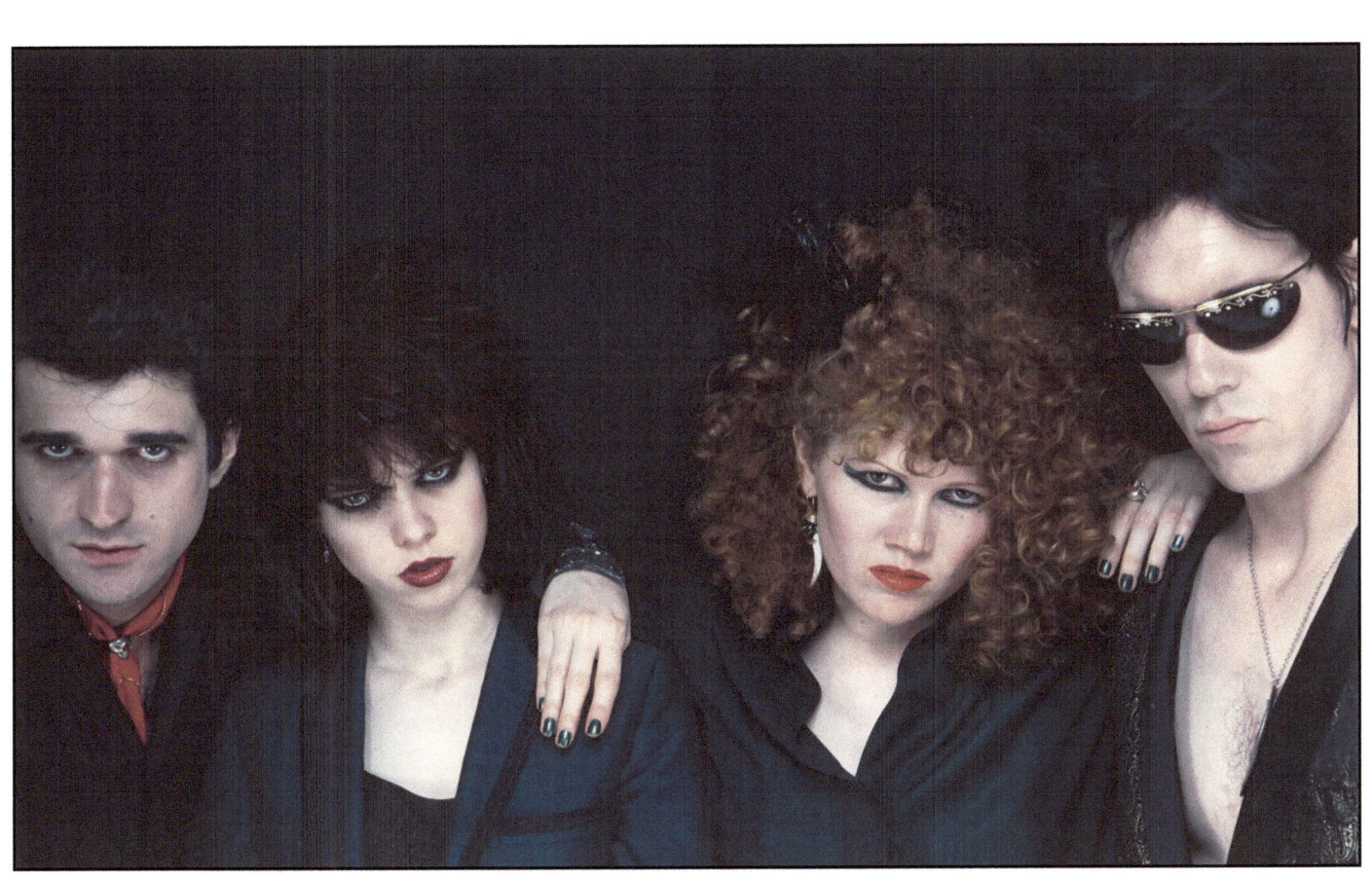

Daniel Ponce

A famous Cuban conga player.
This is the back cover of
"Chango te Llama".
The front cover is religious
artifacts used in the worship of
Chango. Google Chango...

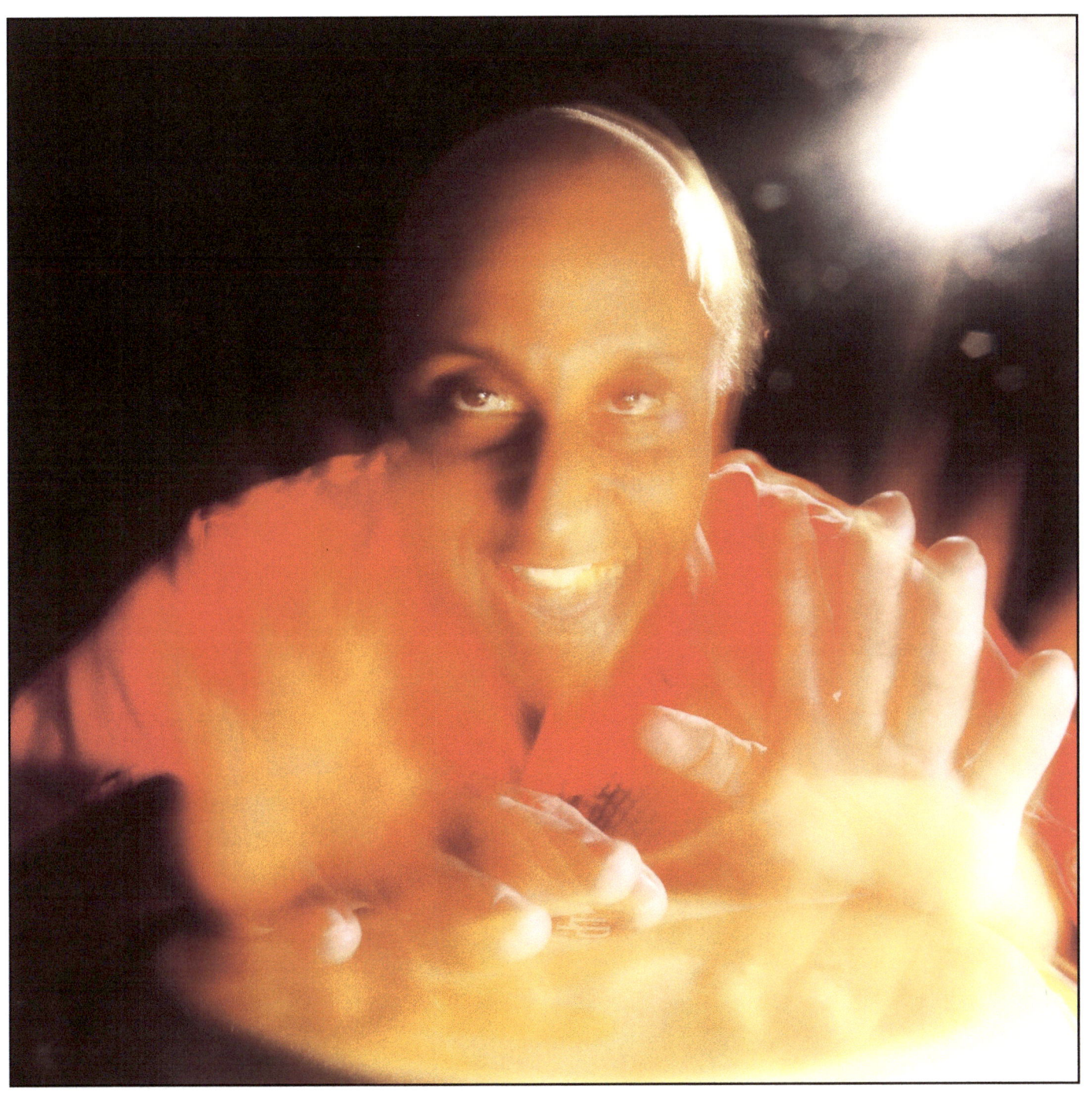

Dieter Meier

I was to shoot Dieter for
"Interview", I built a set
emulating a Dali perspective.
Then I got a phone call from
the label saying that Dieter
had no time.
"All I need is five minutes" I
told the label.
Dieter came, saw the set,
climbed under the table and
when we finished he stayed for
an hour and drank all my Beck's...

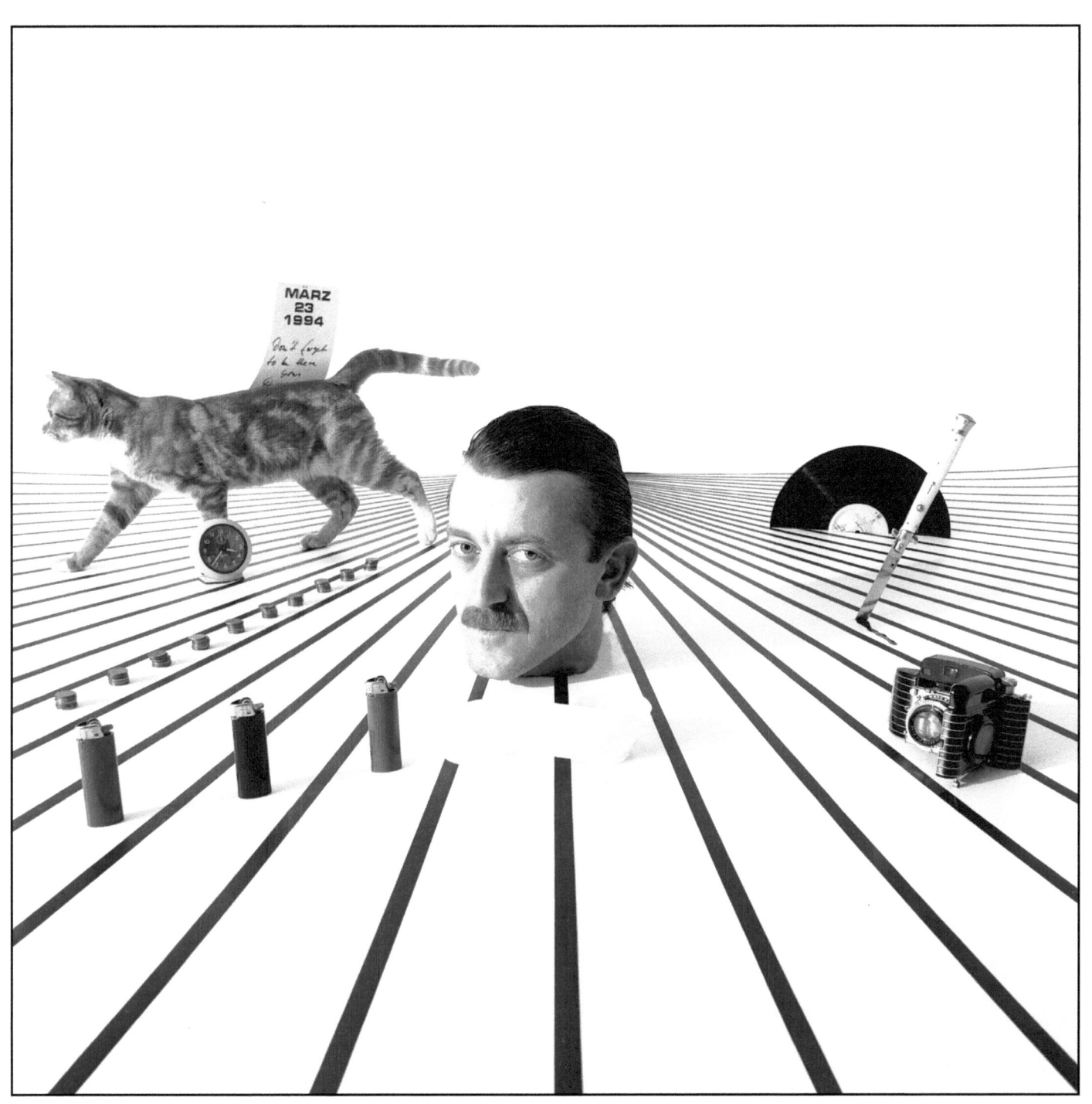

Duran Duran

Another shot for Interview.
Their first single was all over
the radio. When they came to
my studio, they all disappeared
into the bathroom for an hour. I
thought they were doing drugs.
Then one of them came out and
said "Do you have
any more hairspray?"

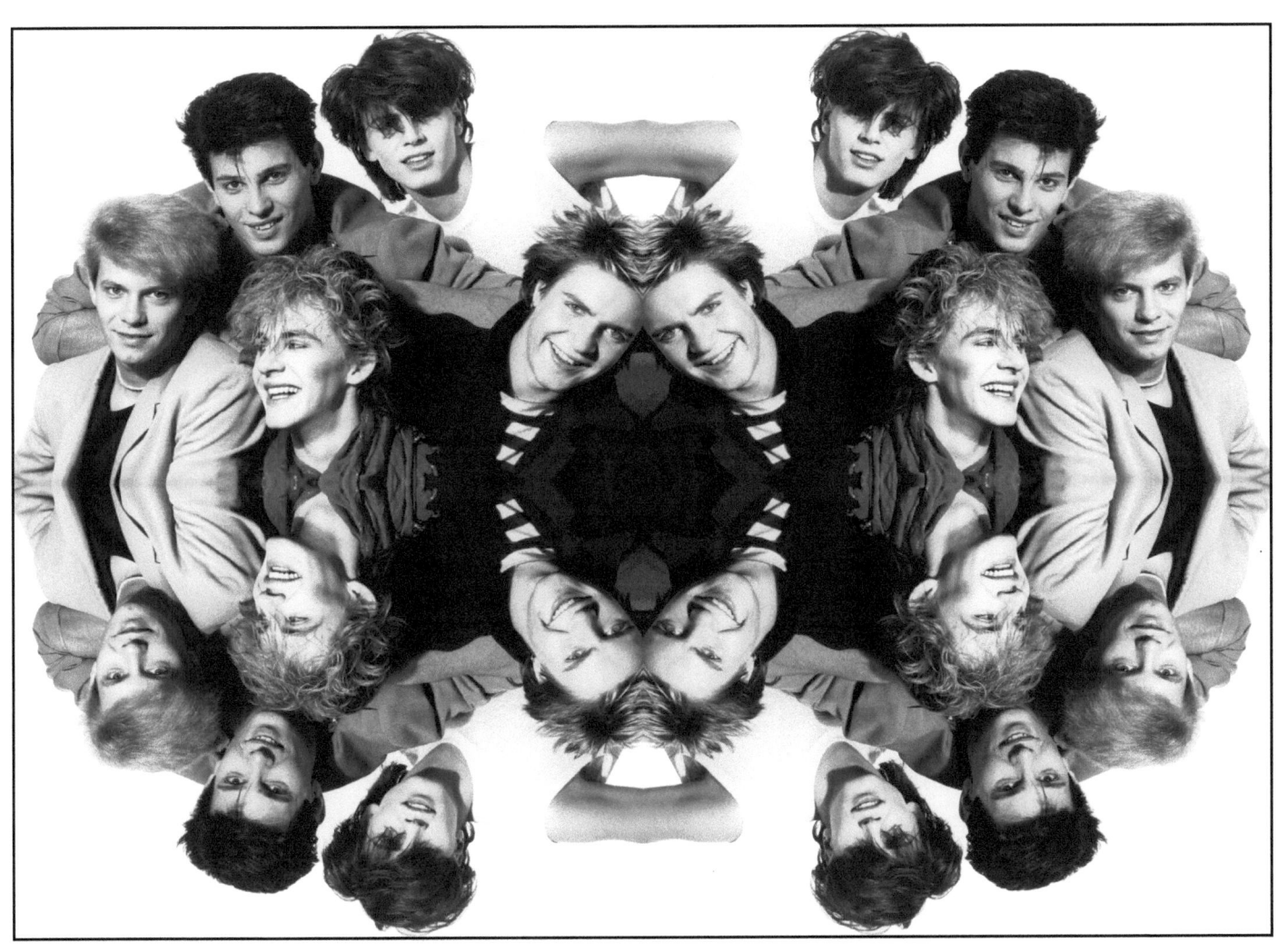

Melissa Etheridge

I think this was her first-ever photoshooting. She was stiff and non-responsive. I asked her if she had any of her new tracks and she gave me a cassette of the recordings in progress. I put the tape in the studio's stereo, turned it up to 11 and said, "Melissa, sing!"

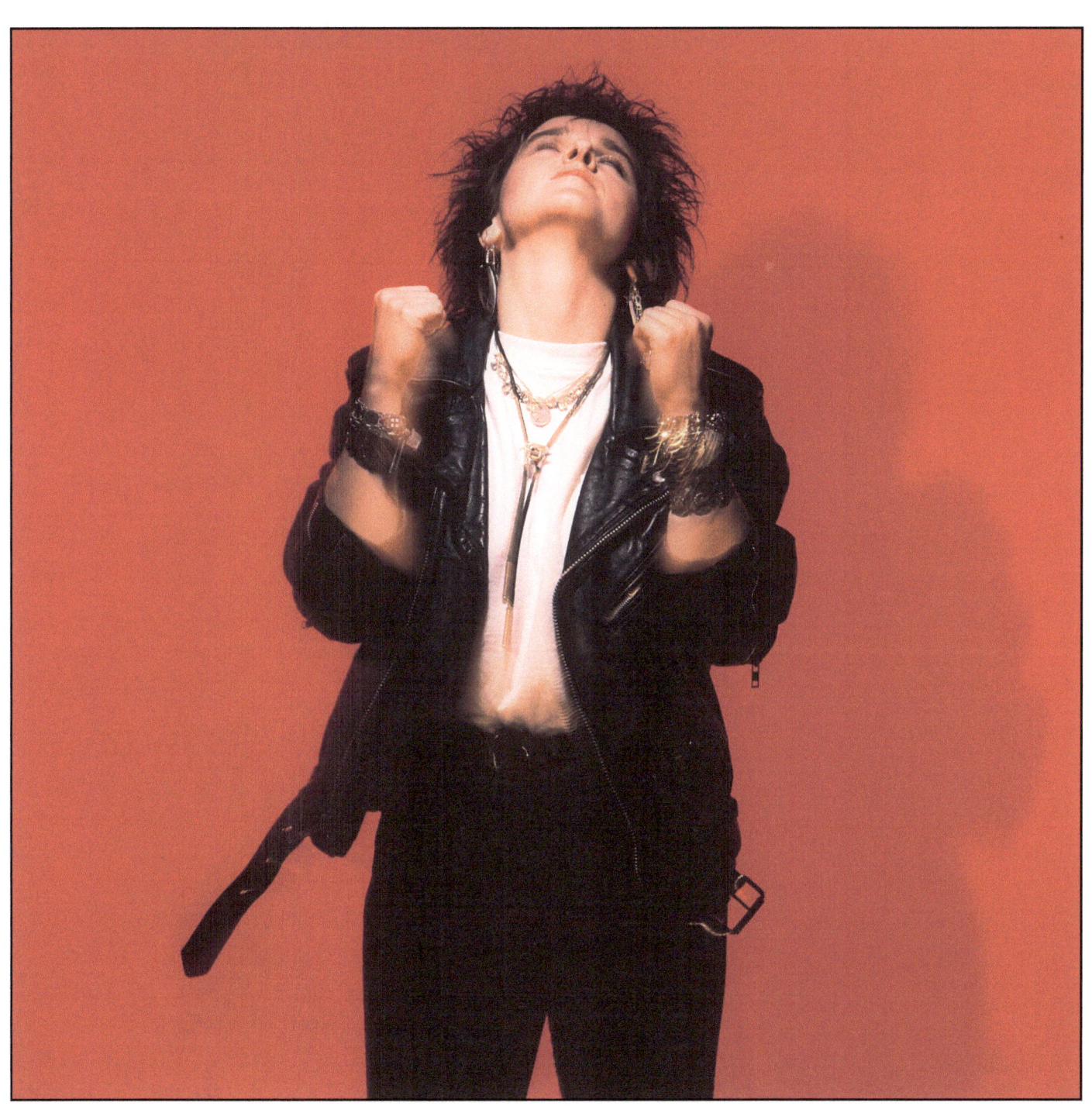

The Fleshtones

This was a publicity shot for the
album "Hexbreaker". I filled
baking pans with lamp oil and
the horns of fire magically
appeared over Keith's head. I
photographed them so many
times and will show more of my
shots of them in a
future volume.

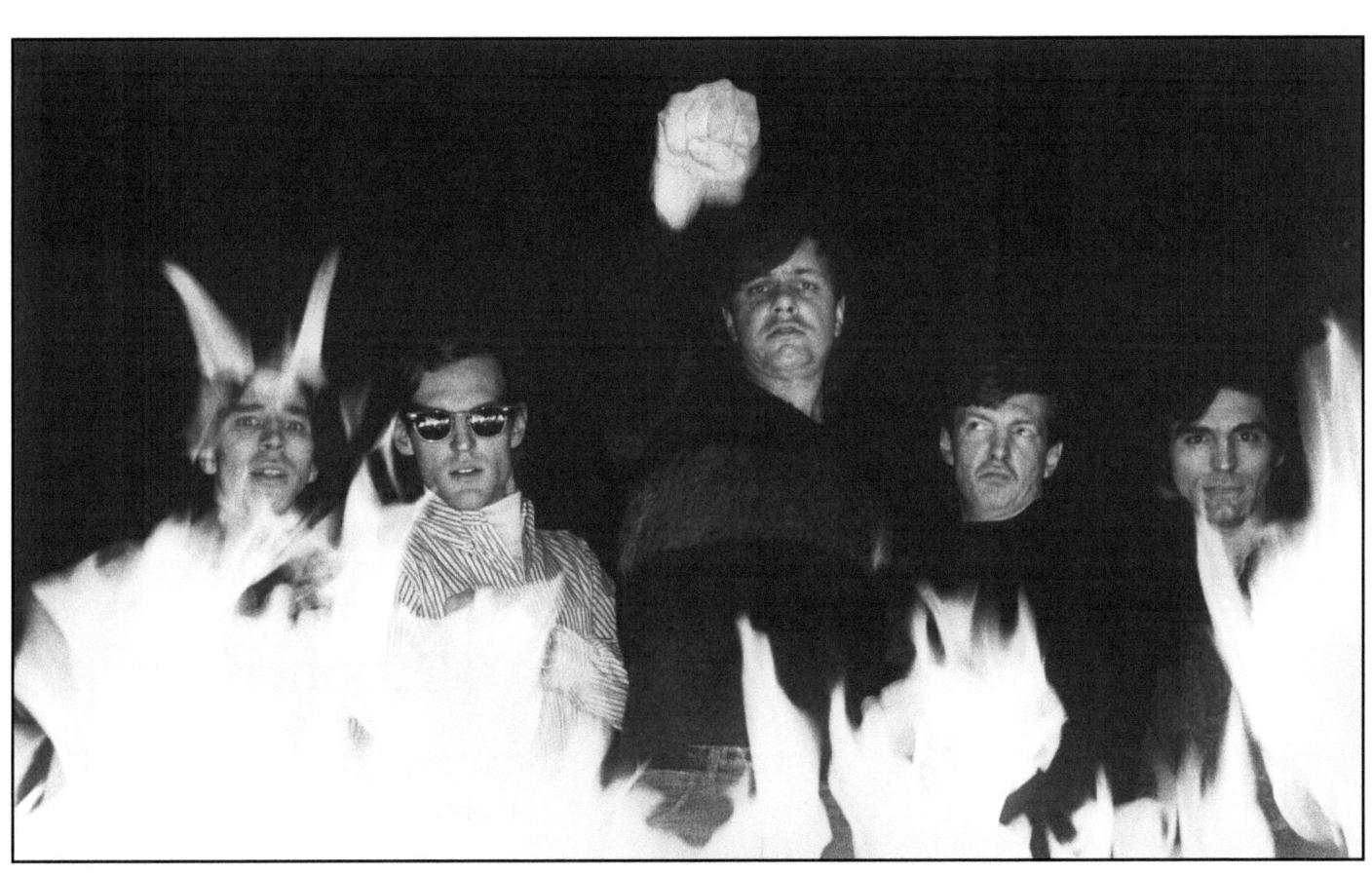

Gimme Danger

At first I didn't know what
inspired me to suggest that
they wear white with red
bandanas. Later, I realized that
"look" was that of the
bull-runners in
Pamplona, Spain.
Only God knows where I get
these ideas...

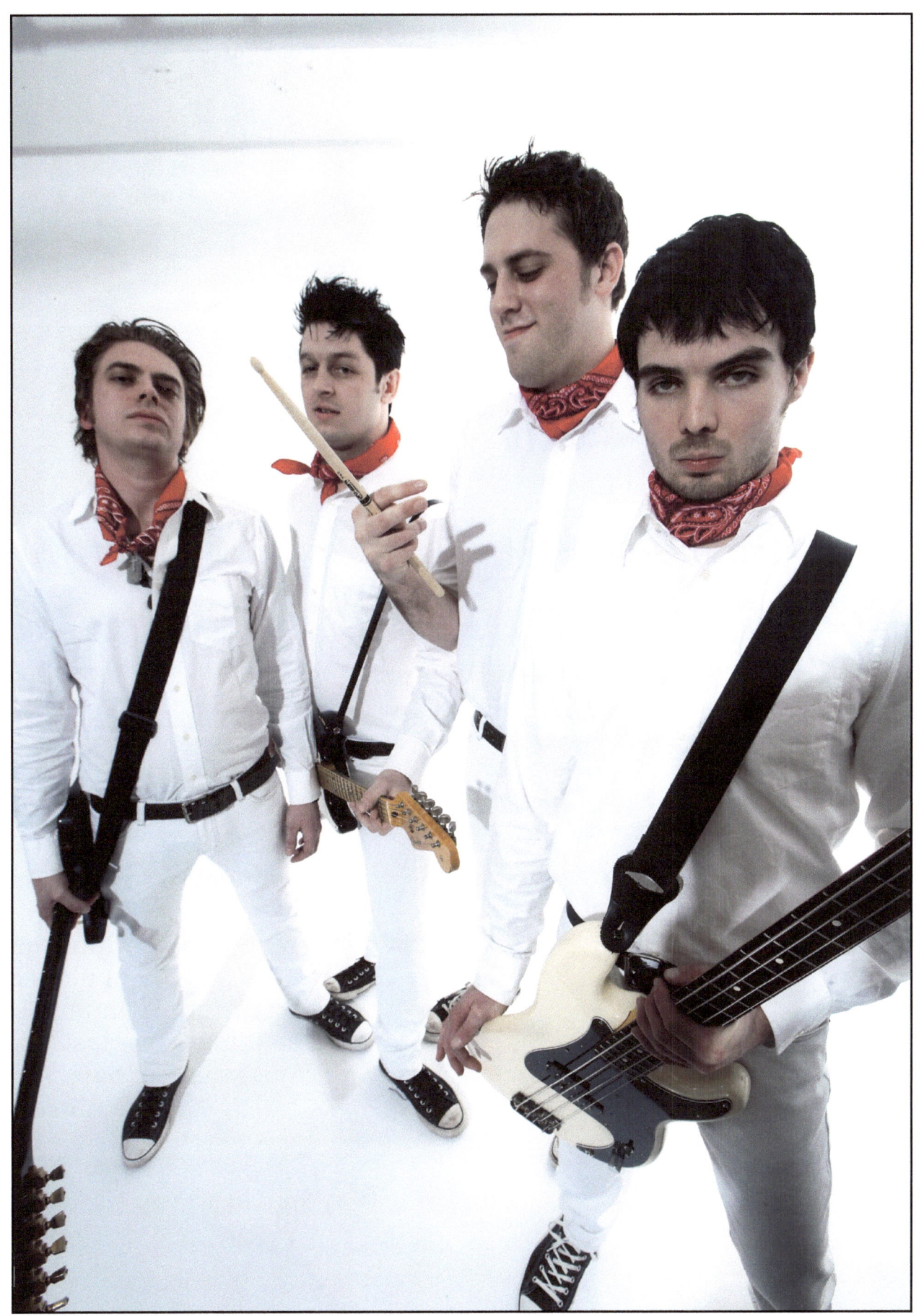

The Go-Gos

I wanted to shoot them for
"Interview", but they were in a
hurry for an album cover.
Lucky me...
My first platinum album.
The films were "lost" for 23
years, I was happy to get
the films back.

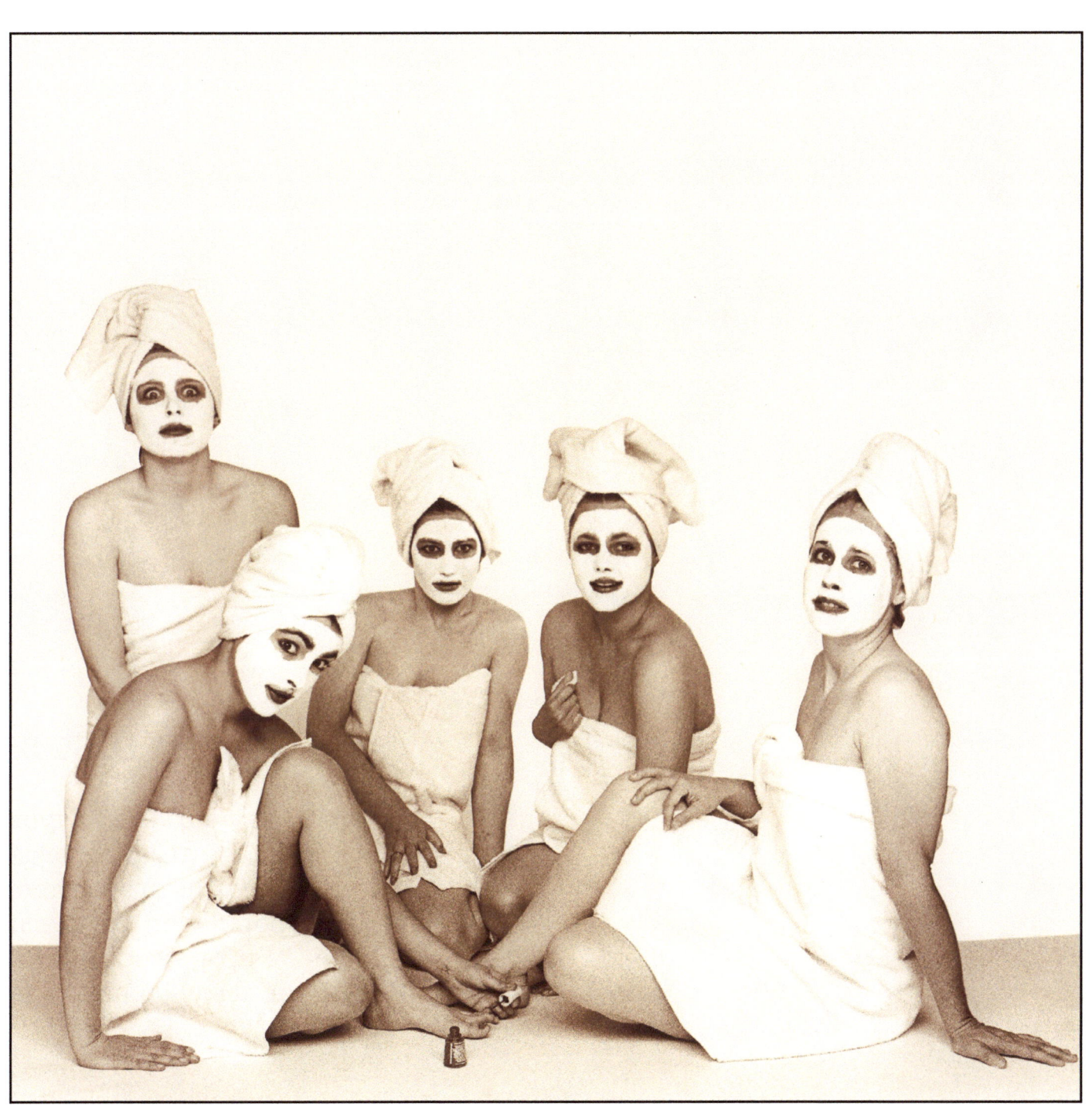

Gothminister

This guy's "day-job" is a lawyer in Oslo. He makes great records in his spare time. Quite popular in northern Europe and the US. He isn't as scary as he looks.

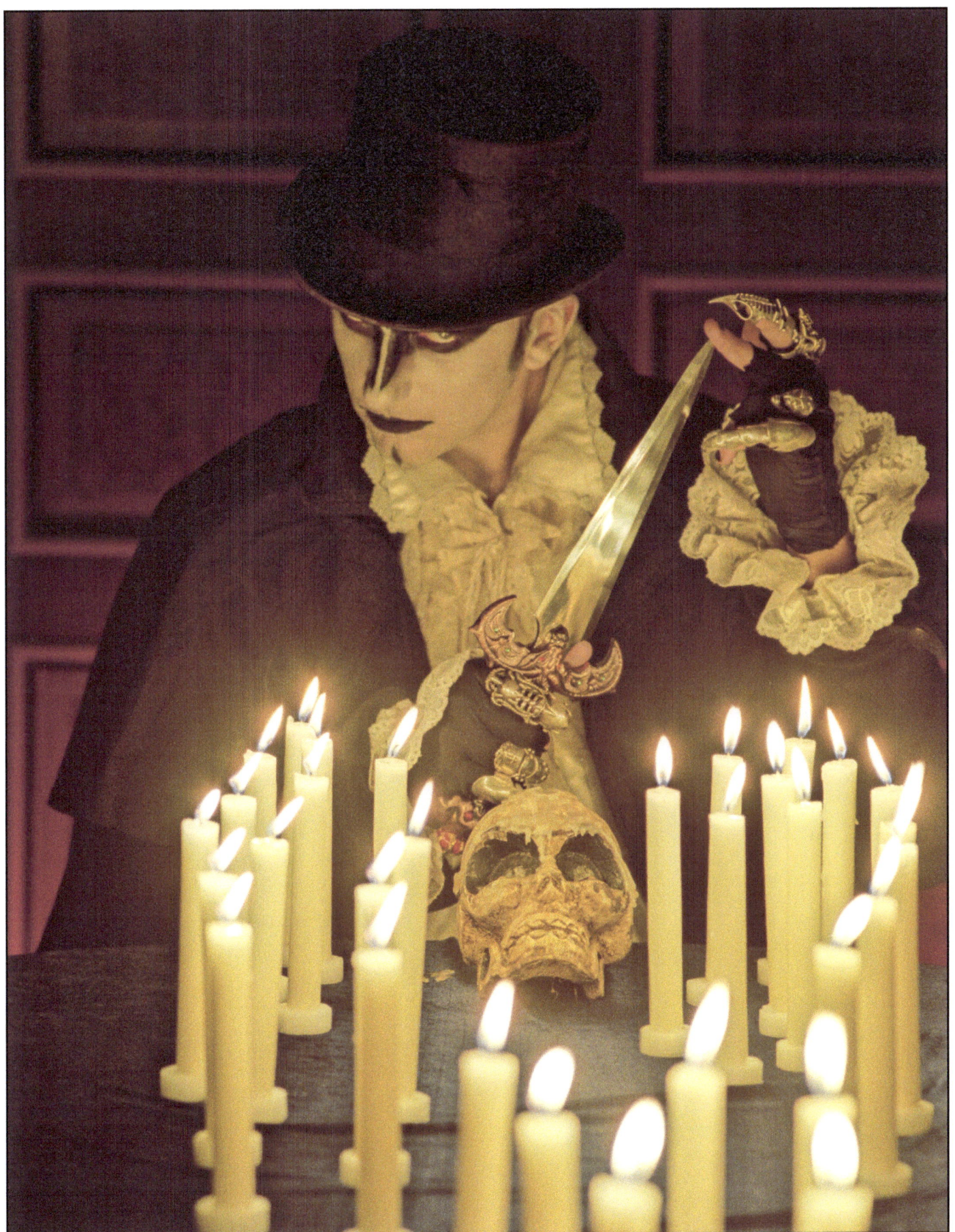

Guitar Wolf

A really great Japanese punk
band from Nagasaki described
as garage rock power trio. I had
the pleasure of shooting them
at their gig in Cologne.

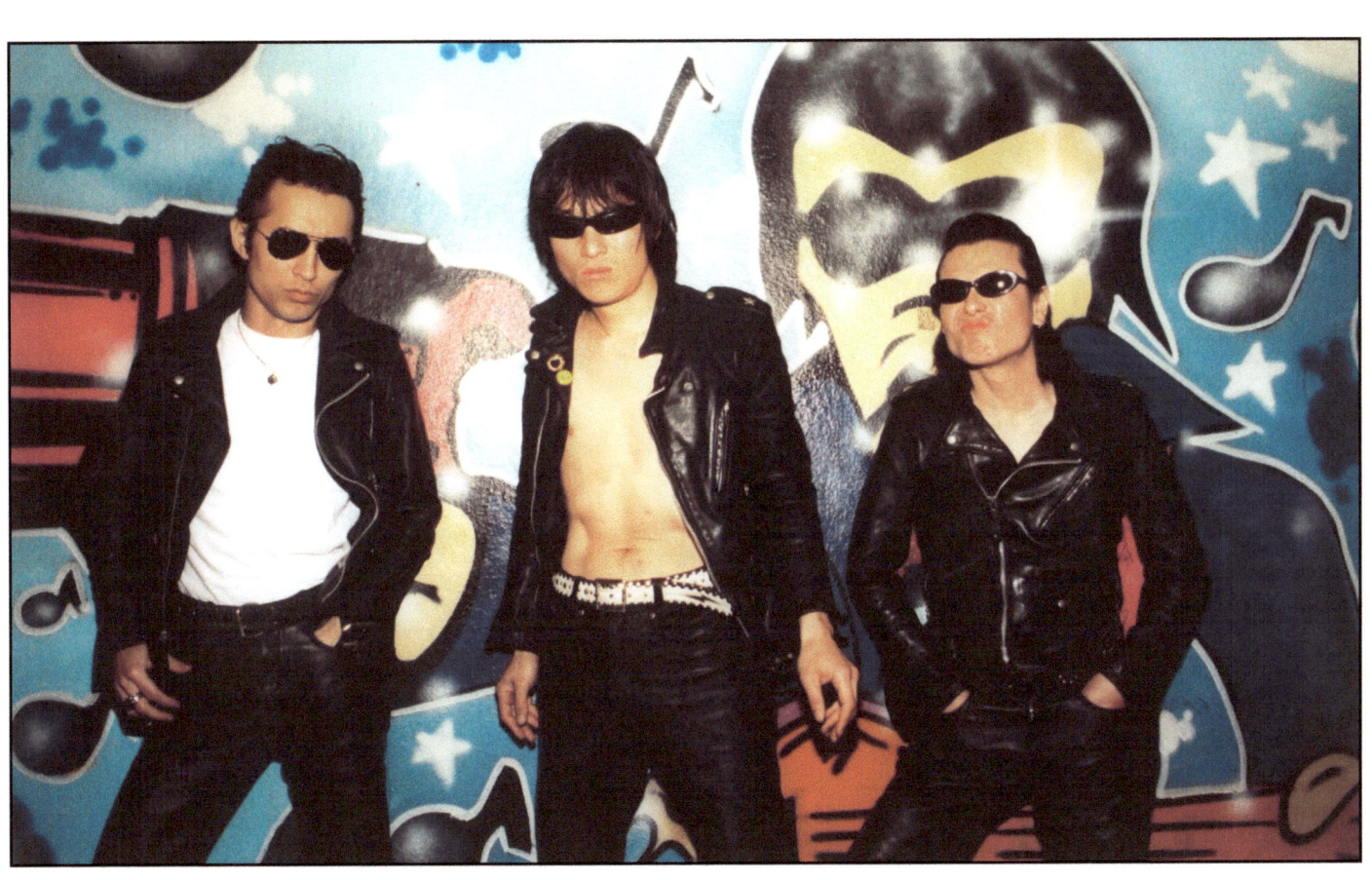

GWAR

I got the assignment to go to a
small city in Germany and
shoot these guys. I had no idea
what I was getting into. They
spray "blood" all over their
audiences who wear white
t-shirts in anticipation.
After the show, I thought I had
been in a war.

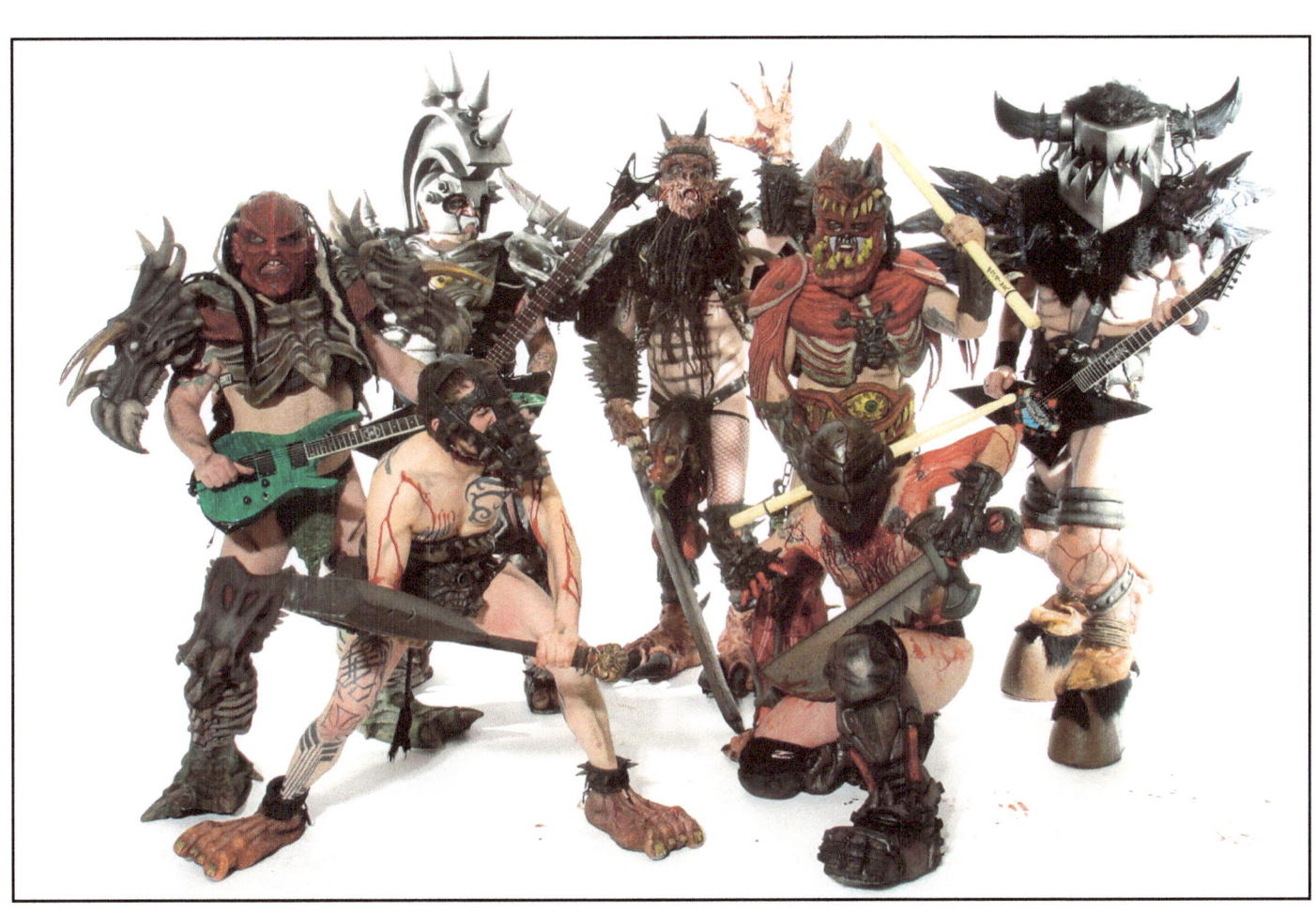

Interpol

Shot in a hotel library in Cologne, I had no idea how "big" this band was until I went to NYC and saw that they were headlining at Madison Square Garden...

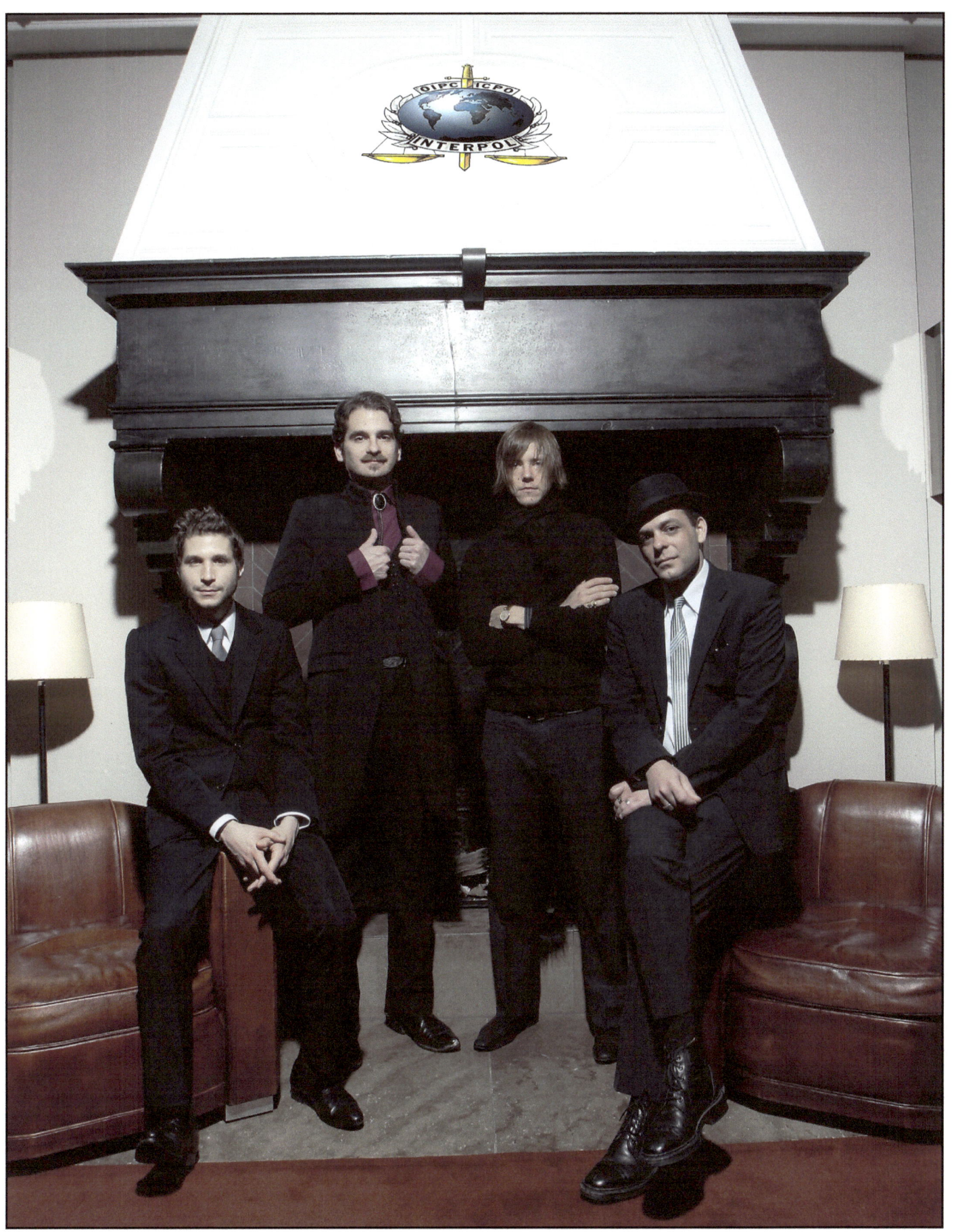

41

Joan Armatrading

Joan is gay and her publicist
assumed that she would want
to be photographed by one of
the female photographers
in NYC.
I had photographed her for a
day during radio promotions
and saw that she was shy.
I was sensitive to that.
She chose me for the
publicity session.

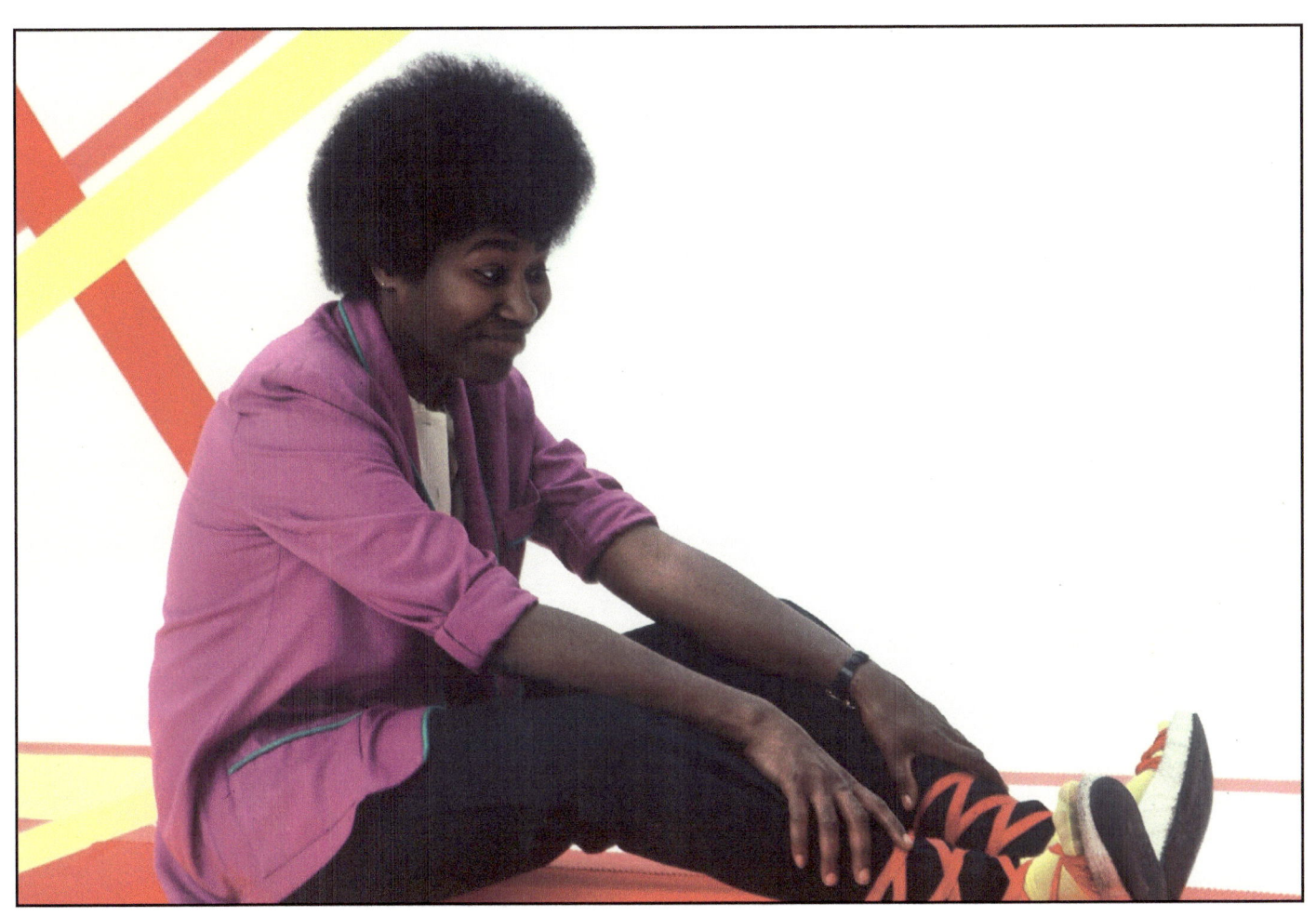

Kid Creole
aka August Darnell

This shot is from the shooting for "Off the Coast of Me". The front and back cover had a cast of about 40 people. As The Kid was still under contract for another label, he had to wear a mask...
Like he was fooling anybody?

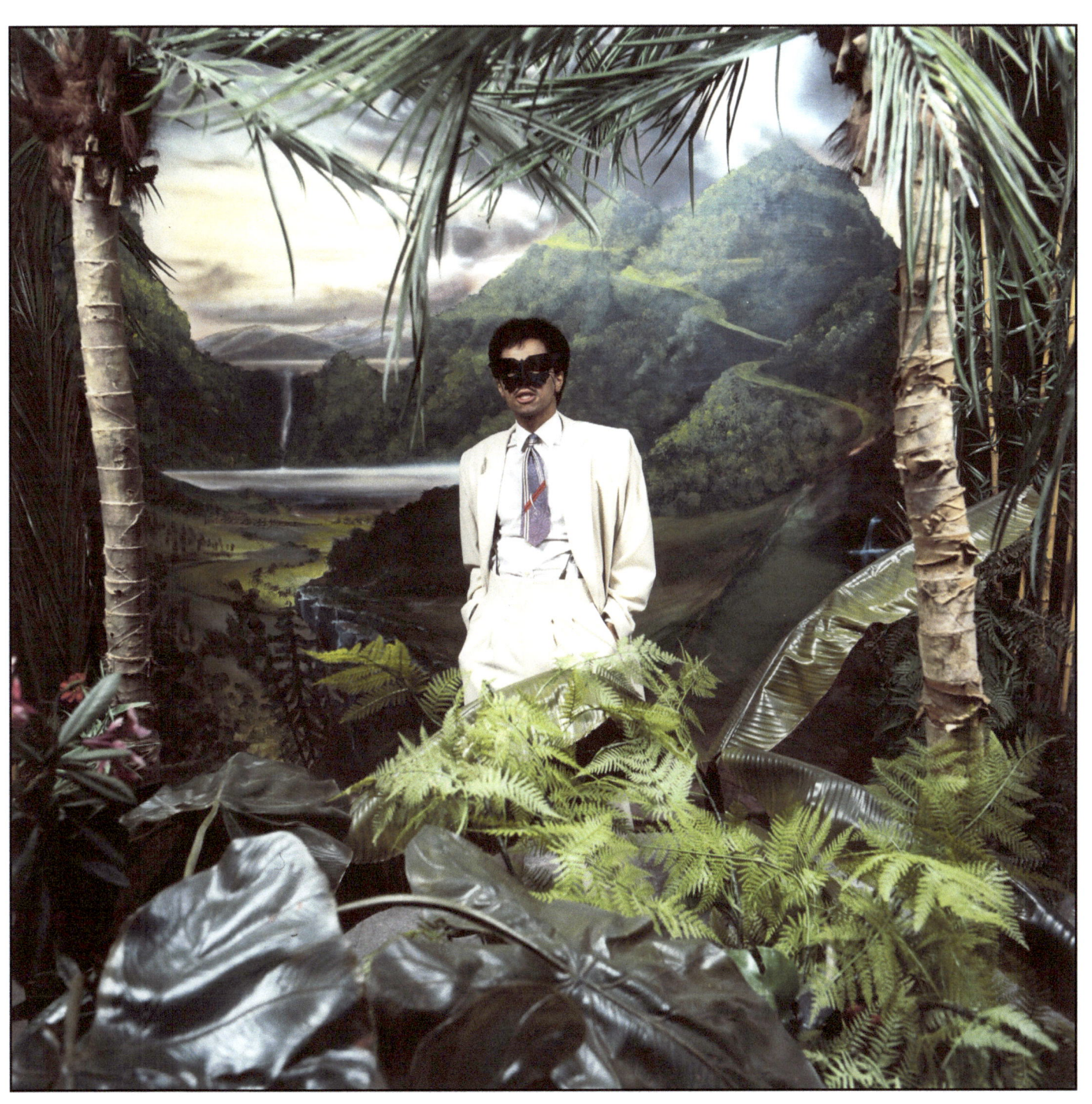

Klaus Nomi

I think I shot every concert
this wonderful New Wave artist
performed in Manhattan.
I think this was his debut at
Max's Kansas City.
His contra-tenor was something
wildly different at a time
when different was "in".
He made me a lemon tart for
my 40th birthday.

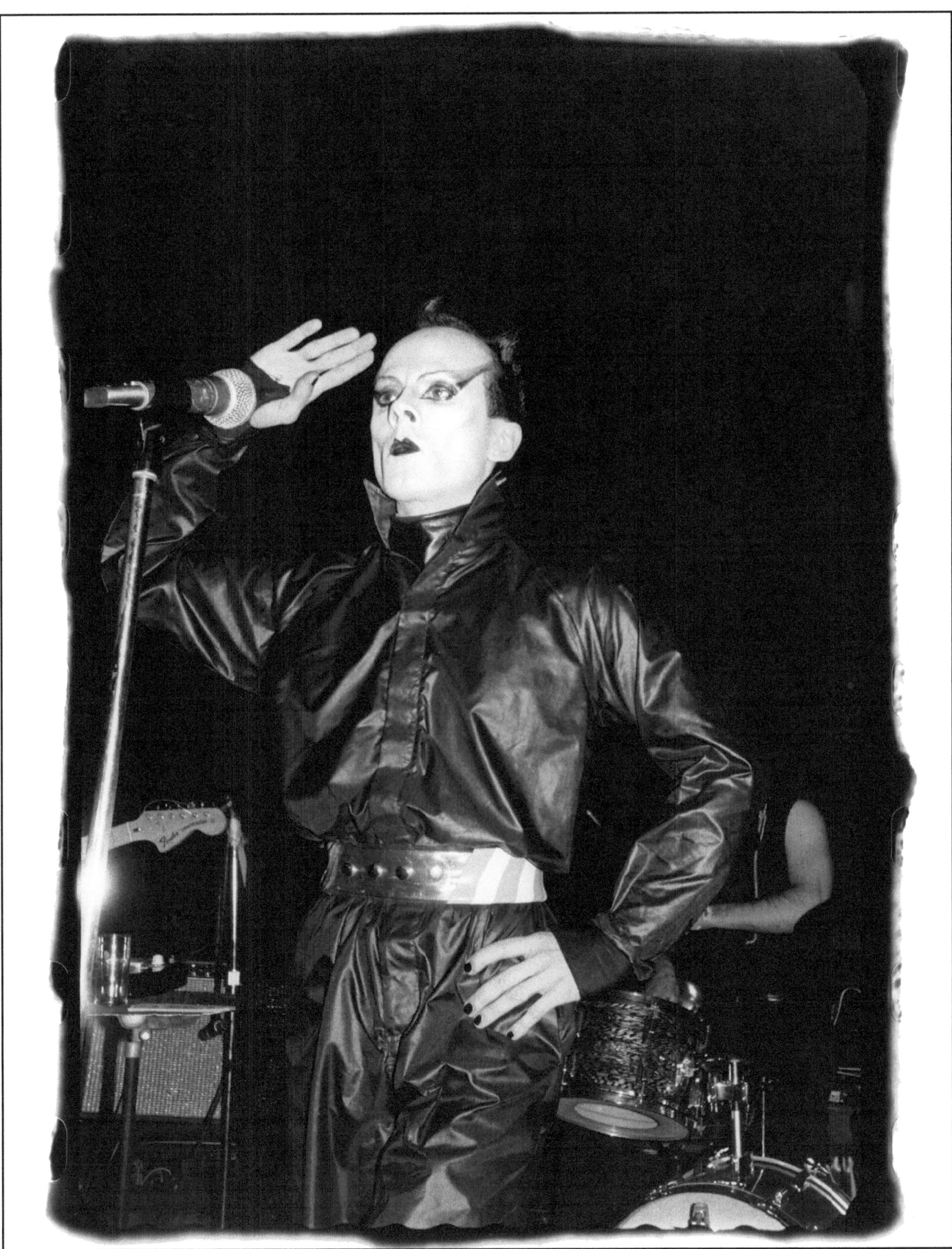

Love Delegation

A spin-off of the Fleshtones featuring Keith Strang, Peter Zaremba, Wendy Wild and two other characters.
I put too many filters on the lens and then smeared Wendy's lipstick around the edge of the filter.
I love psychedelia...

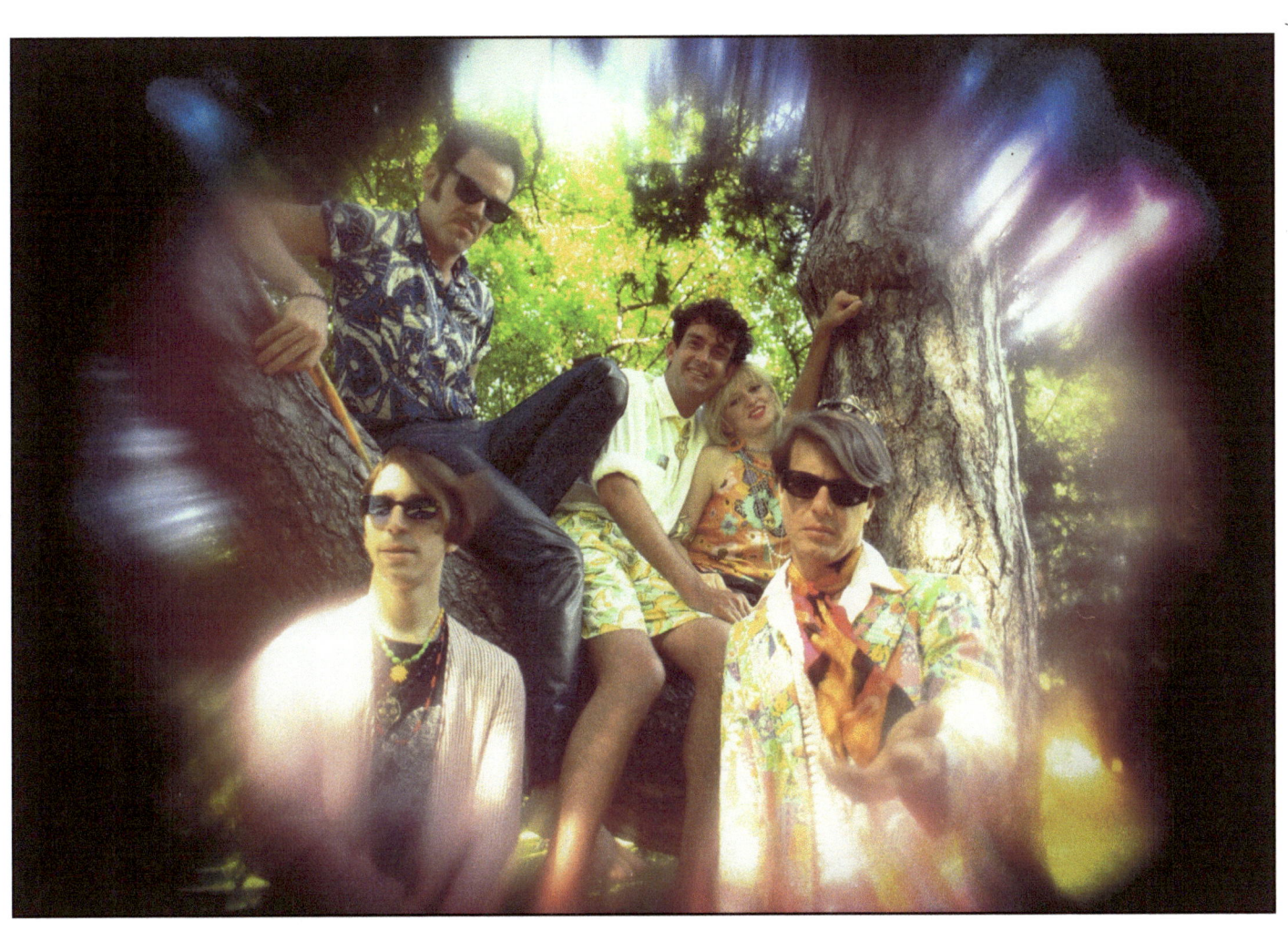

Lydia Lunch

She opened for the B52s the
first time I saw either of them.
At that Max's concert, I
didn't really know what
punk rock was.
I photographed her for her
debut album and her single
"Atomic Bongos". I will show
those images in another book.

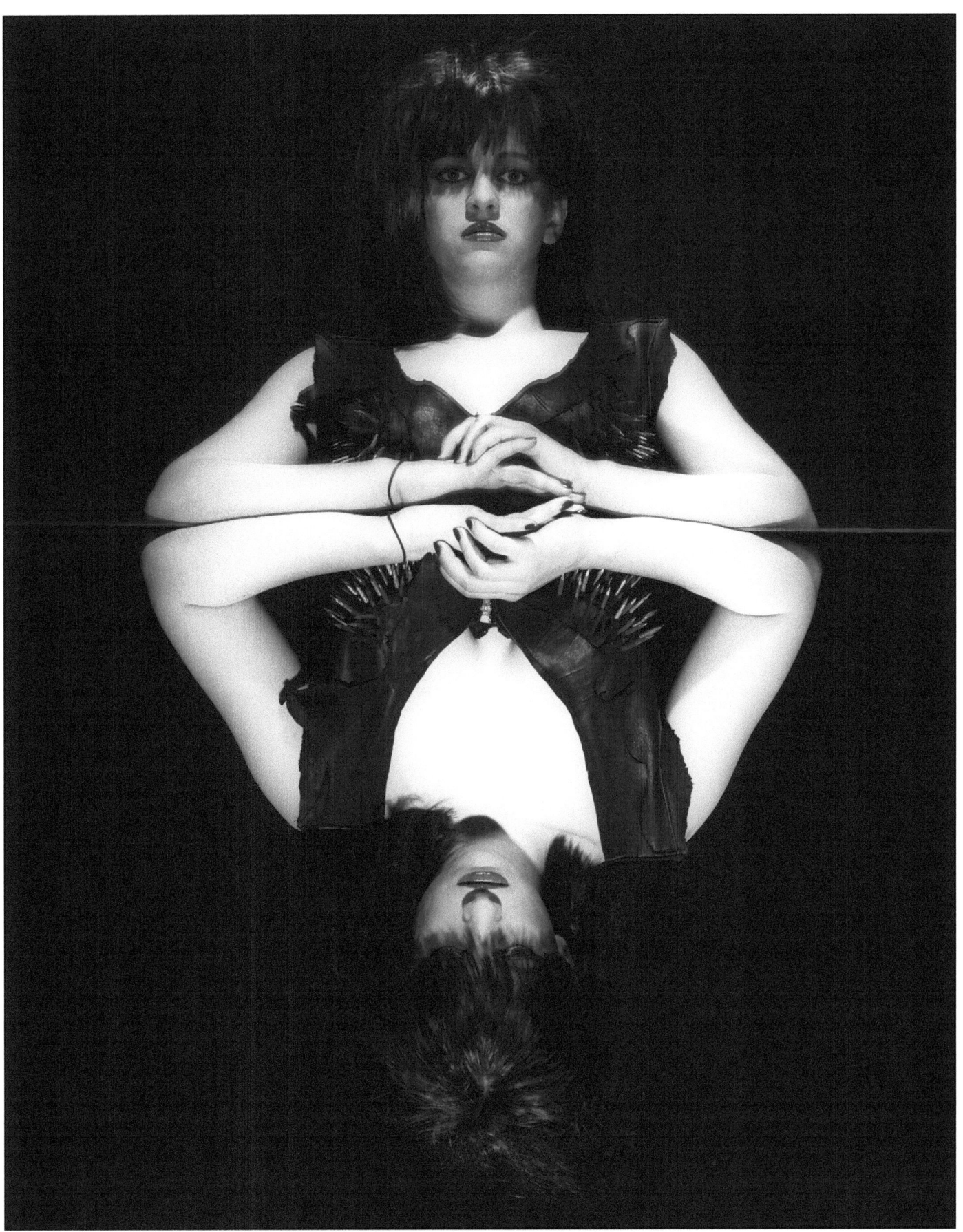

Madonna

I was lucky enough to be hired
to photograph what was
probably Madonna's third
concert as an unsigned artist.
Didn't get paid...
The full story can be found in
my book "Madonna...Raw"
available on Amazon in
five languages.

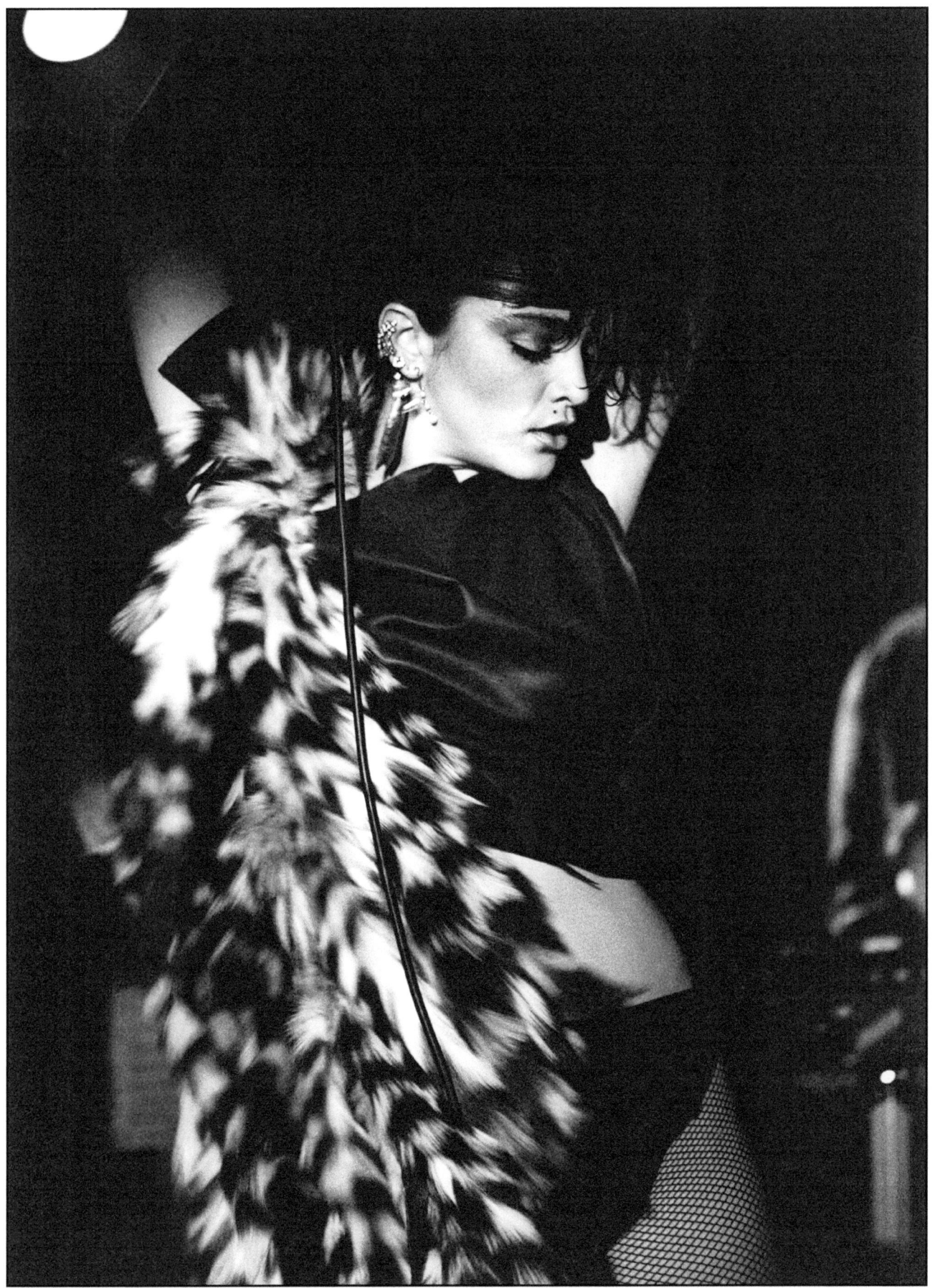

Man Parrish

Manny was the epitome of New
Wave. He was a techno-pioneer
who mixed in the new Hip-Hop
sounds to his techo tracks.
His debut album was released
on a Belgian label and he is still
a cult icon today.

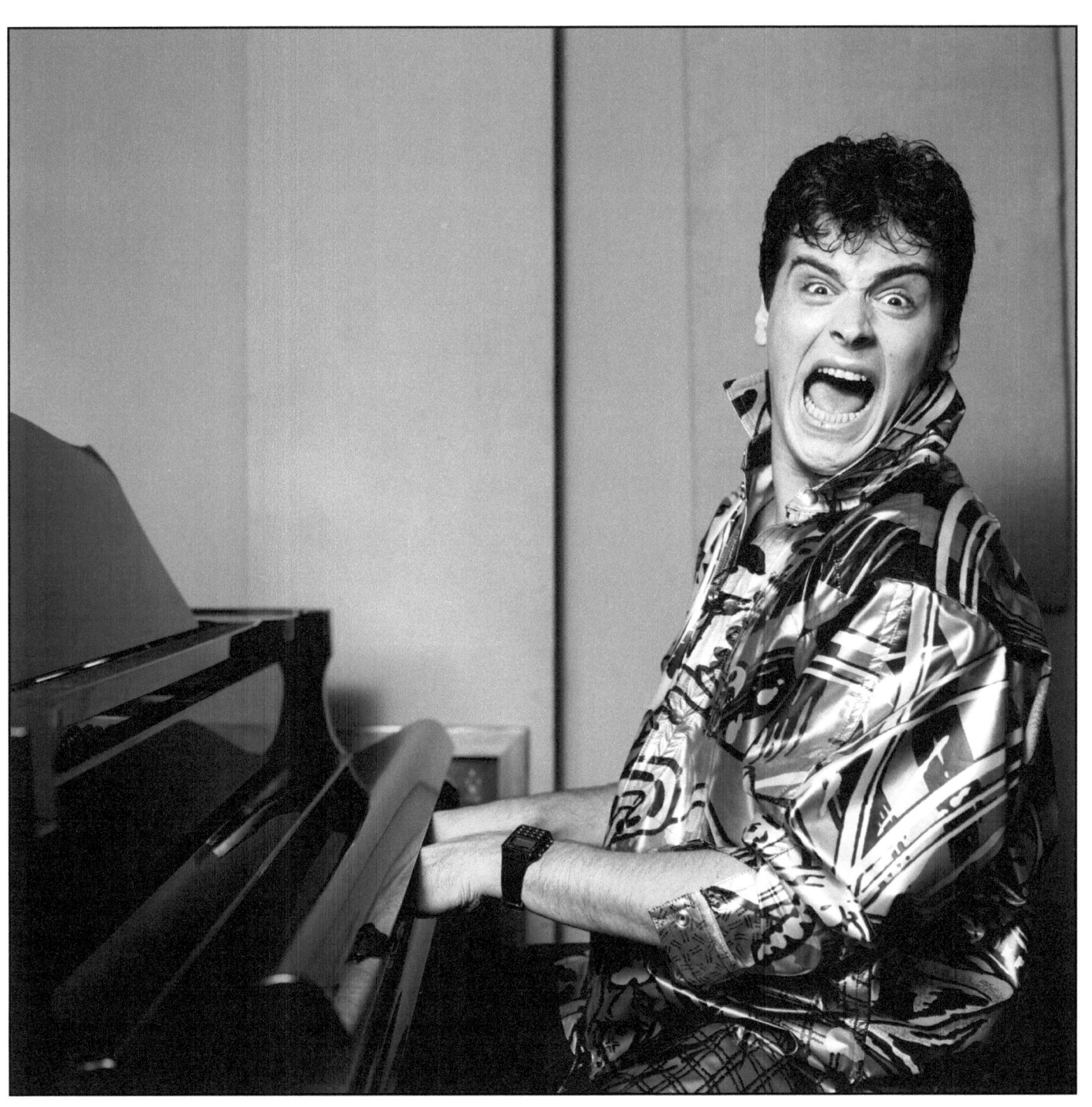

Marty Venker

Marty was a former Secret
Service agent who was so
distressed by the assassination
of John Lennon that he
quit the Service.
Here he is in his second career
spinning at The World nightclub
in NYC.

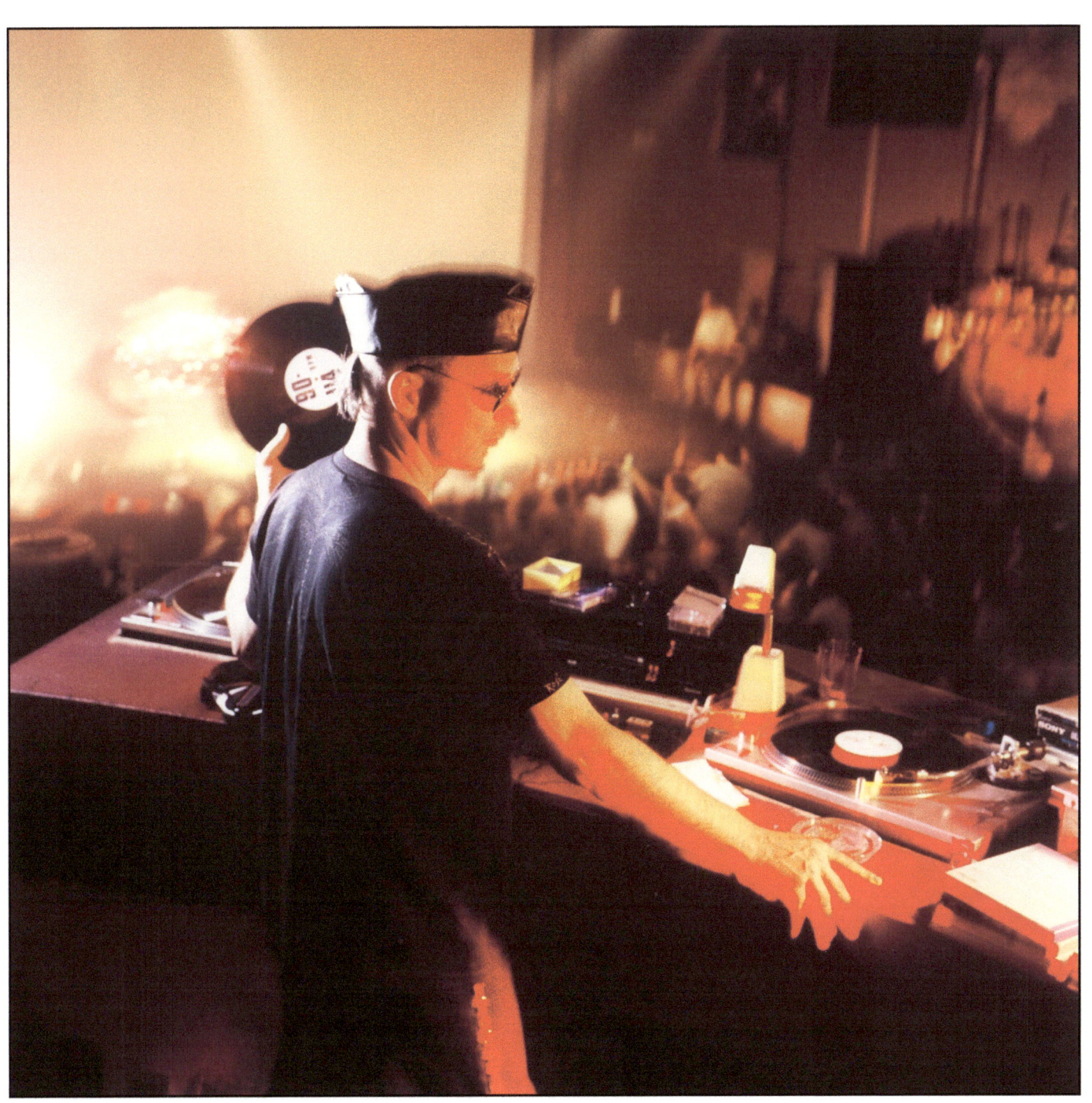

Michael McLintock

This is the cover photo for his
posthumous LP "Sex".
He rounded up transvestite
prostitutes in Manhattan's
Meat Packing district and paid
each of them $100 to pose with
him and Kevin Tooley
the drummer.
It was an interesting evening to
say the least...

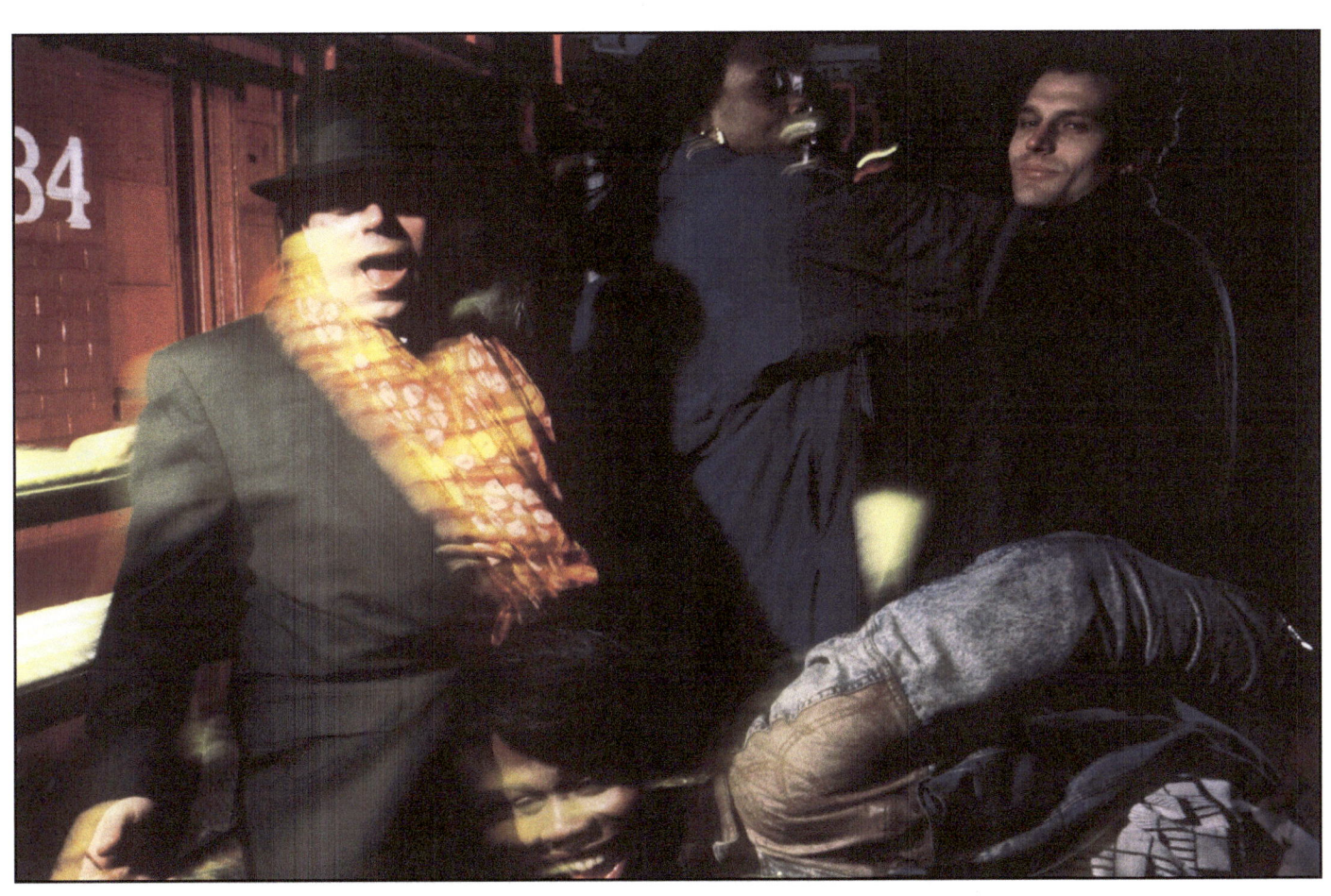

Michael Monroe

Formerly with Hanoi Rocks.
Here Michael is with his band
"Demolition 23". I designed a
massive CD booklet and after I
showed Michael the Pantone
color book, I really shot myself
in the foot. He kept changing
the color schemes daily for over
a month.

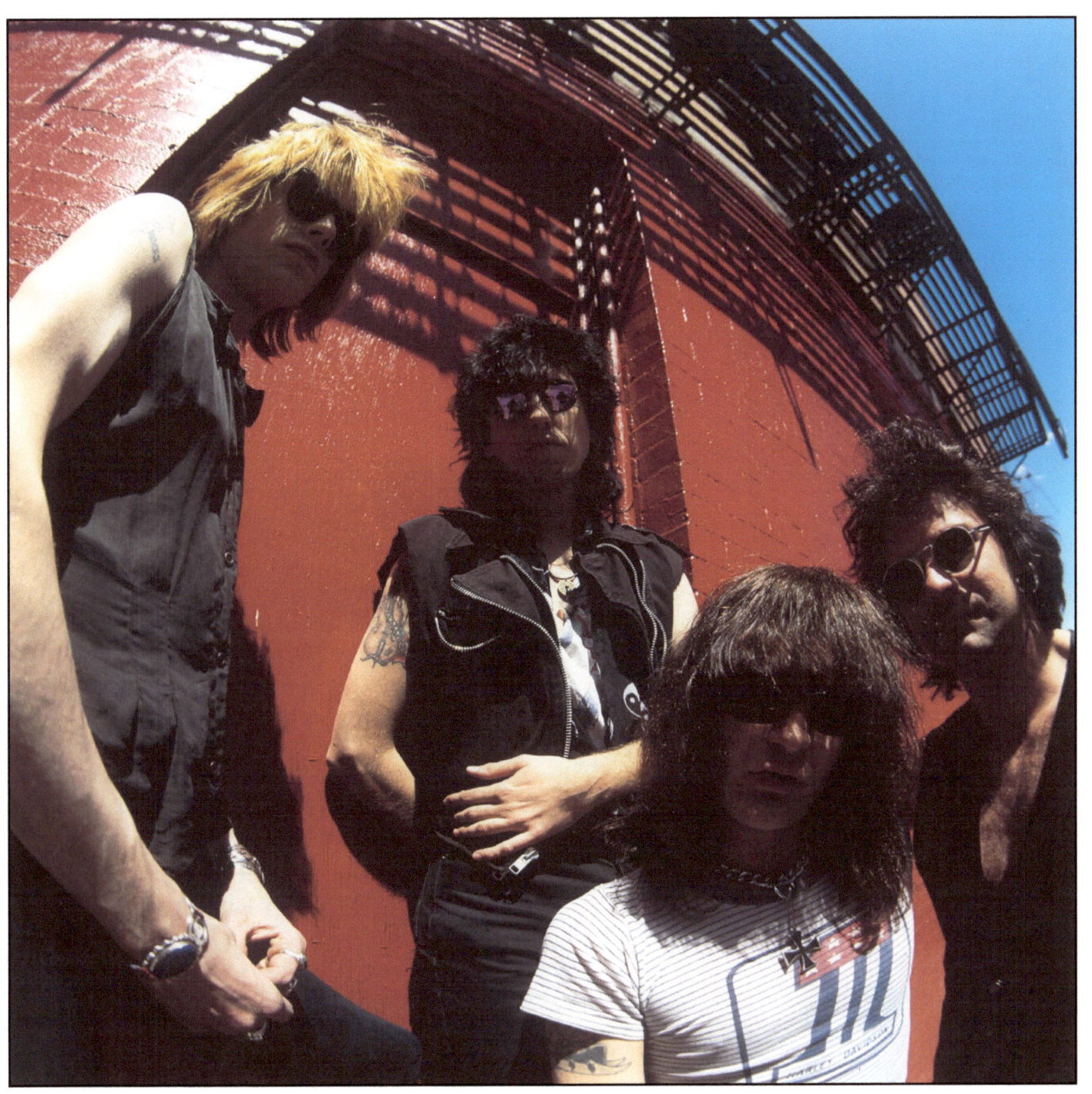

Min Xao Fen

A Chinese classical pipa player. A
pipa sounds like a banjo and
I always wanted to hear her play
"Foggy Mountain Breakdown".

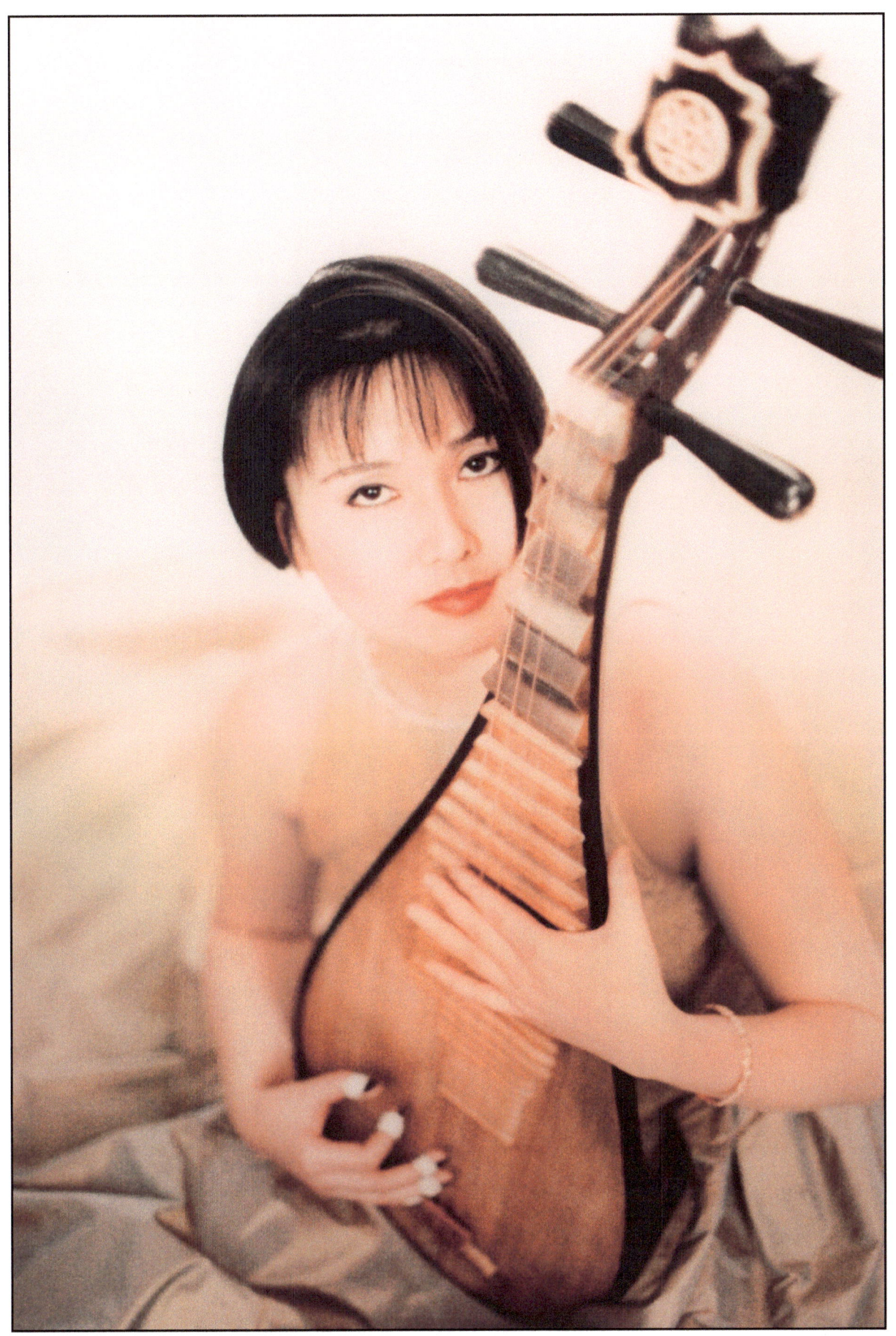

Jerry Only

A founding member of the
Misfits, Jerry is really a sweet
guy and great to his fans.
Here he is raising the devil.

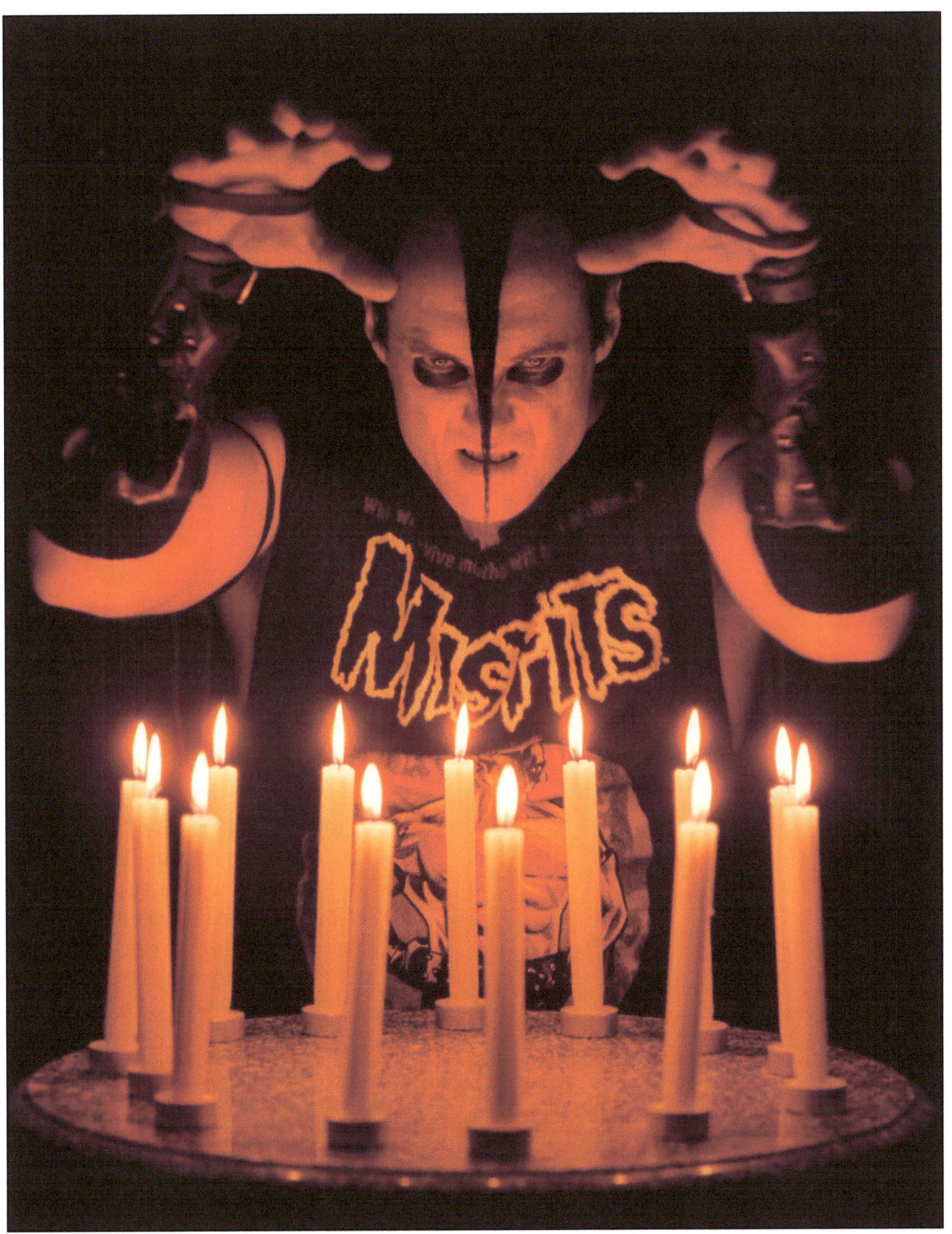

Phil Collins

Shot for "Interview" in a hotel
conference room. The broken
glass is a nod to Memorex
recording tapes ads where an
opera singer breaks a glass
with her recording.
His publicist got a bit upset
about the broken glass.
All for art...

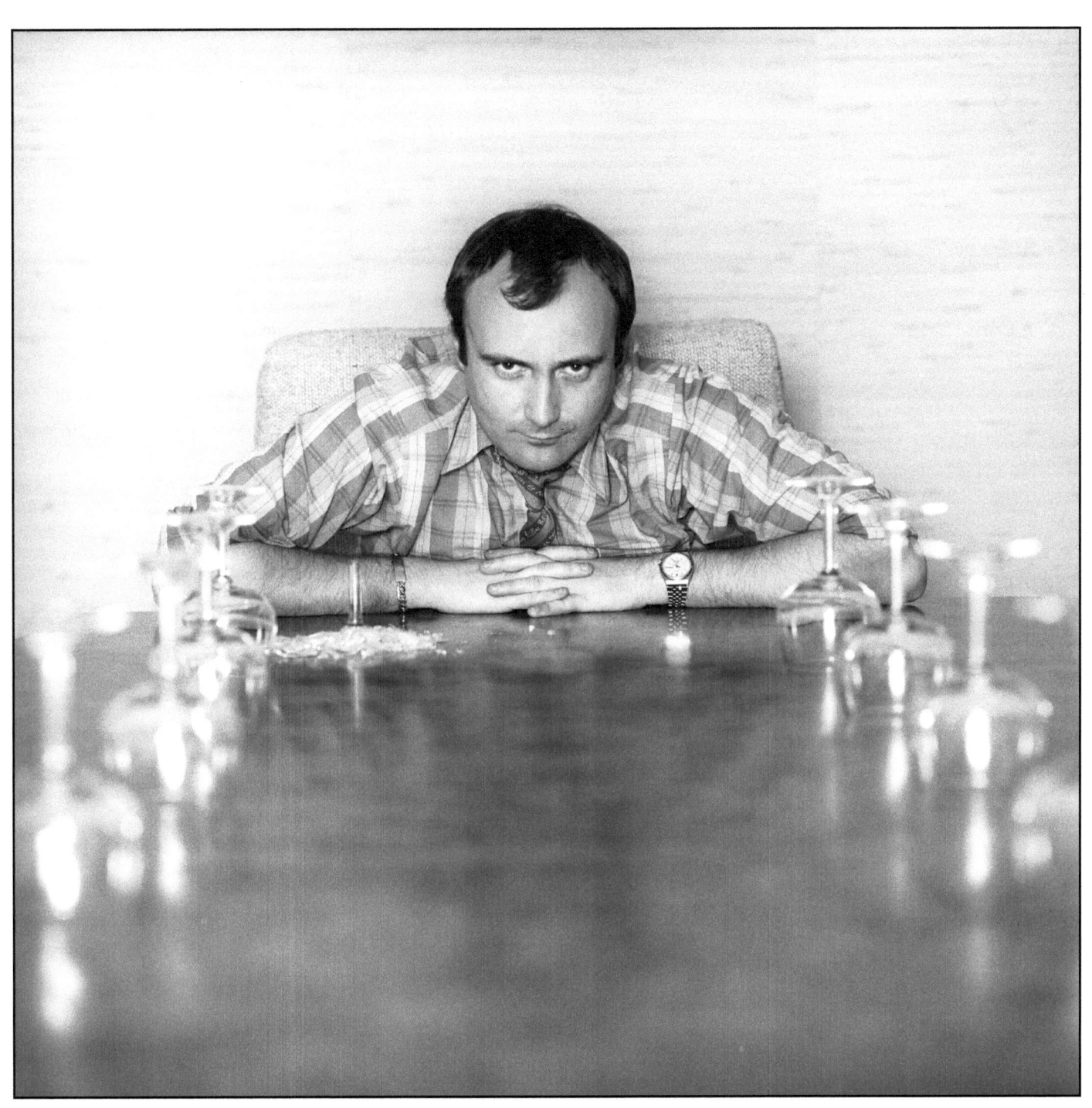

The Plasmatics

Another assignment for
"Intervew". Sometimes
classified as a punk band,
the Plasmatics were
something else.
There live shows were some
of the most exciting I have
ever seen.

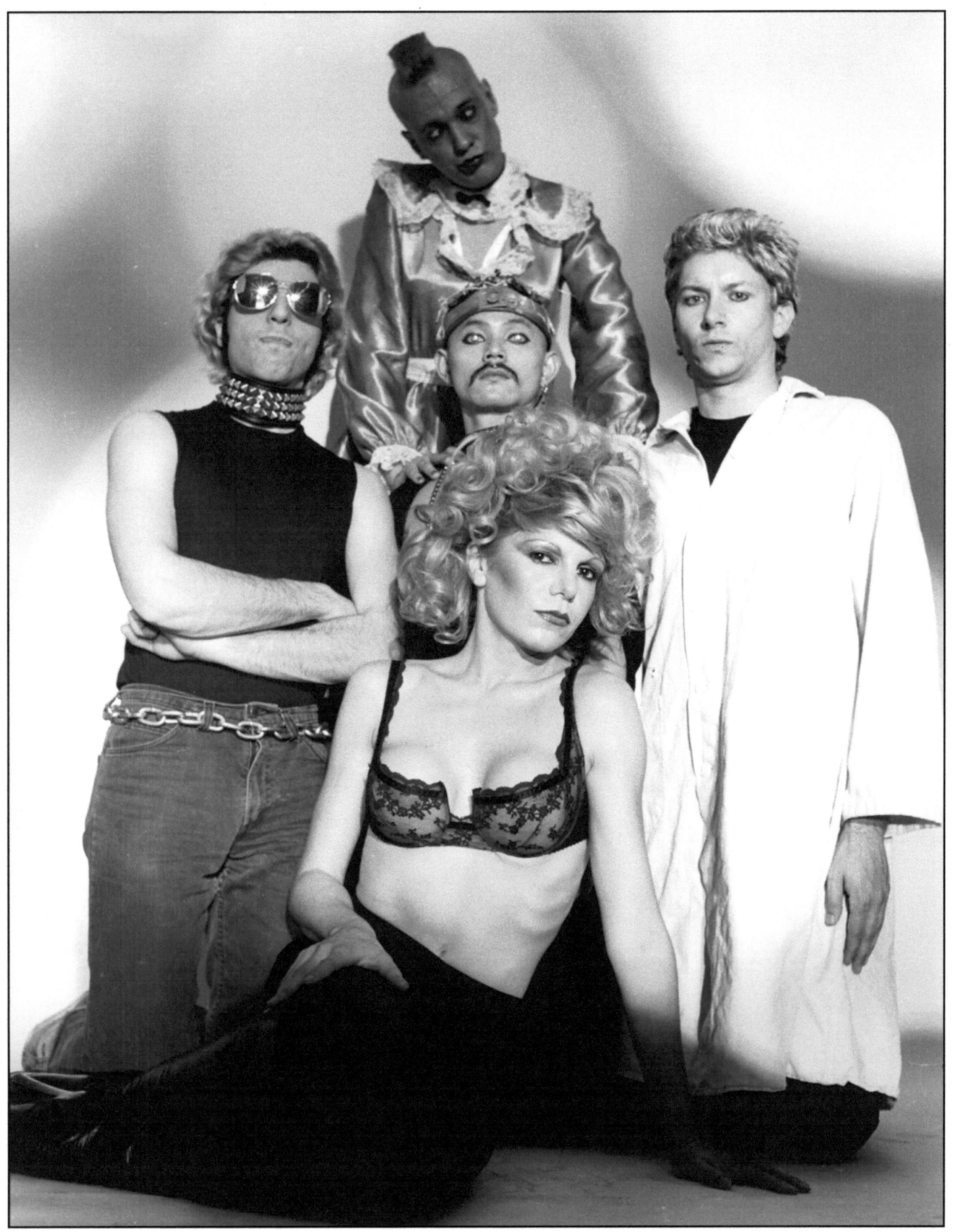

The Police

I shot this with a 200mm lens
from the balcony of the
Diplomat Hotel ballroom.
My timing was so spot on that
I caught Sting at the exact
apogee of his jump and all his
strings are sharp.
I try to shoot on the beat.
OK?

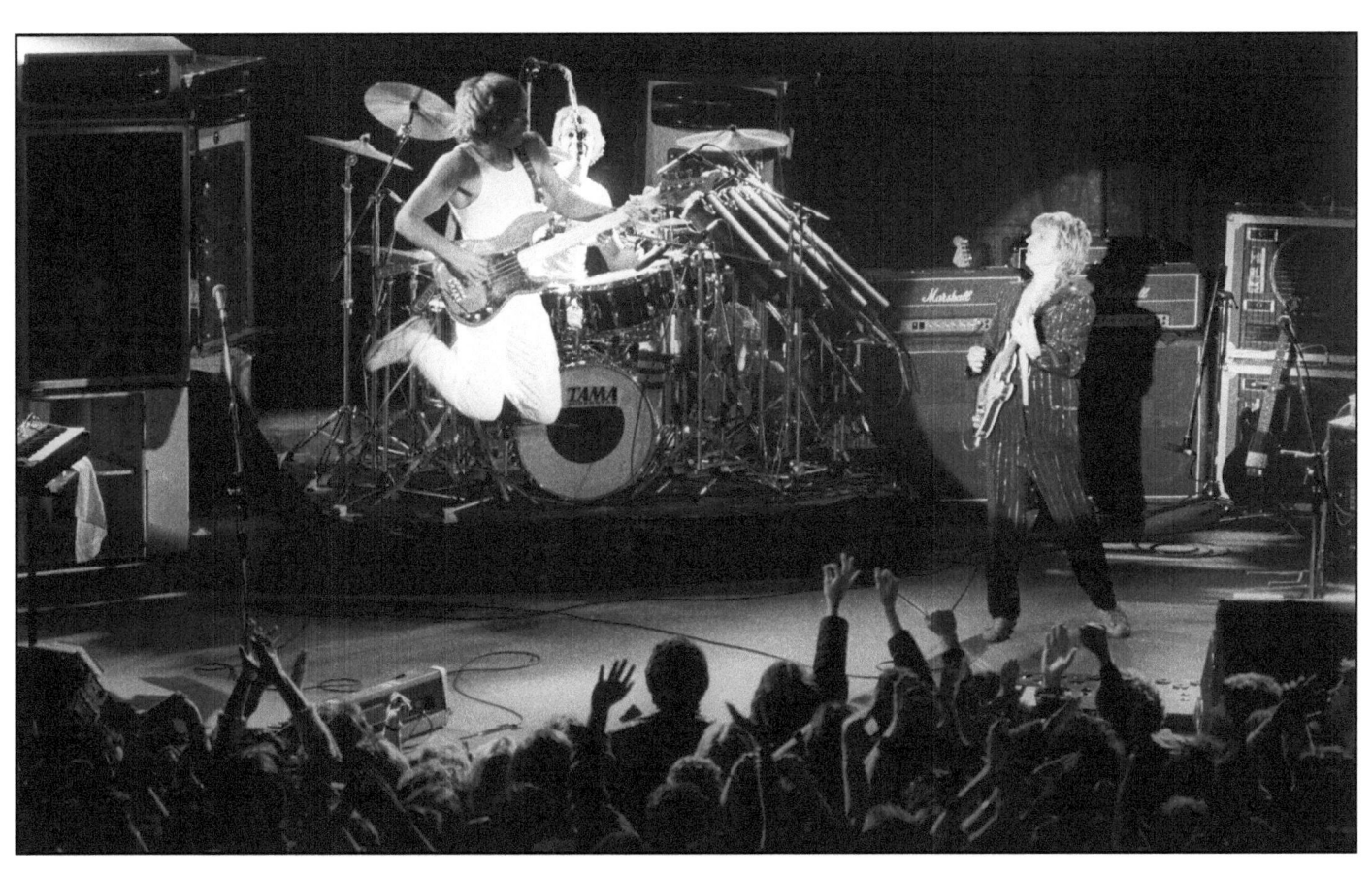

The Psychedelic Furs

I shot them for Interview and
they asked if the lighting
director could stand in.
Since he really wasn't a
band member, he jumped
out of the picture.
I am showing the edges of this
negative as I had run out of film
and used the last color negatives
shots with my little Paxette camera
which has an unusual frame.

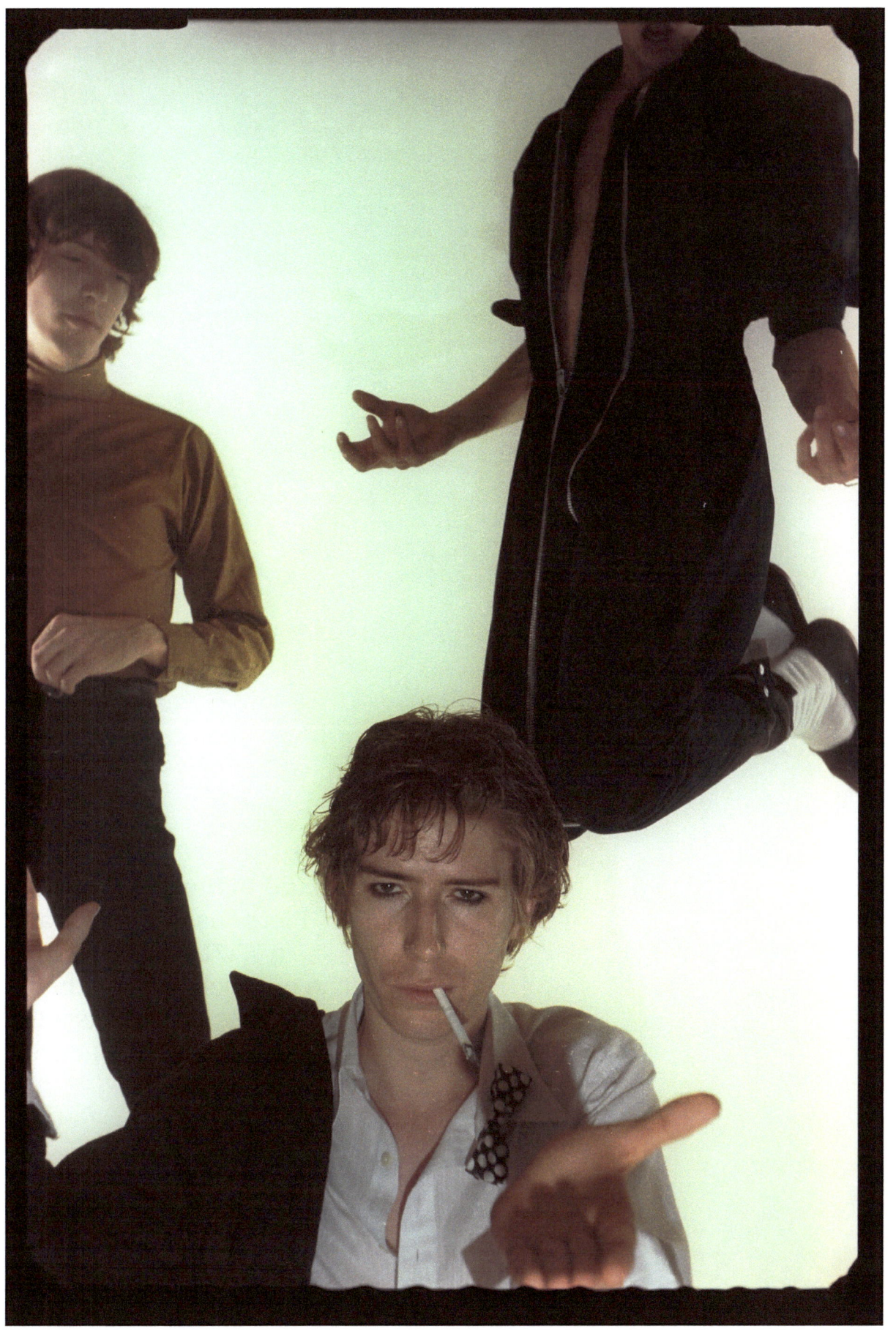

RAAR

A band of blue-skinned Scottish
Picts that I photographed in
a WWI cemetary in Berlin.
The big rock behind them is not
a standing stone, it is a German
general's grave stone.

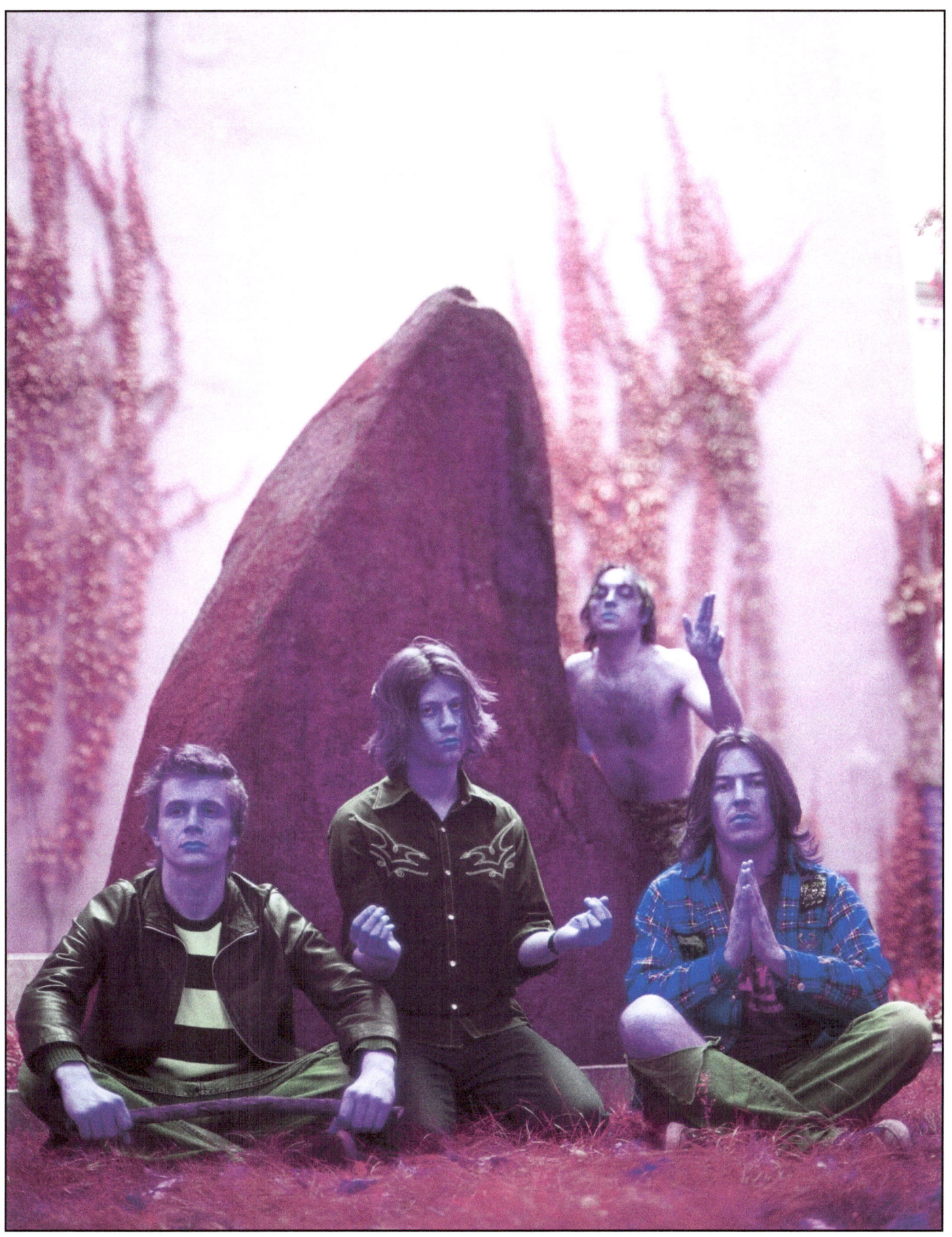

Ramones

I don't know if this is my best
shot of the Ramones, but it is
my take on the caterpillar in
"Alice in Wonderland".
I have so many shots of the
Ramones that I like I made
a book about my 12 year career
with them. The photos and
the stories behind them.
"I Speak Music - Ramones"

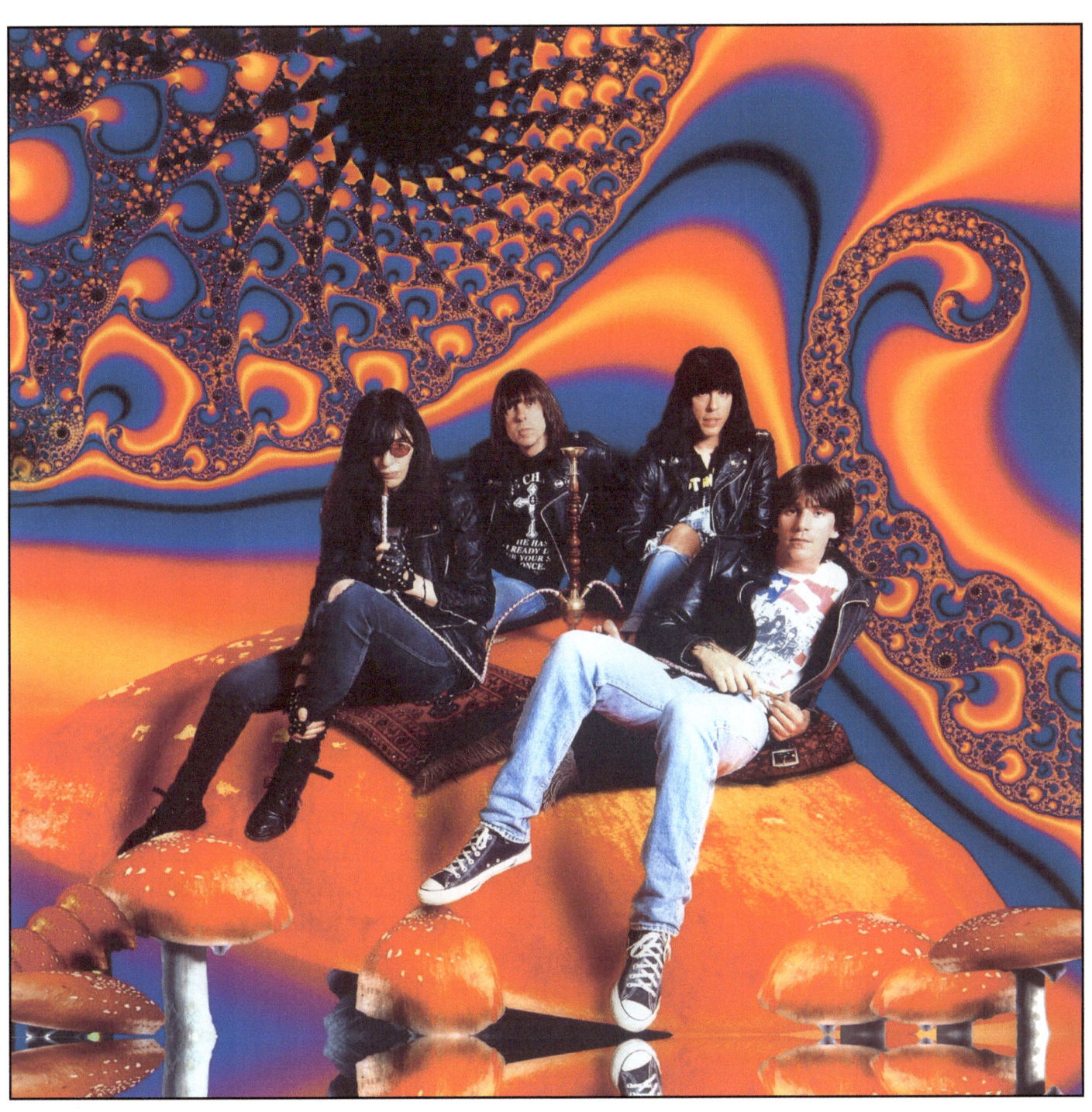

REM

This might be their first studio
photo shoot. It was during their
first visit to NYC. Buck, Berry
and Mills stayed in my studio.
I tried to interview Michael, but
he mumbled so much the tape
was unintelligible.
I got them a gig at the Mudd
Club, but when only 12 people
showed up on a Monday night,
Steve Mass didn't want
to pay them.
They played for free...

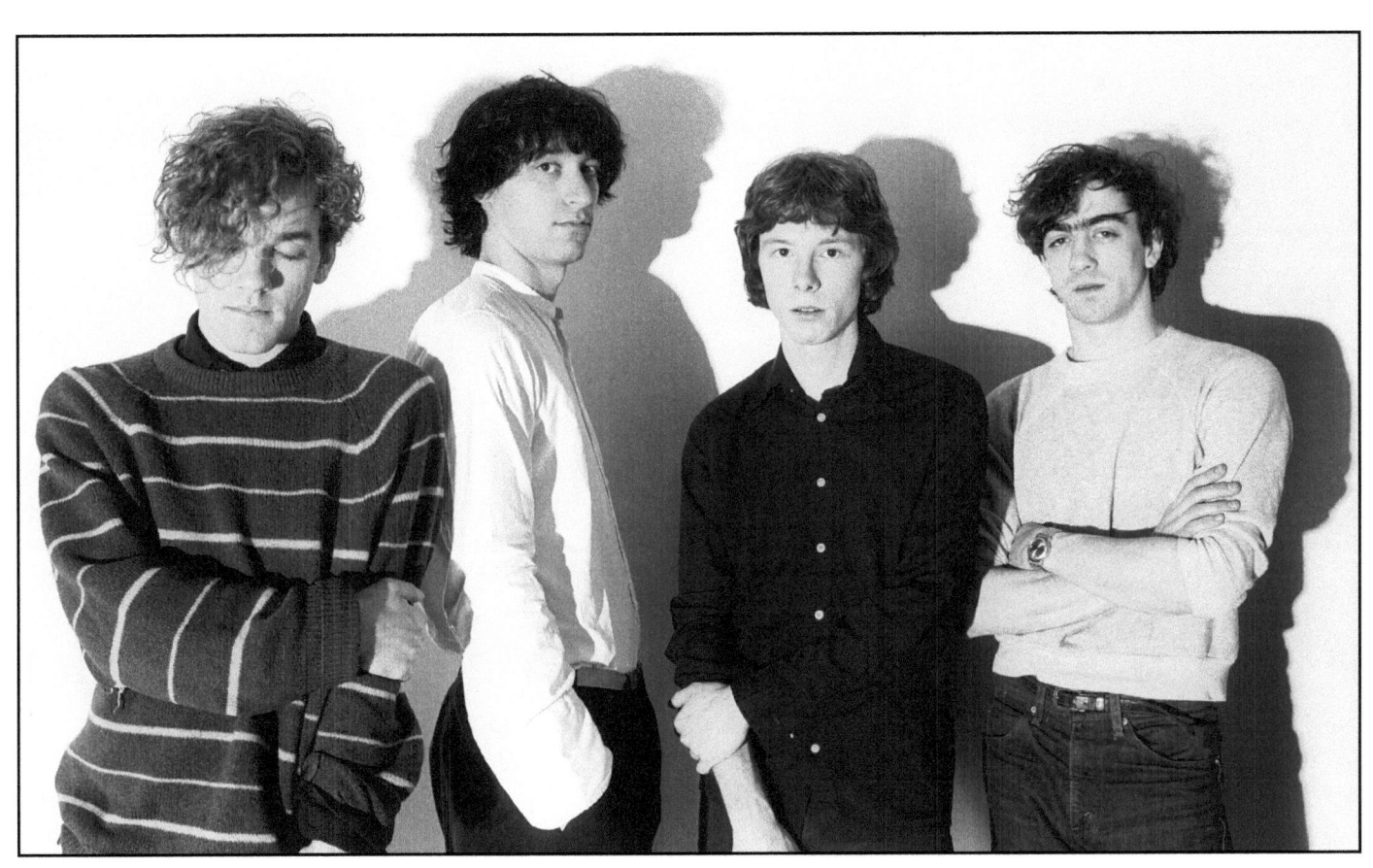

Rockweilers

This shot was for a cover of the Rockweiler's single. A Spanish rock band that were fans of my work with the Ramones, they contacted me by email and we worked out a concept and got a German model for the shot. The wingtips represent a businessman.

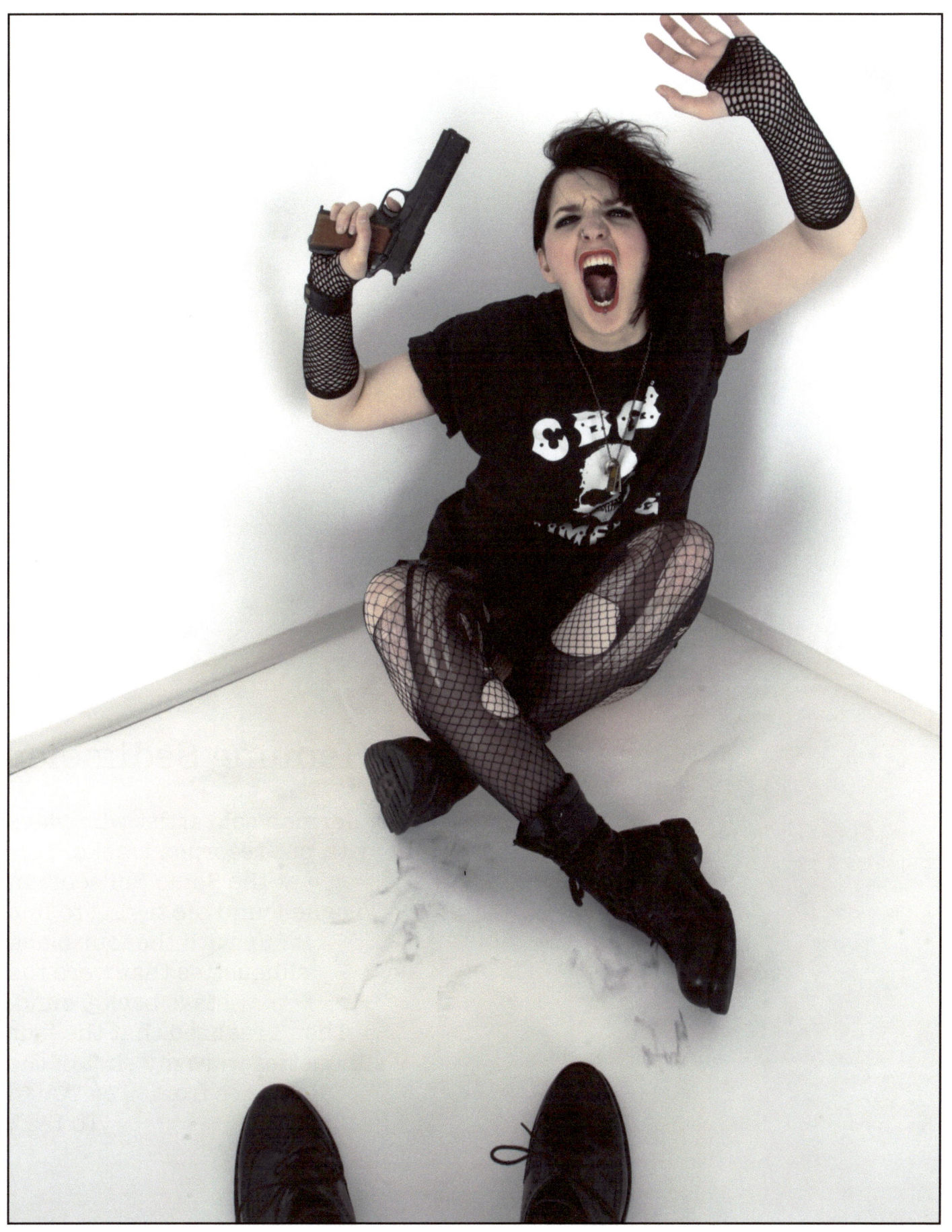

81

Henning Sedlmeier

A German solo artist who plays with pre-recorded tracks. This gig at the Sonic Ballroom in Cologne found me trying to line him up with the four black silhouettes that were the stage background.
Then I realized that the four silhouettes were my shot of the Ramones from "Too Tough To Die".

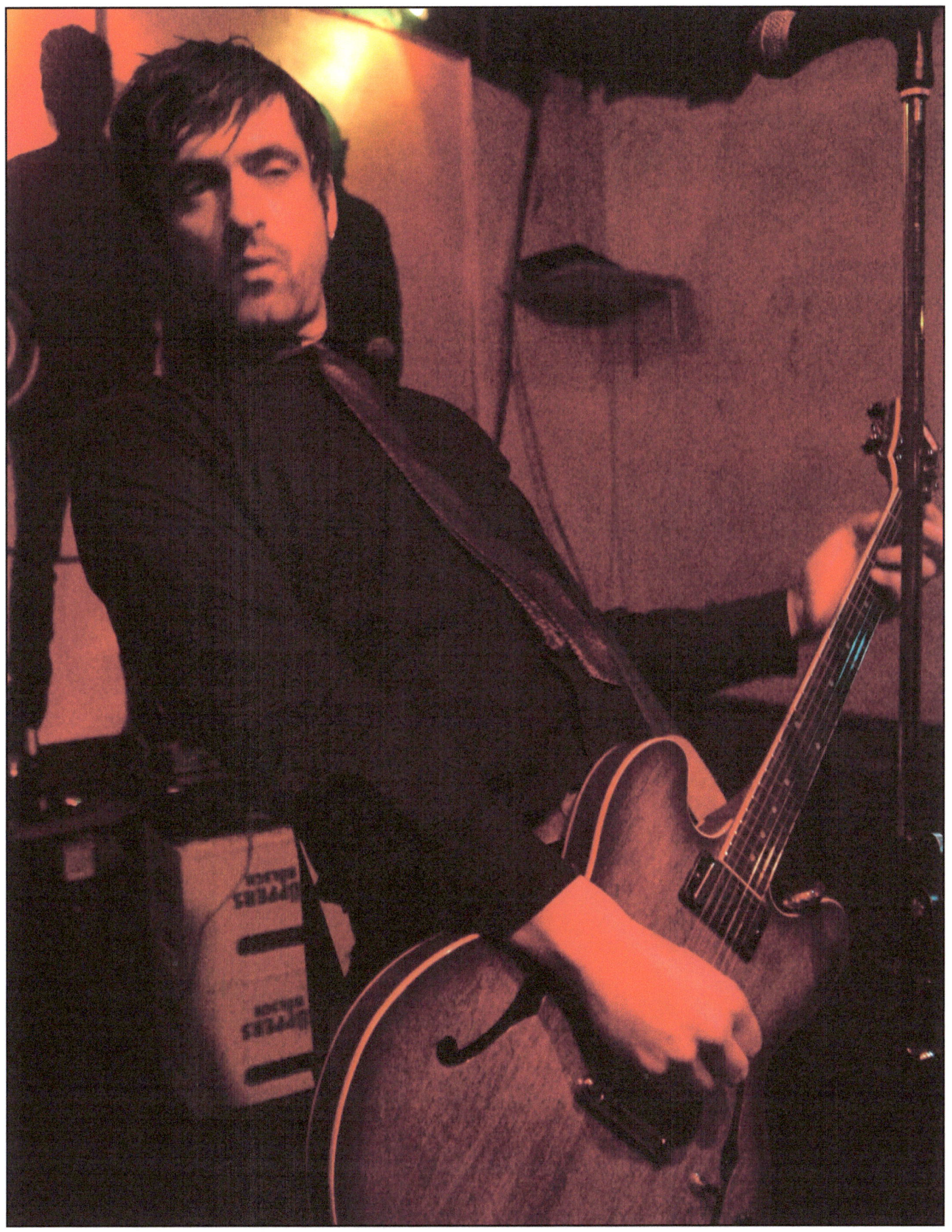

Smoke Blow

A German rock band I shot
for the cover of Ox Fanzine.
Smoke Blow was going to
play an unplugged concert
so I had them burn their
electric guitars.

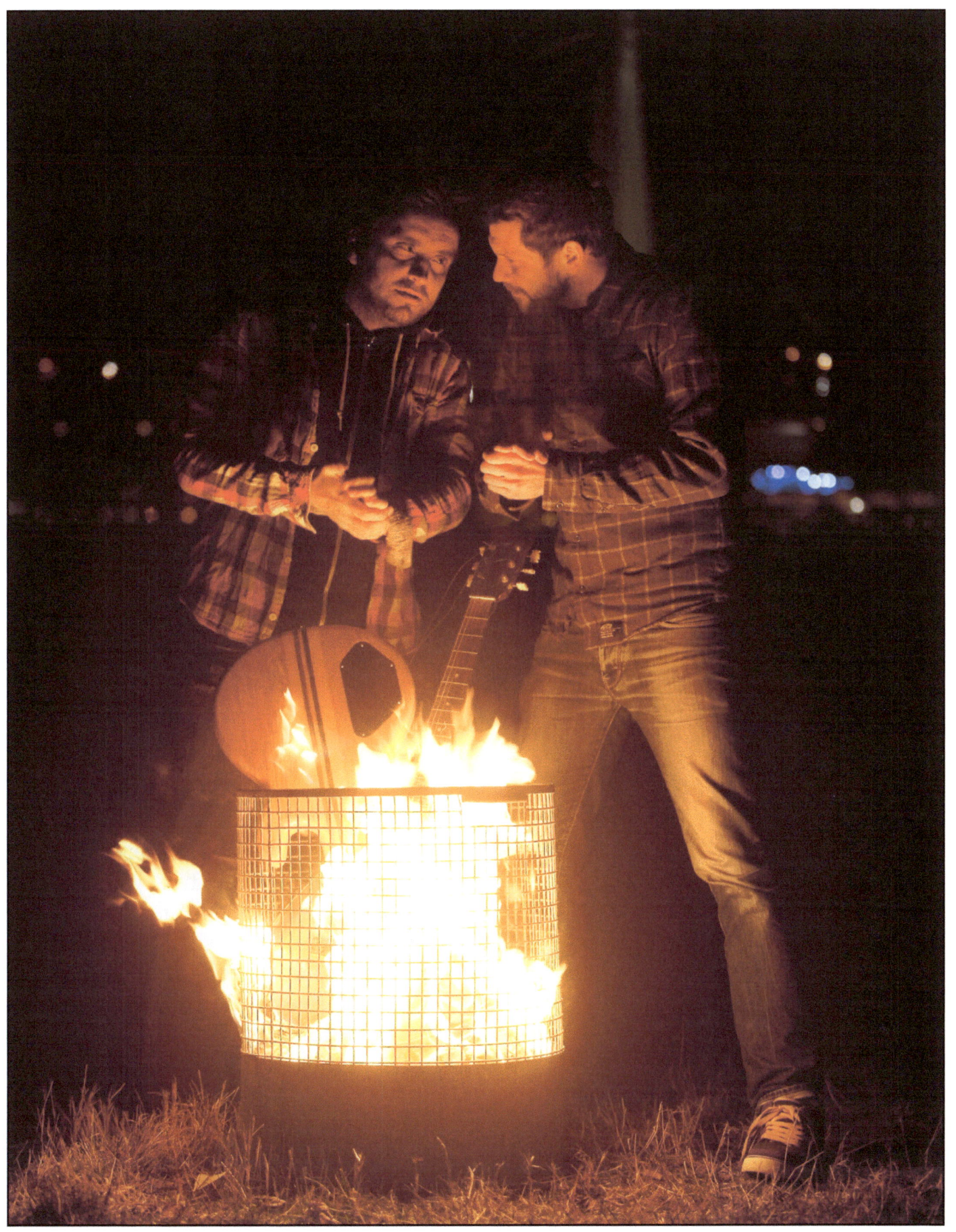

Chris Spedding

One of the best guitarists in the world. His song "Guitar Jamboree" has him playing the signature riffs of many famous guitarists. I saw him perform that song with only an ancient Les Paul Junior and a tiny Fender amp. No special effects. This print is a failed darkroom manipulation. I think it looks cool anyway...

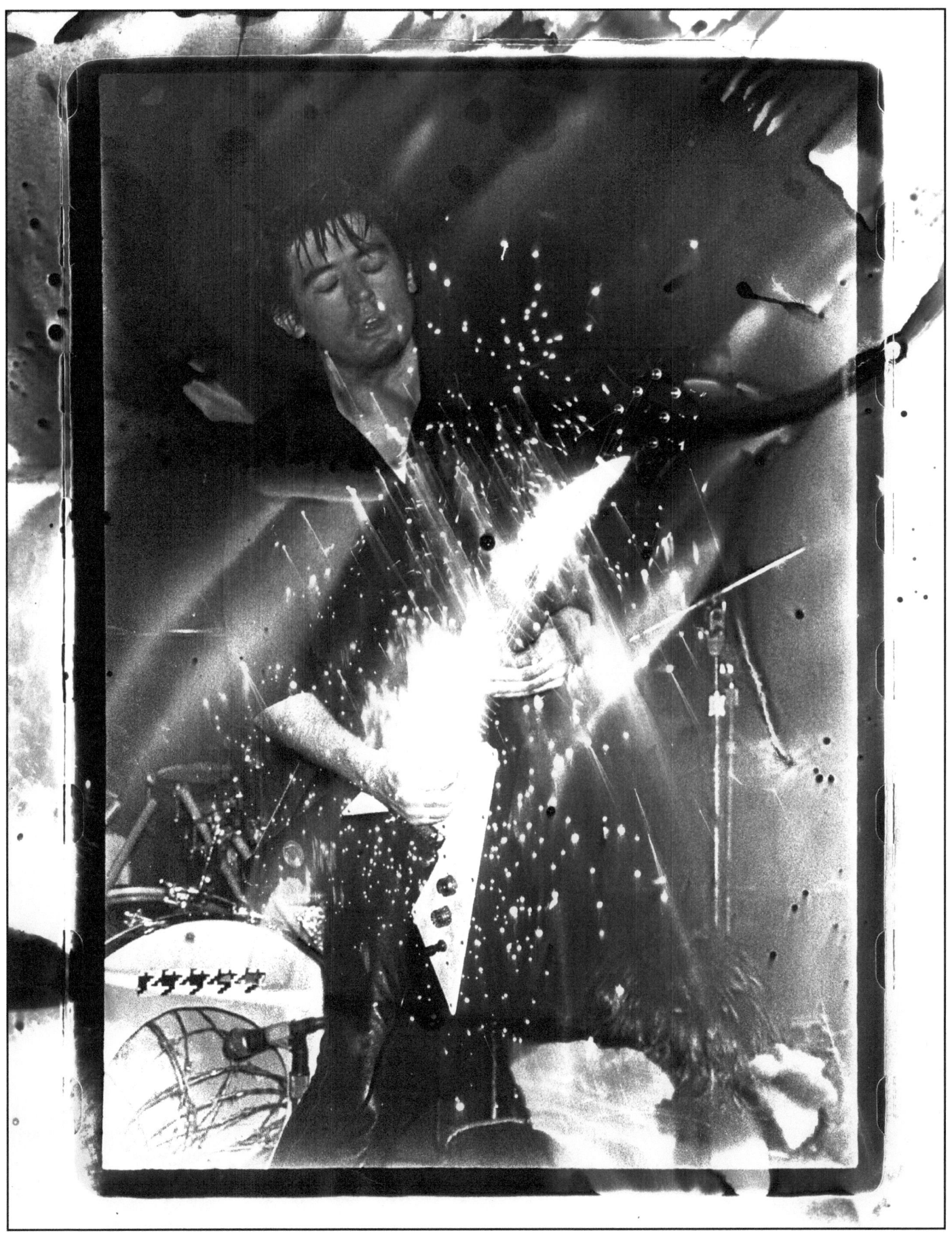

87

Stephen Sprouse

The fashion designer as a punk
rock guitarist. This photo was
for Tama Janowitz's book
"A Cannibal in Manhattan".

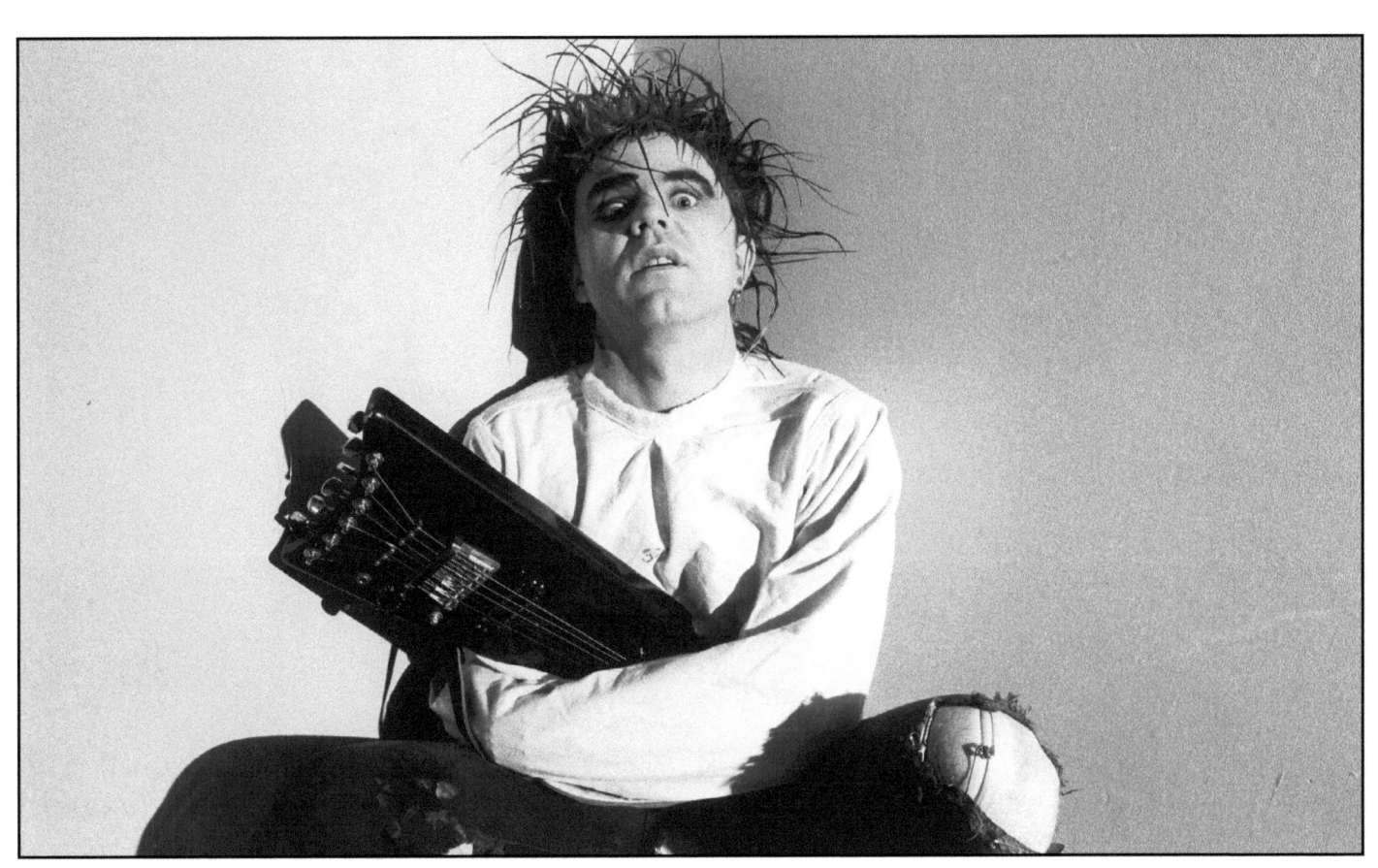

Suicide

Shot at a Manhattan club called
"The Eighties". Alan Vega had
thrown his mike into the
audience and someone threw
it back

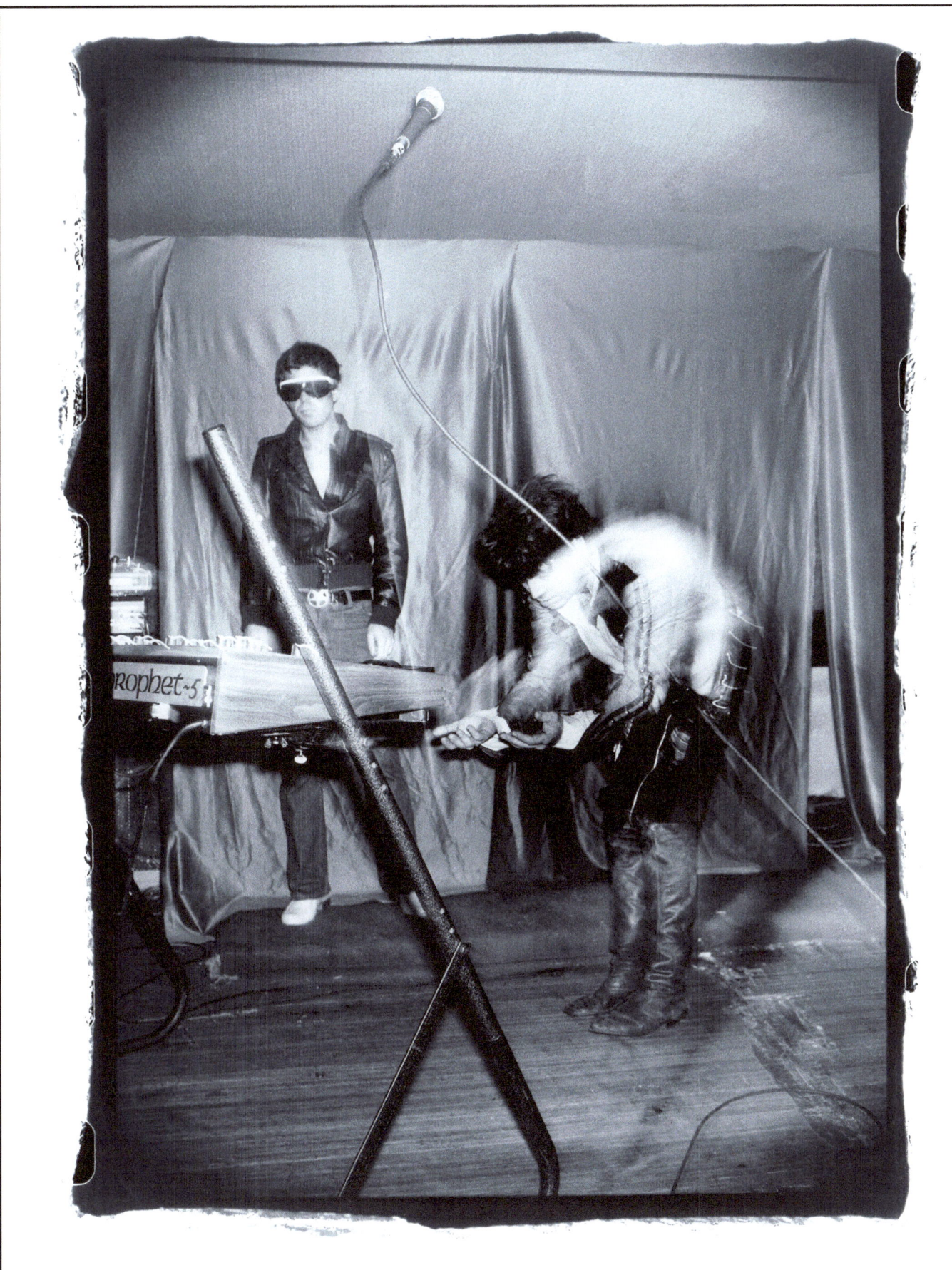

Tina of

Talking Heads

Although I photographed The
Talking Heads several times for
SPIN magazine, this is my most
favorite of all the shots.
I will show the full band shots
in another book.

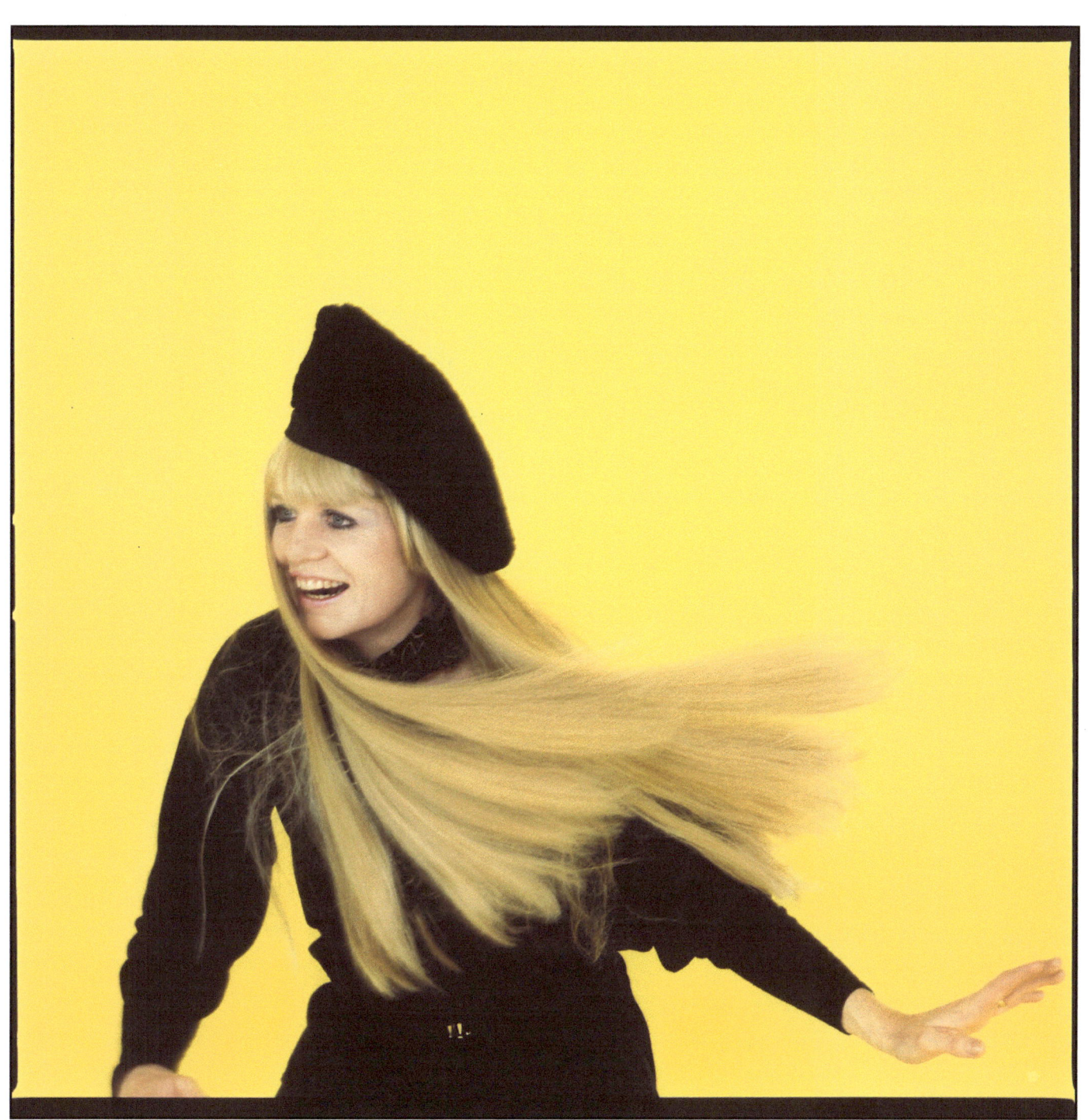

Toots Hibbert

This was a shot for the album
"Toots in Memphis".

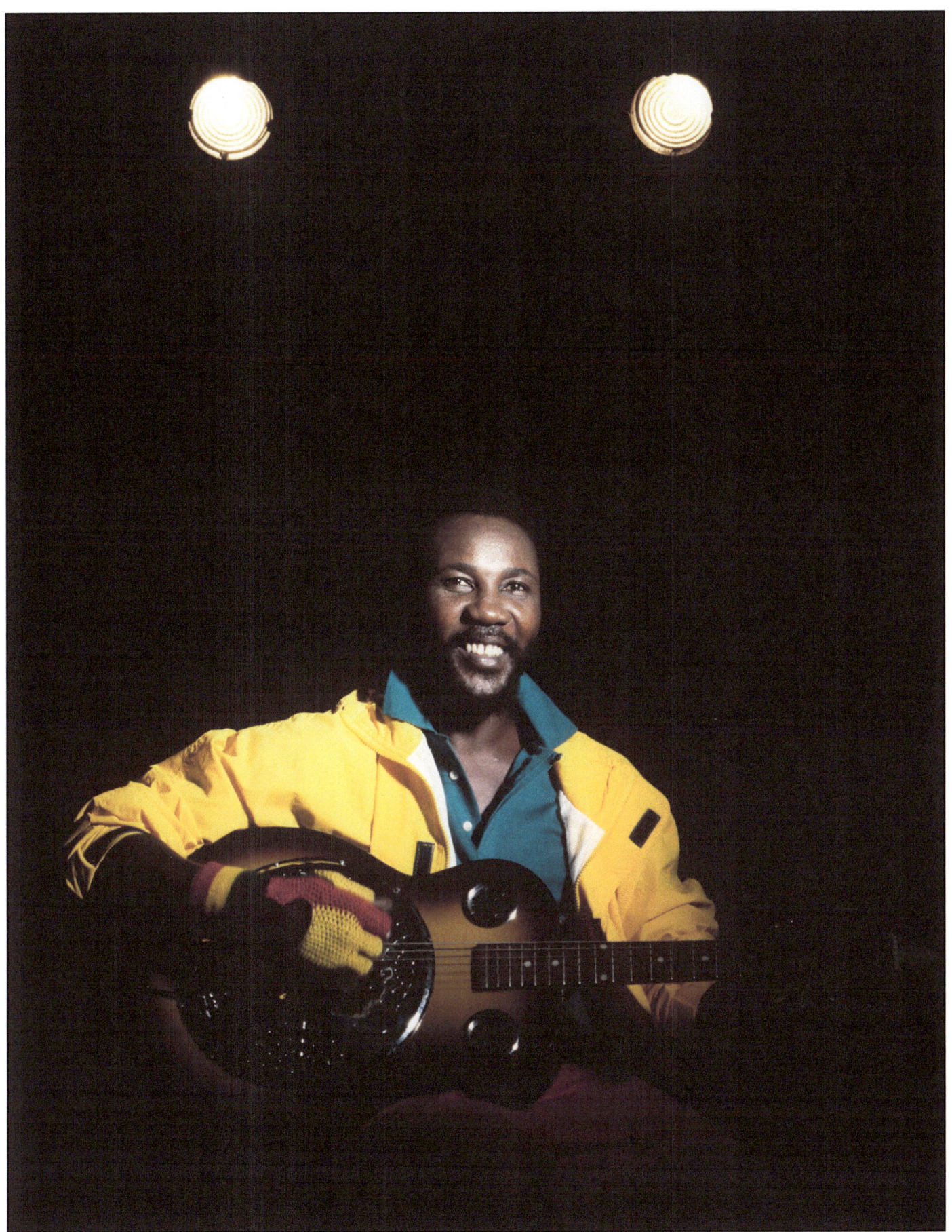

Tom Waits

I shot Tom twice, once for
Interview and once for SPIN.
Tom is a joy to shoot. Here he
is in the kitchen of a restaurant
in Chinatown, NYC where
he knew the owner and we
made a break for lunch.
I have so many wonderful shots
of Tom that he is going to get
his own book. Eventually...

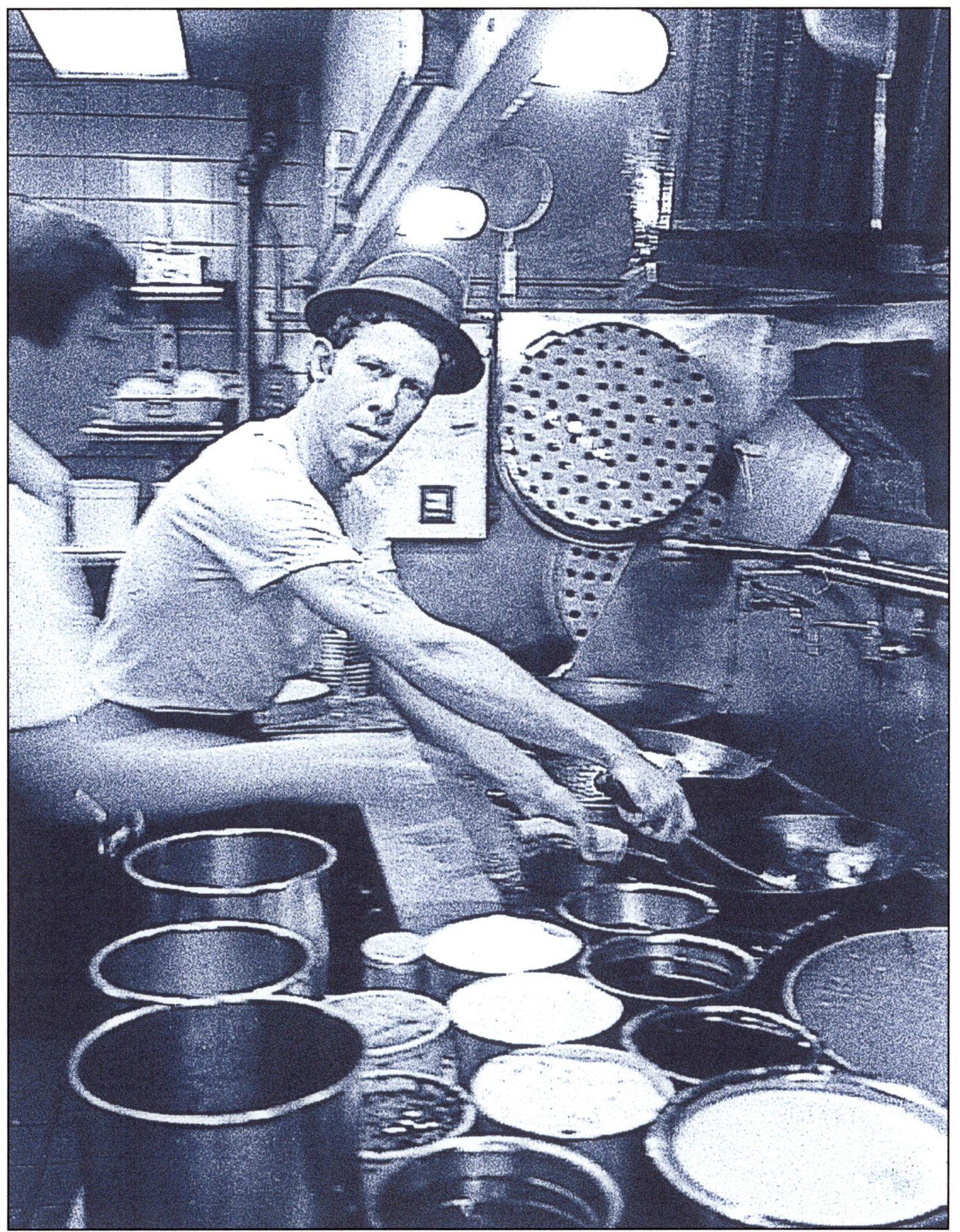

Andy Warhol

Here he is at Studio 54 looking shy. He knew damned well who I was. I worked for his magazine "Interview" and processed his personal films.

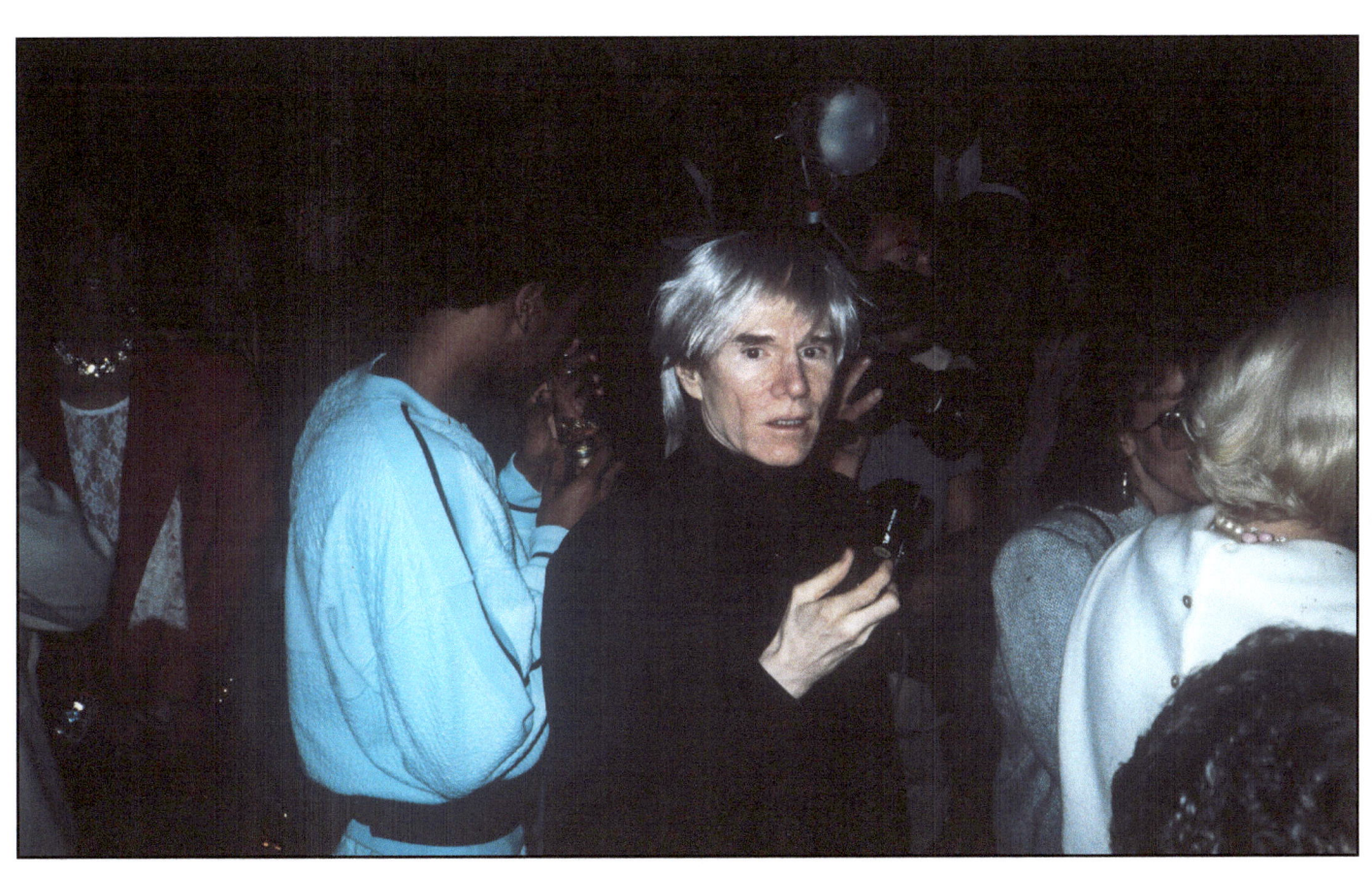

Webb Wilder

The last of the full-grown men.
A rocker from Nashville. This
shot was an early film assembly
before the daze of Photoshop.
We had to end the shooting
when the background paper
caught fire. Luckily, the
sprinklers didn't go off...

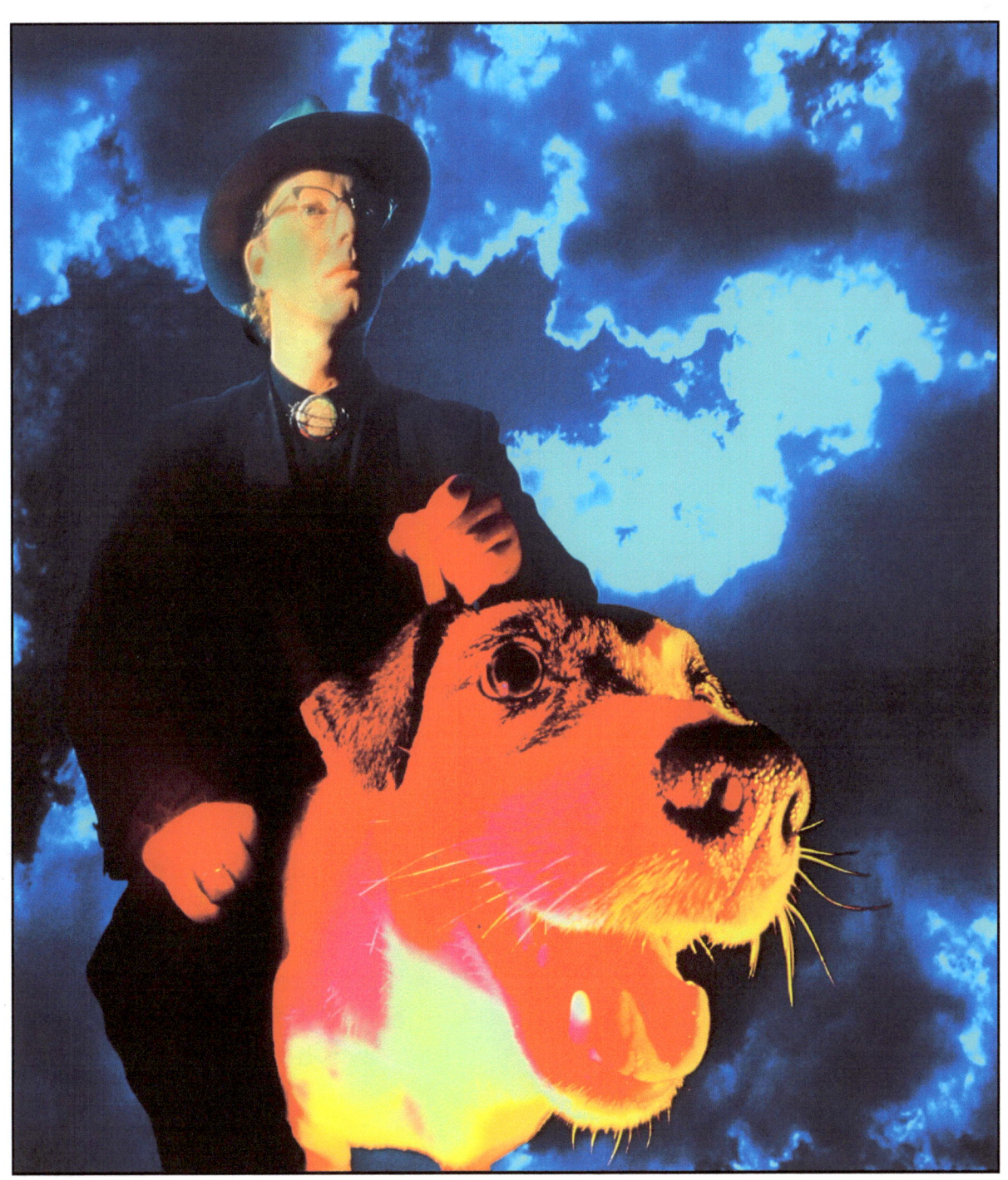

Billy Gibbons

It really isn't fair to Dusty and
Frank of ZZ Top to only show
Billy, but he is one of my
favorite guitarists. I snuck into
a 1970 concert in Pensacola, FL
when I was in the Navy and
have been a fan ever since.
It was a high point of my career
when I shot ZZ Top for
SPIN magazine.

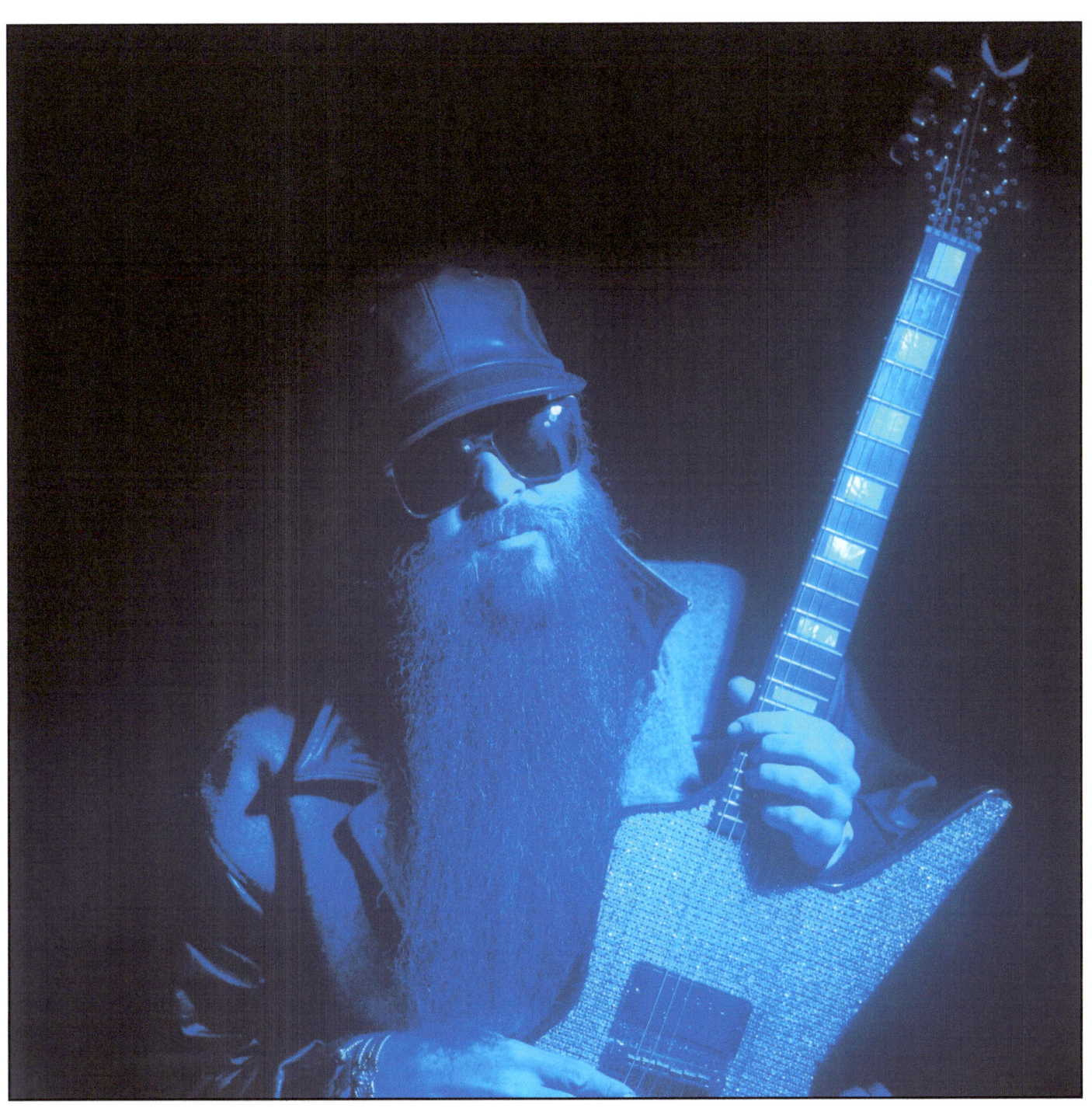

THIS IS HIP-HOP

So I was standing in the middle of Herald Square, Manhattan, where 34th, Broadway and Sixth cross. By Macy's. There was such a traffic gridlock that I was contemplating going down into the subway and just go under all that mess.

As I was considering the options, I heard music blasting out of one particular car that was stuck in the jam. I recognized the music to be "TransEurope Express" by the German new wave band, Kraftwerk. I knew that tune from my nights at the Mudd Club, my favorite hangout. At that late-night joint, one heard all the punk rock and new wave hits.

What! There were new words to the blasting music...

Rock! Rock! The Planet Rock!

I had heard "Rapsody" by Blondie', "White Lines" by GrandMaster Flash, but thought those songs were just more New Wave.

A month later, I had an assignment to photograph Afrika Bambaataa and Soulsonic Force in my studio. Four very large black men arrived carrying large garbage bags.

What was in those bags? I was hoping it was weed and they were going to pay me with it...OK...

They proceeded to pull out four very elaborate costumes and dress themselves as a Viking, a Roman soldier, a globe? and an indian chief.

It was a wave alright, a tidal wave. Hip-Hop is the longest running popular music trend in the history of recorded music.

I am Ameri-African. I was born in Morocco. Since that day in 1982, I worked with the whole Cold Chillin' label, RunDMC, Christoper Walker aka The Notorious B.I.G, Big Daddy Kane, Biz Markie and many others.

Hip-Hop! Be-Bop! Don't Stop!

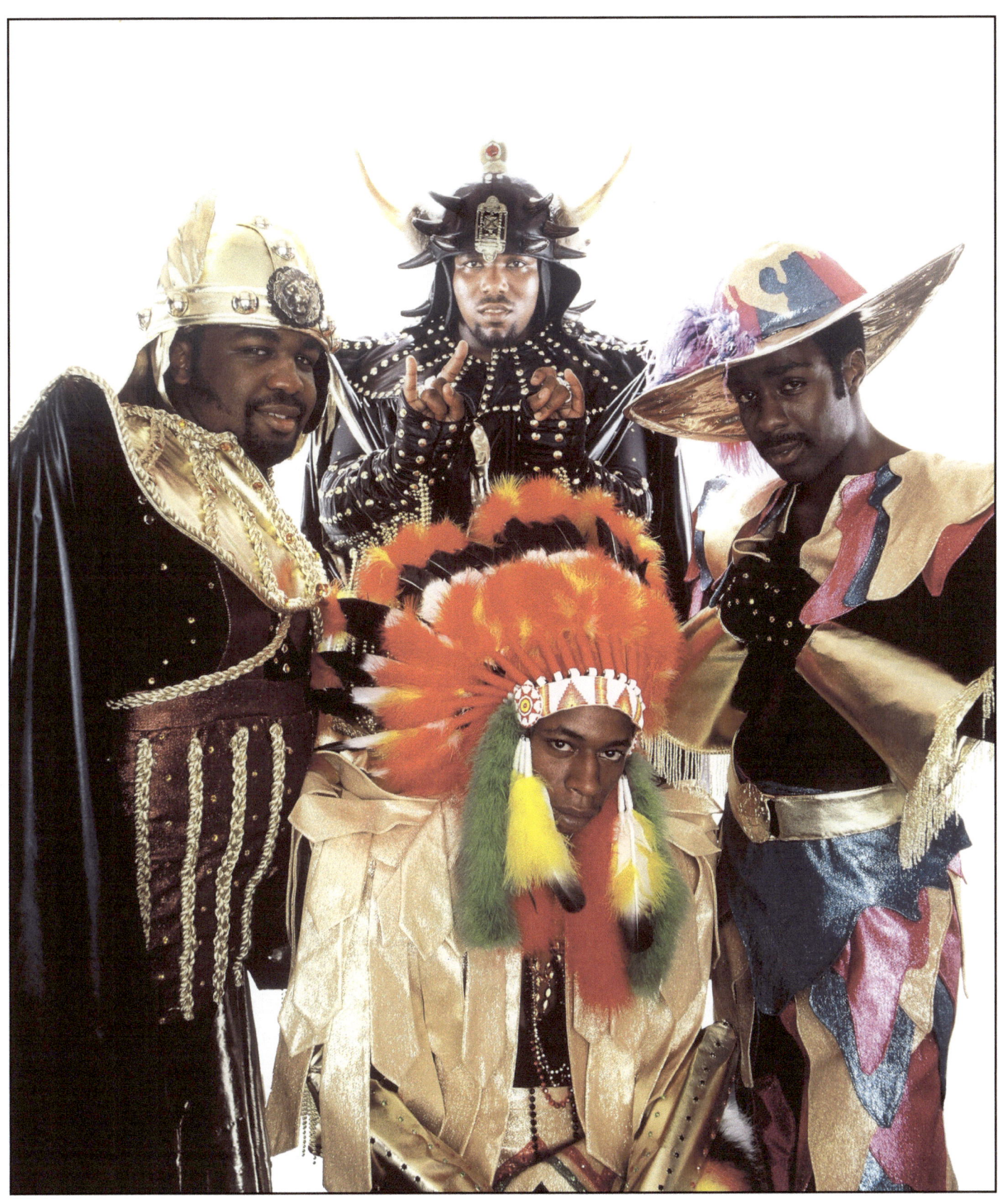

Alphonso Ribiero
aka
The Tap Dance Kind

This young Broadway star had
a dance album recorded.
He needed a cover.
Michael Jackson gave him the
red jacket. The guy with the
ladder was an accident

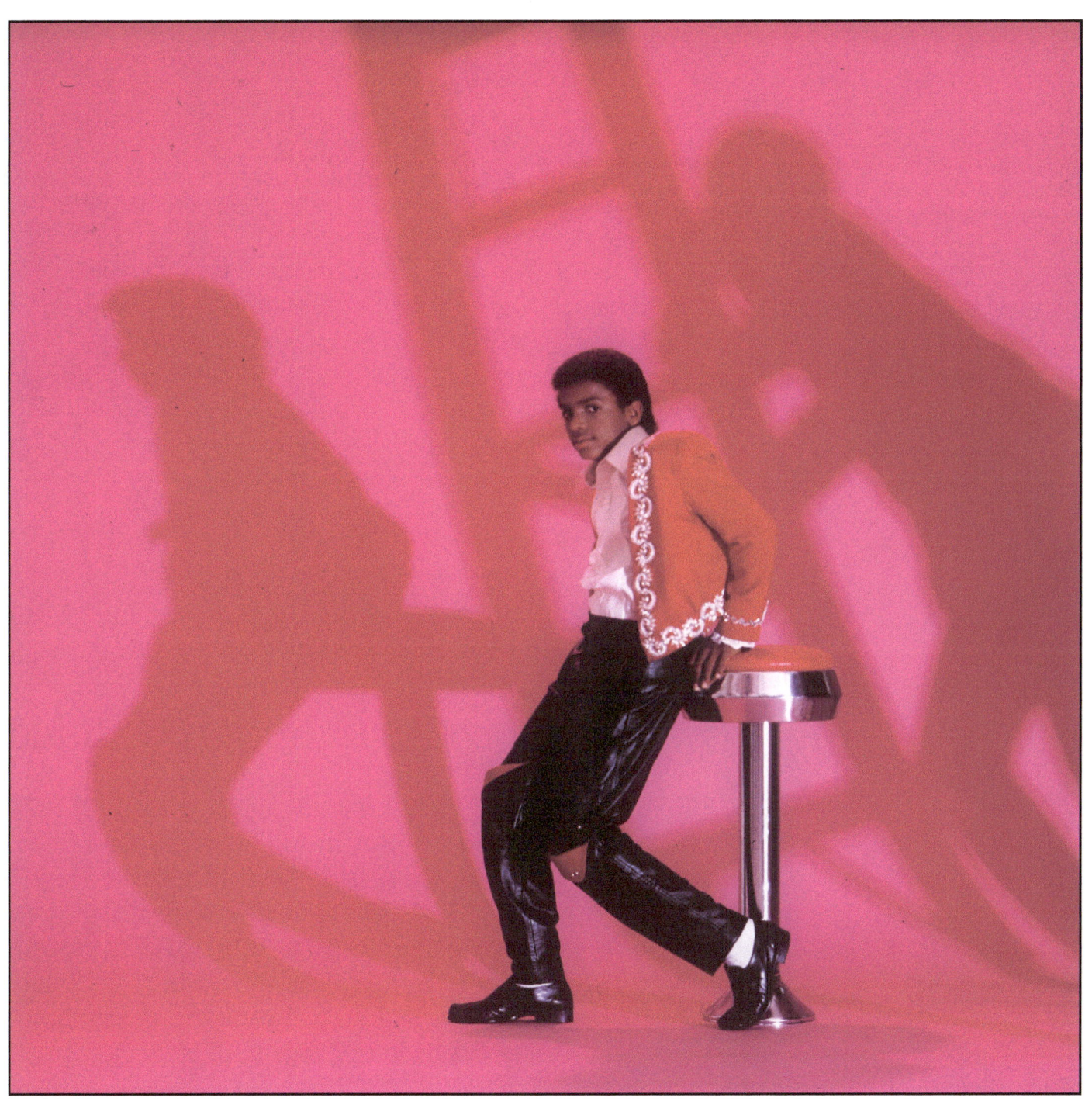

Christopher Wallace

Before he was the Notorious B.I.G.,
I photographed him in his 'hood in Bed-Stuy.
This shot is "Gimme Yo' Money!"
He's got a knife in your stomach
and DJ 50 Grand is saying
"Yeah! You better do it!"
The full story is in my book
"The Big Book of Hip-Hop Photography"

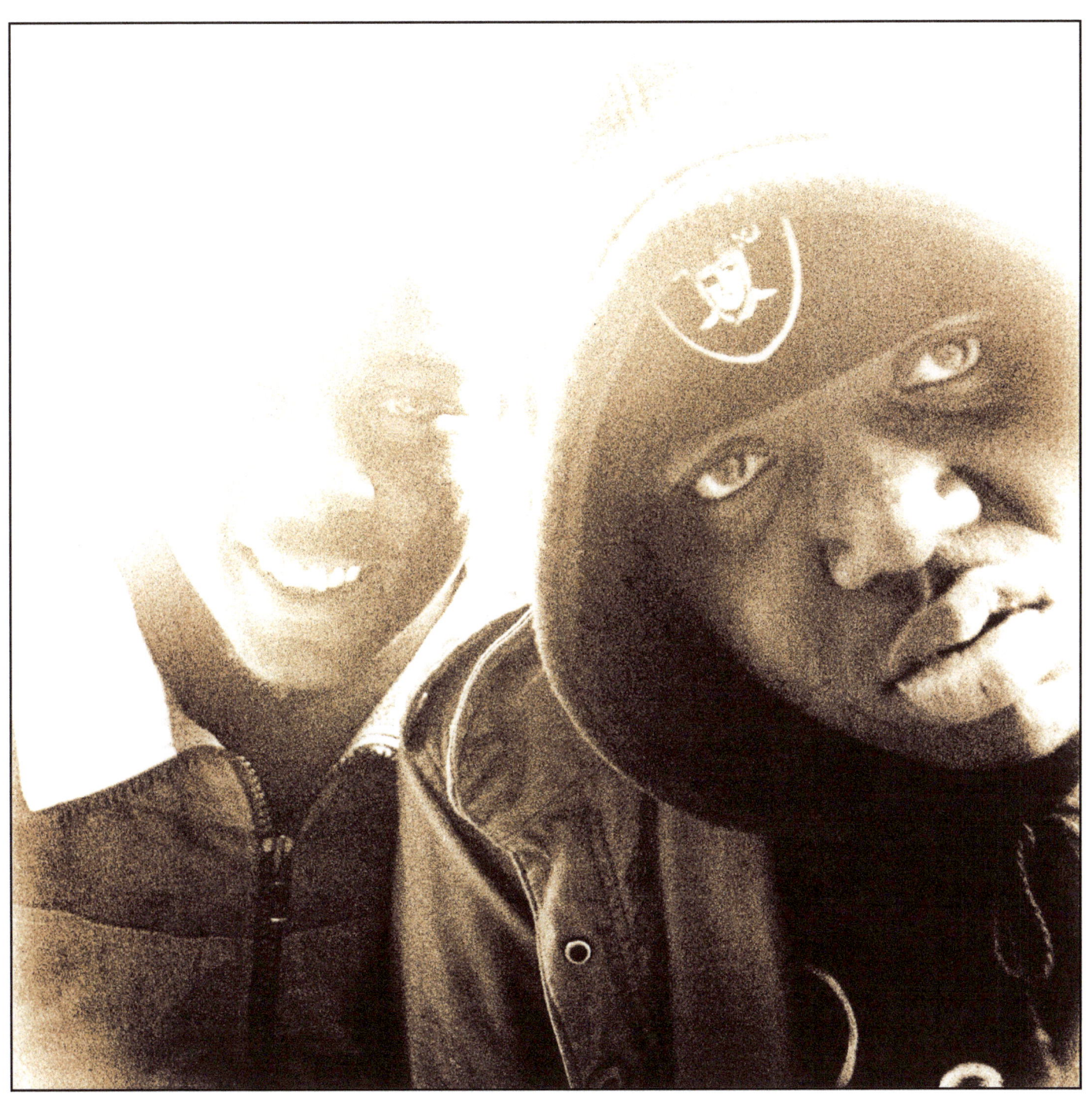

Biz Markie

Biz was always a blast to work for. I could really enhance his ideas and we always came up with good ones. He would give me the tip and I would blow it up.
Here, the Diabolical Biz is posing for the cover of his breakfast cereal, "Diabolical Crunch".
You gotta see it to believe it.

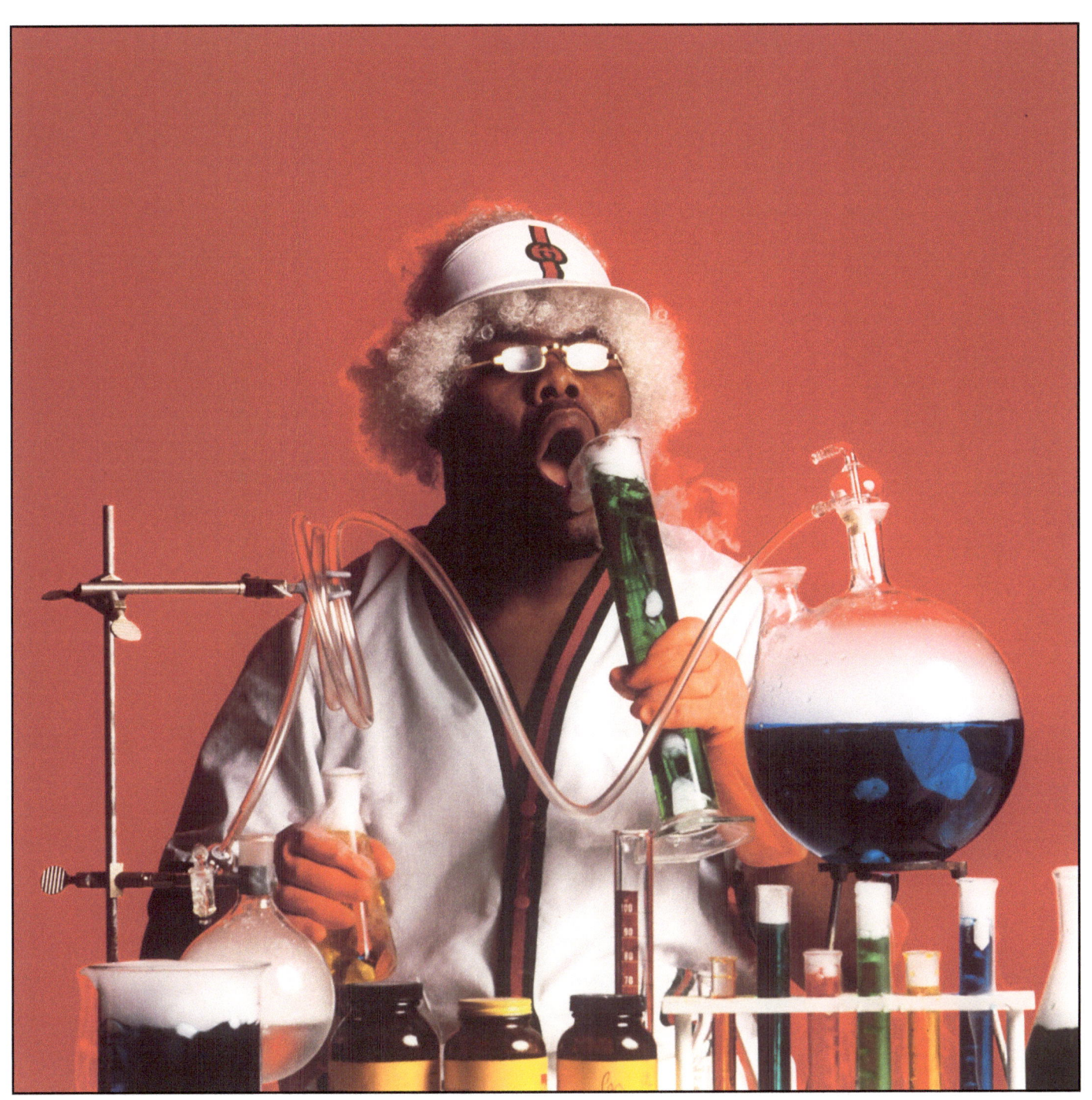

Bootsy Collins

Master Bassist.
I shot some publicity shots for
Island Records. This outdoor
shot was on the helicopter pad
of the old World Trade Center
built before the Twin Towers.

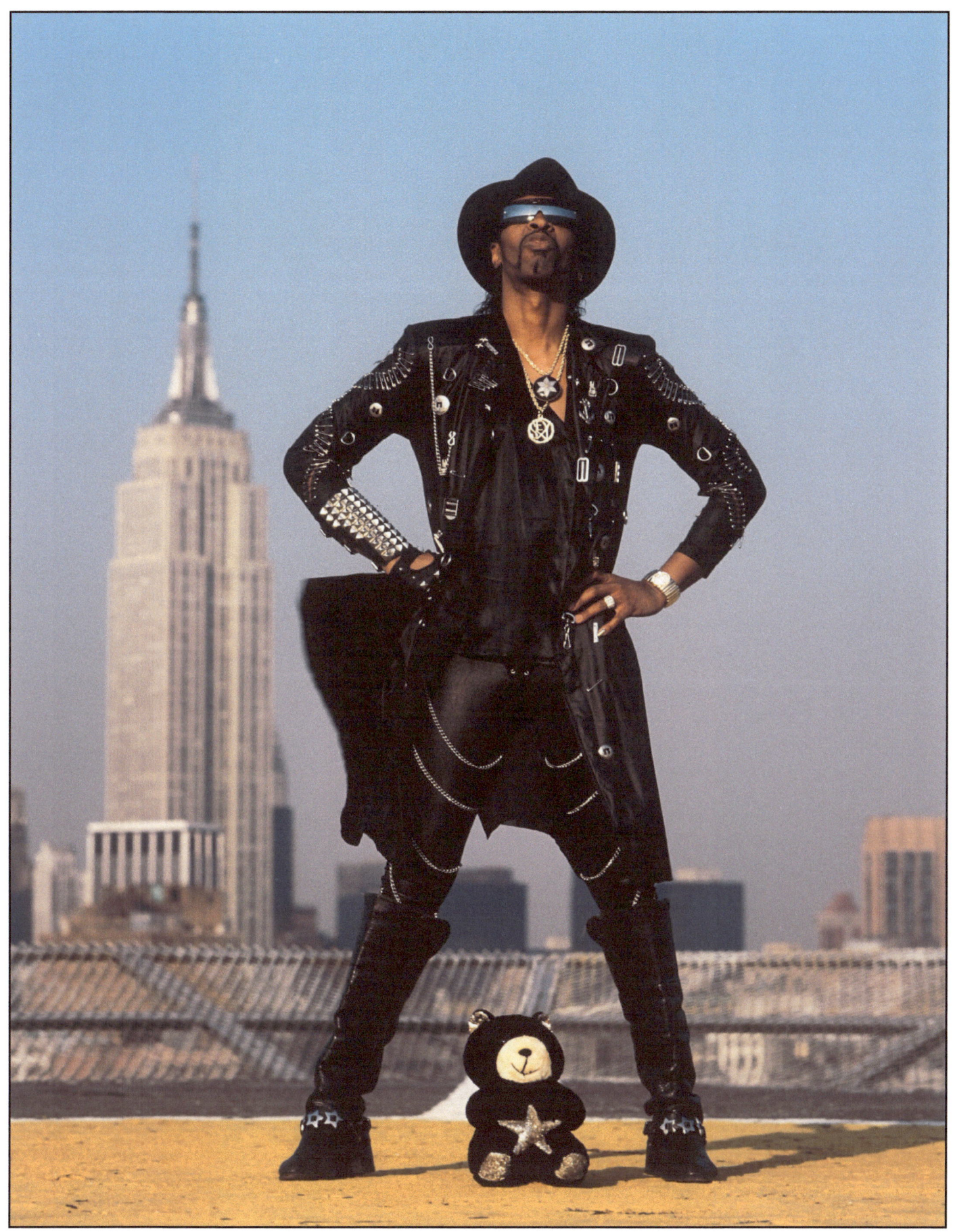

Bubba Sparxxx

I shot him in the hallway of
a German television studio
in Cologne. Where is he now?

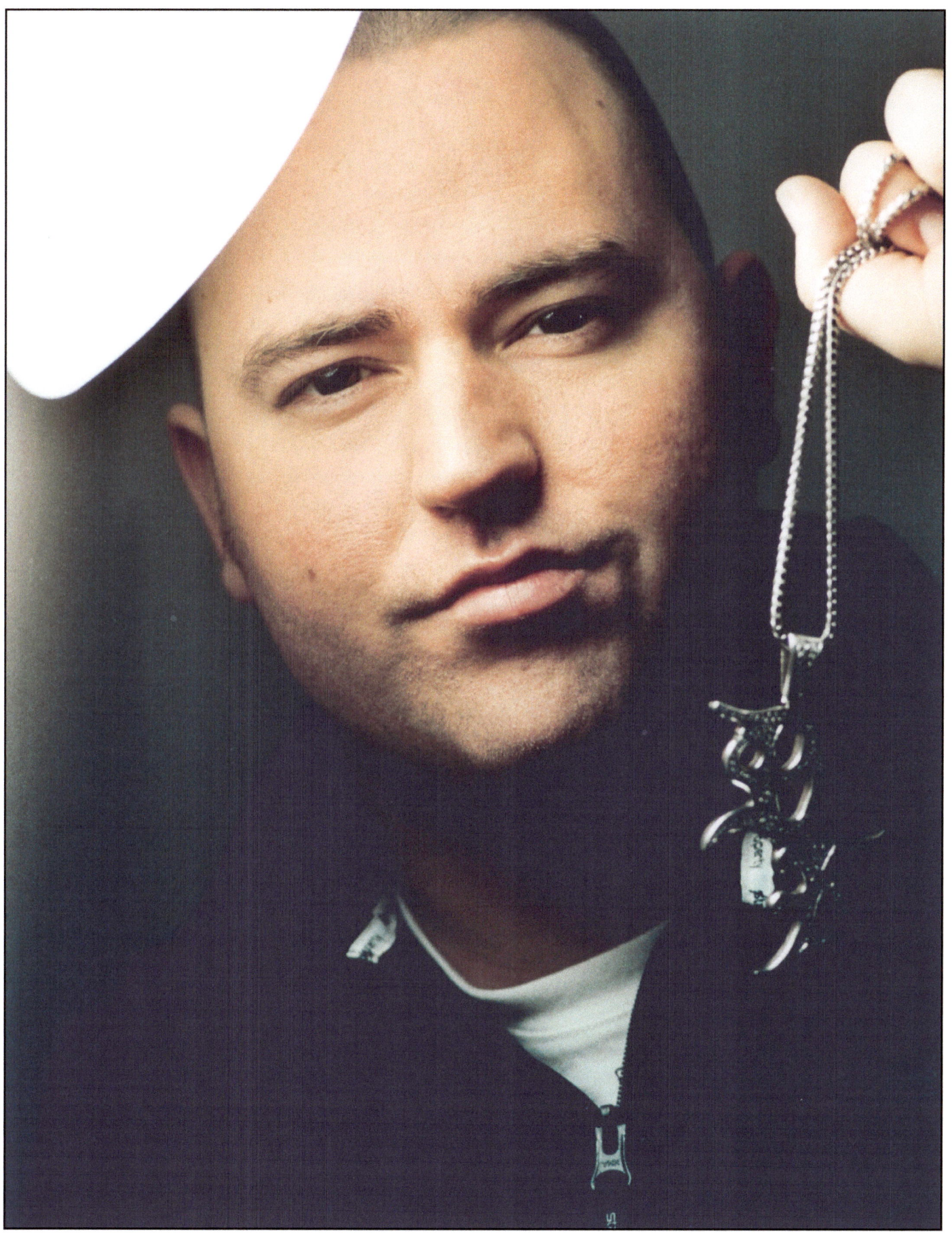

Craig G and

Marley Marl

Marley is a major producer of
Hip-Hop, Craig G is one of the
best freestylers I ever heard.
This shot was for a cover of
Craig's debut LP.

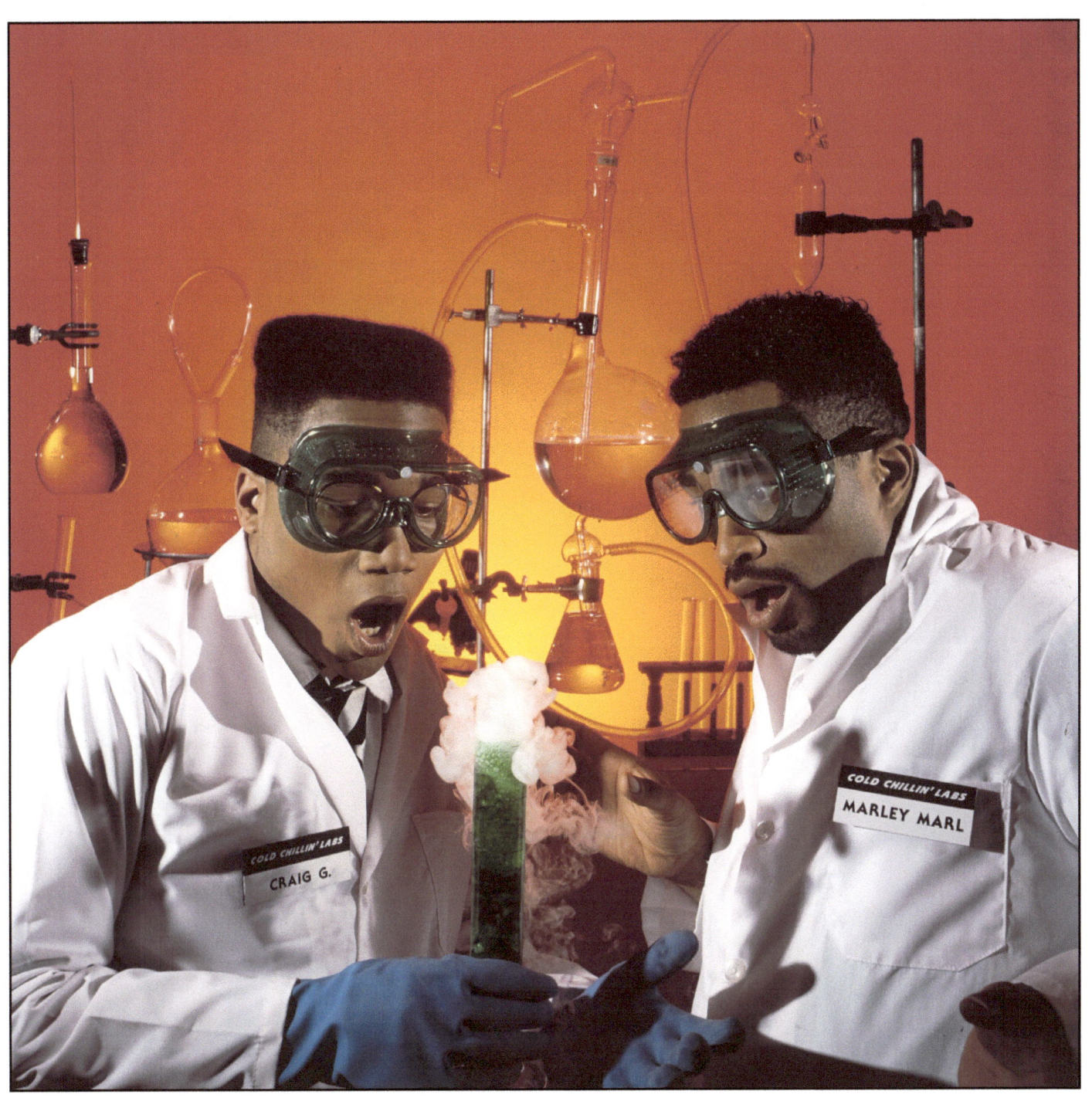

Cypress Hill

Used to say,
"Is that your age or your IQ"?
Shot them in the same
Cologne TV studio.
Short session, five shots,
15 seconds of fame...

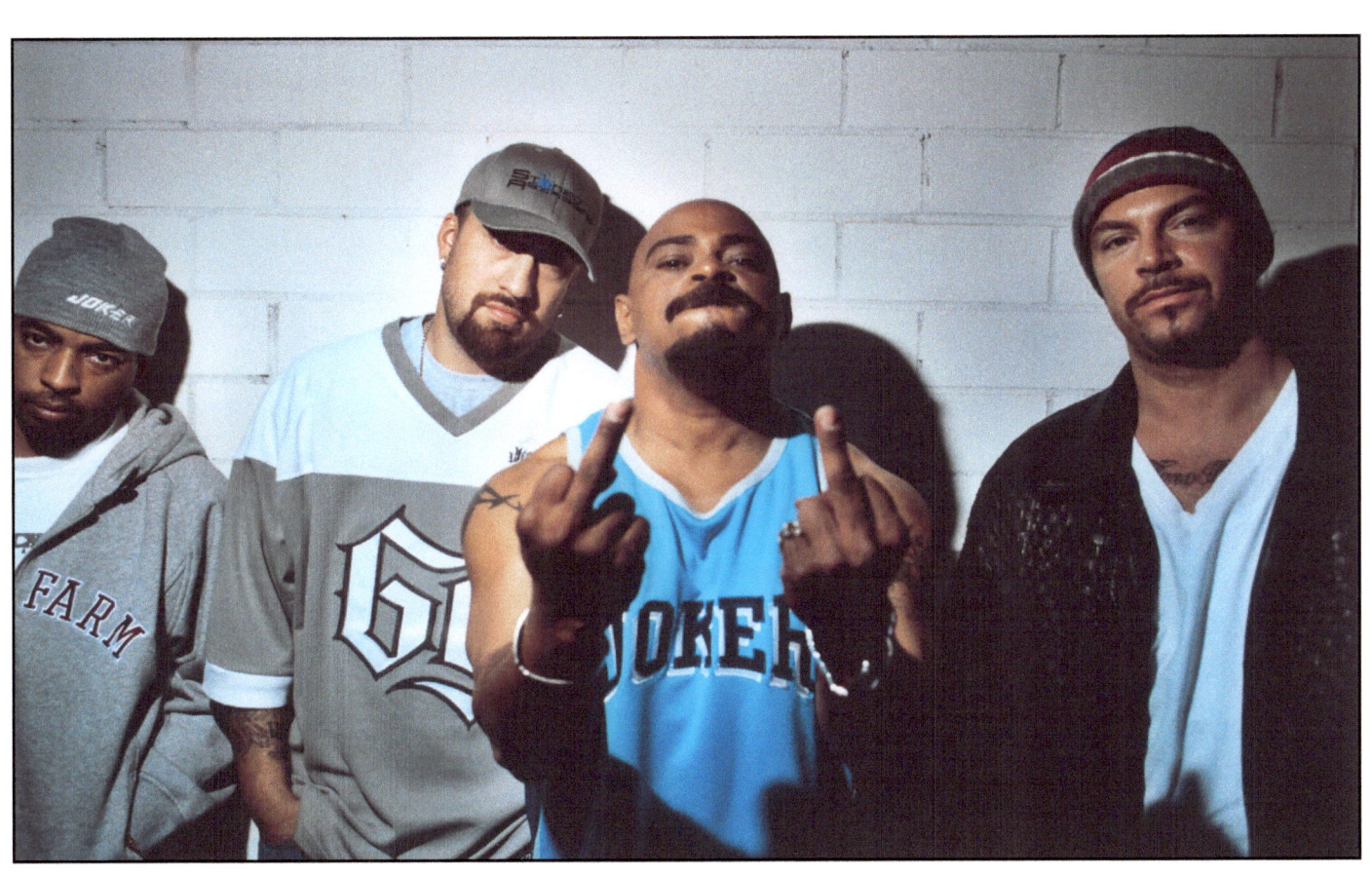

DeeDee King

aka

DeeDee Ramone

He actually quit the Ramones to
become a Hip-Hop artist.
"Funky Man"

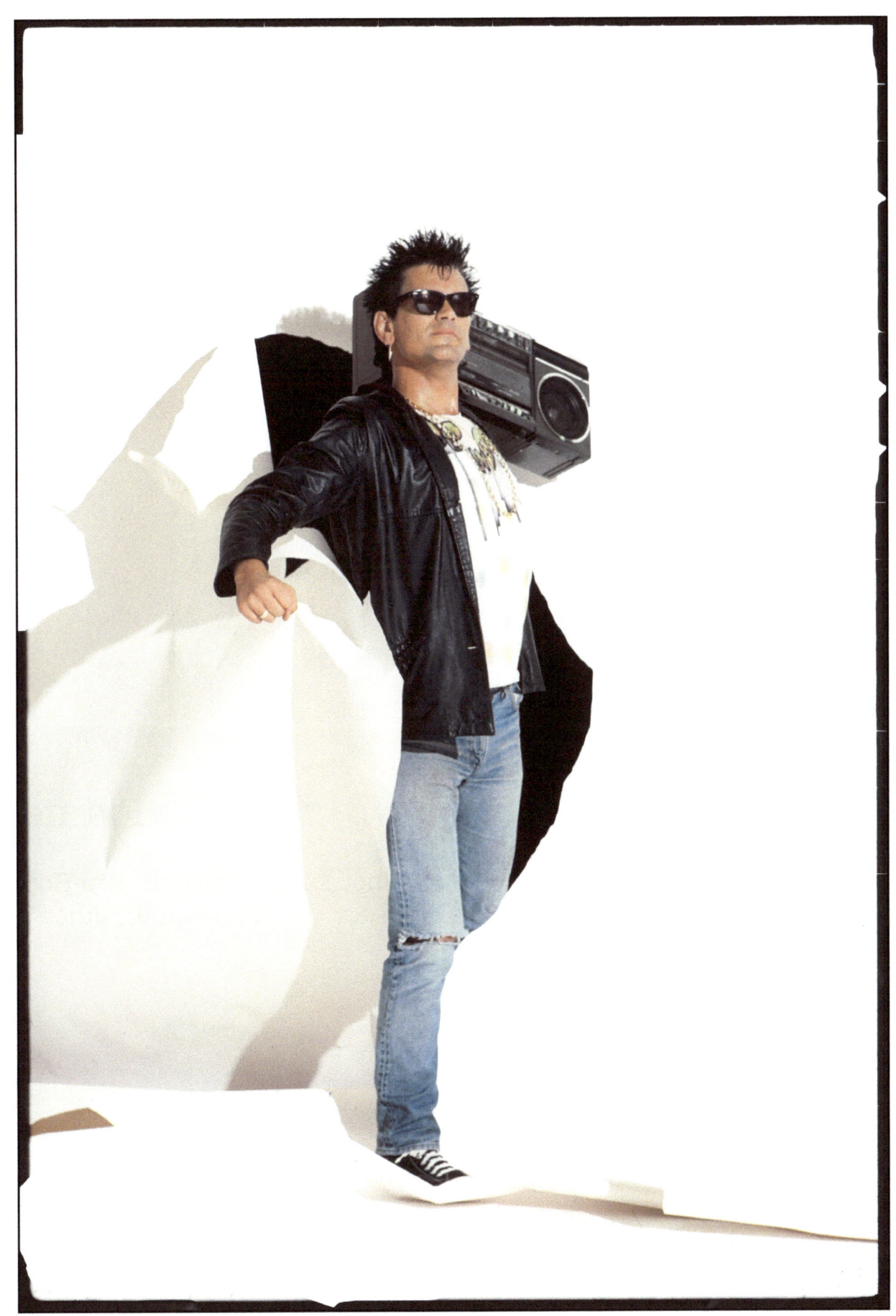

D-Flame

Shot for the German Hip-Hop
magazine, "Juice".

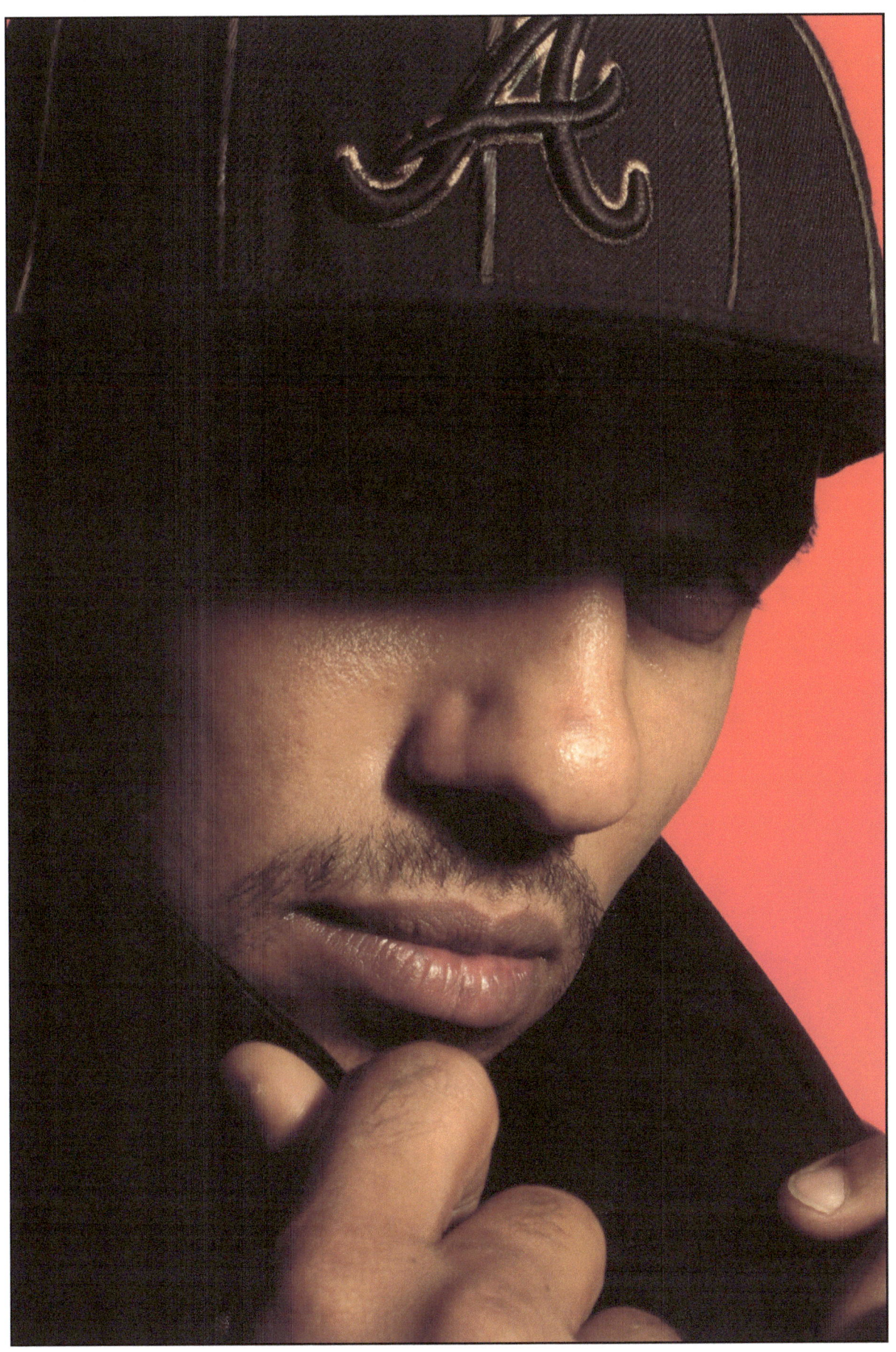

Tatwaffe

means murder weapon. I let
him use a shot from this shoot
for the cover of a single.
He couldn't pay me as he said
he had no money. The single
went platinum. Now he's got
money and I don't...

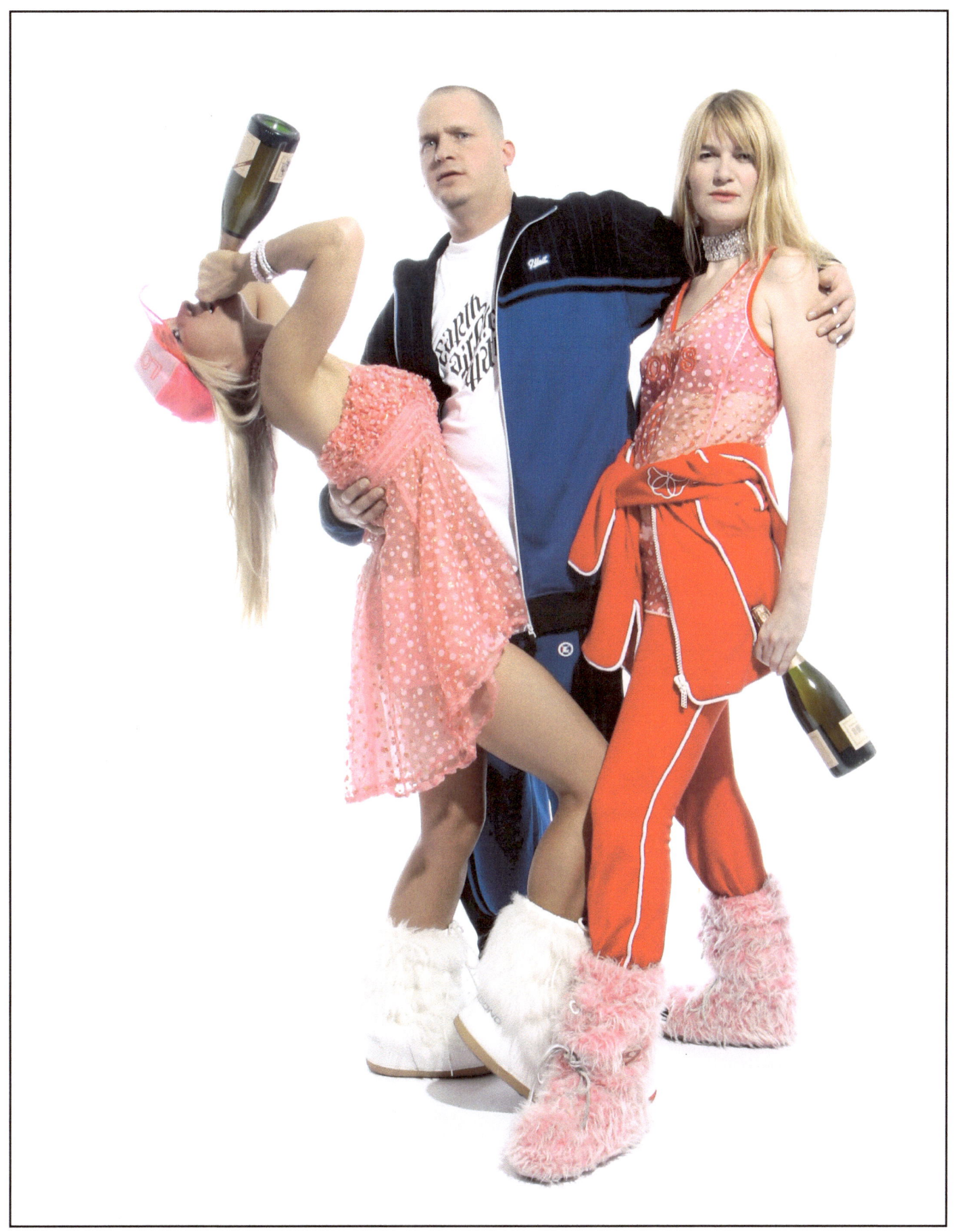

Double J

The hit maker, I mean hit man.

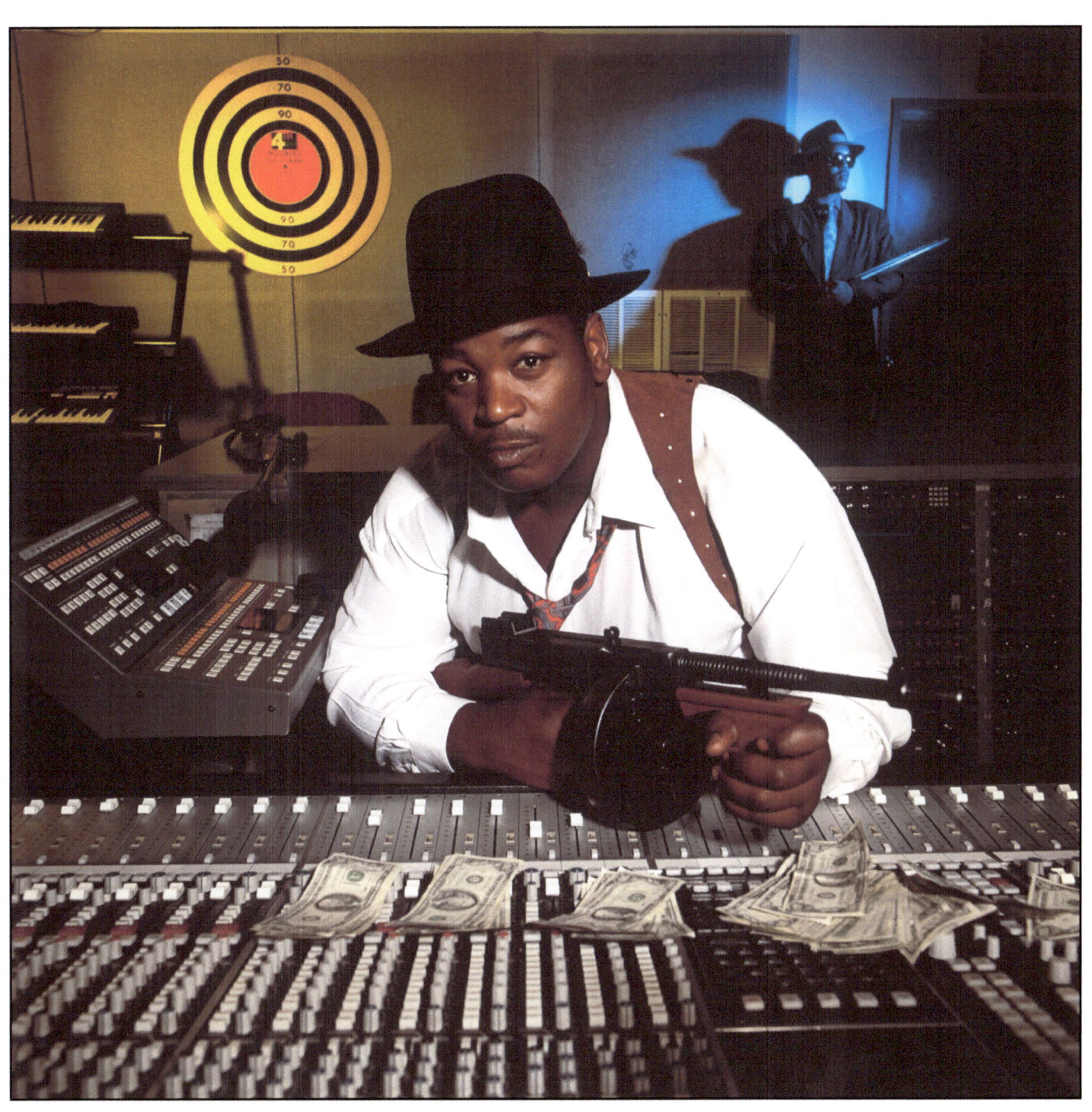

Eko Fresh

A German rapper.
I shot this for Juice magazine.

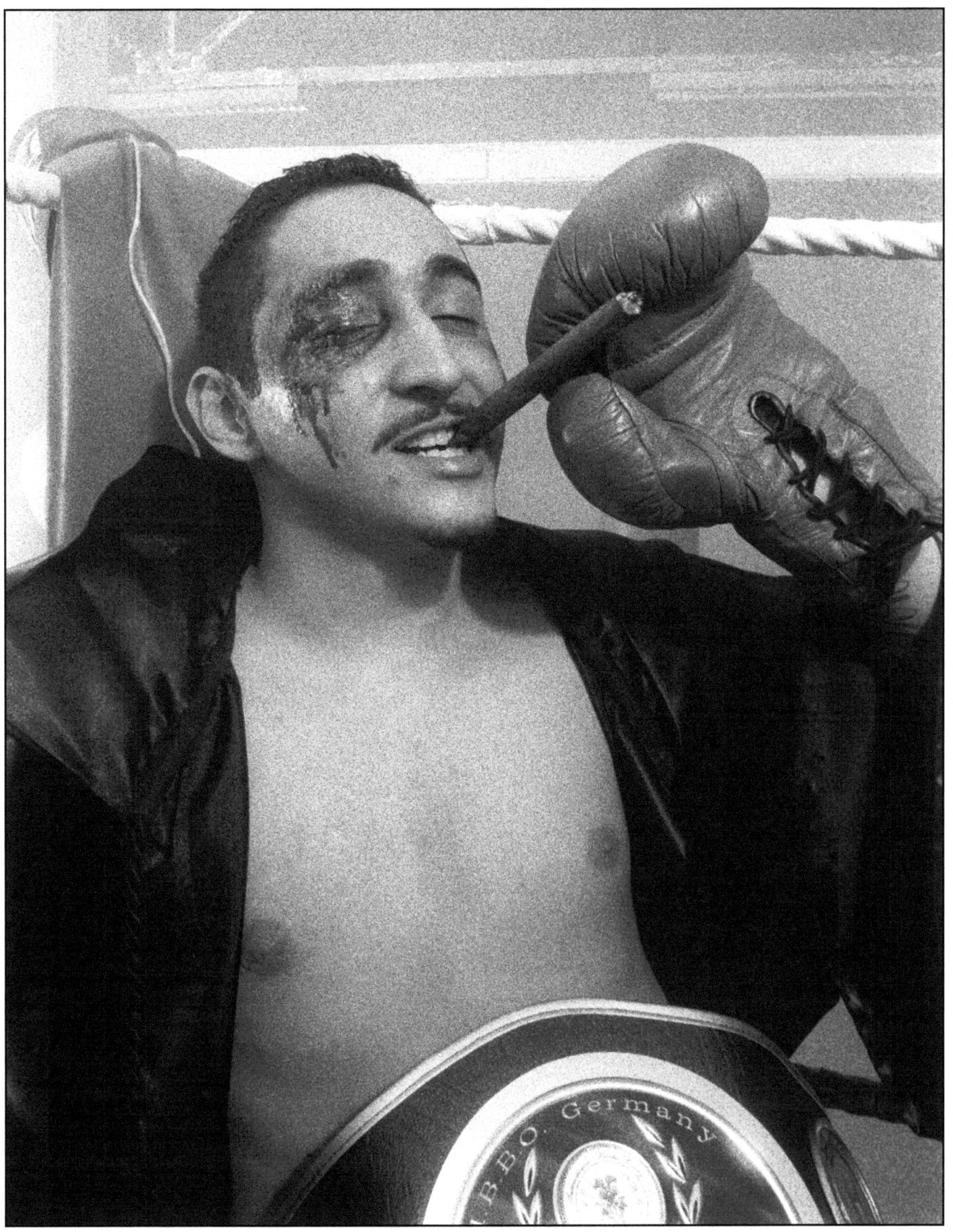

EPMD

Shot in Amsterdam for Juice
magazine. I had them "lagging"
or pitching quarters.
A primitive form of gambling.
Whose coin lies closest
to the wall.

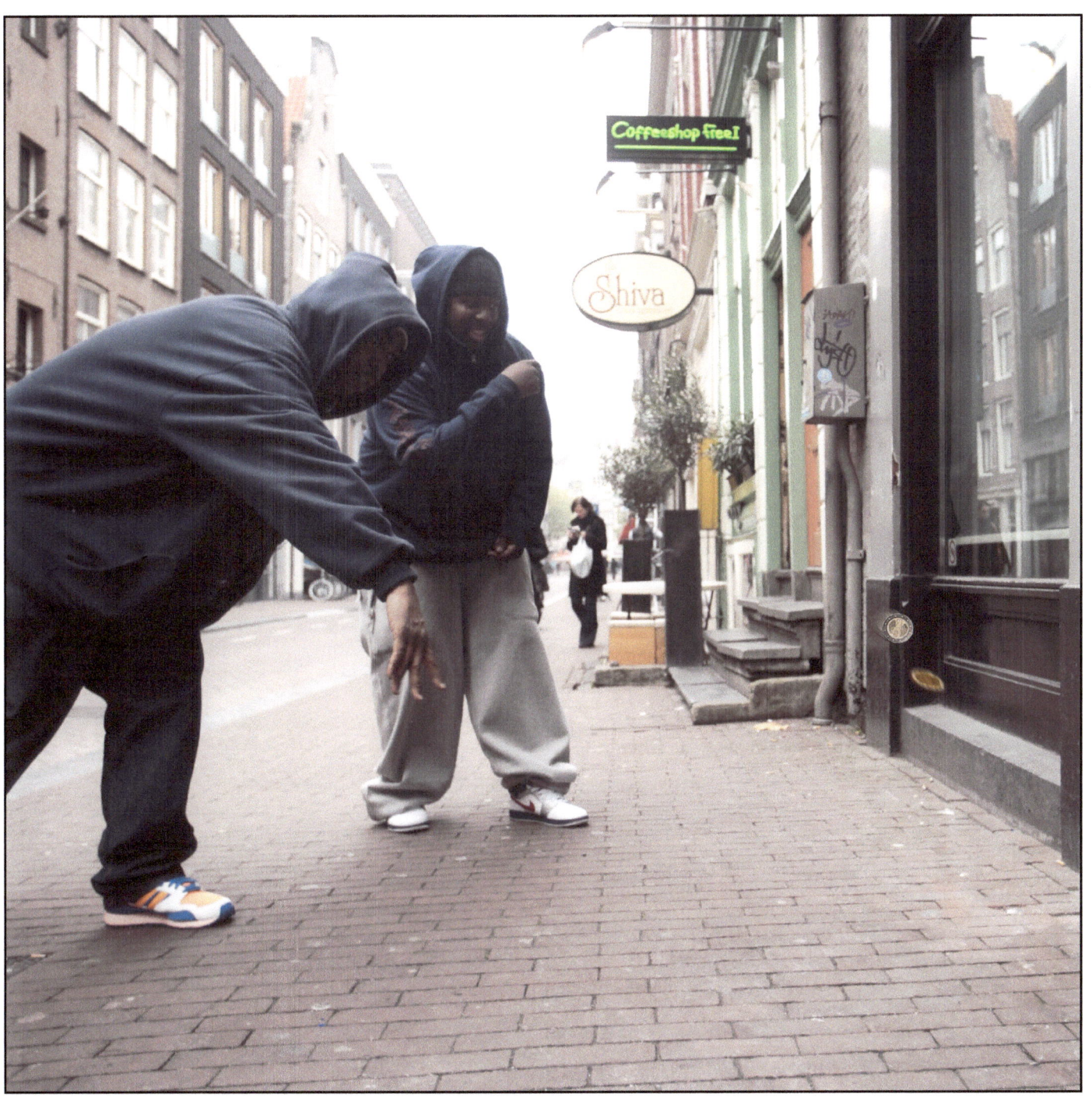

Eric Soul

A French DJ channeling the
ether onto the platter.
He was sharing the evening's
turntables with Bambaataa.

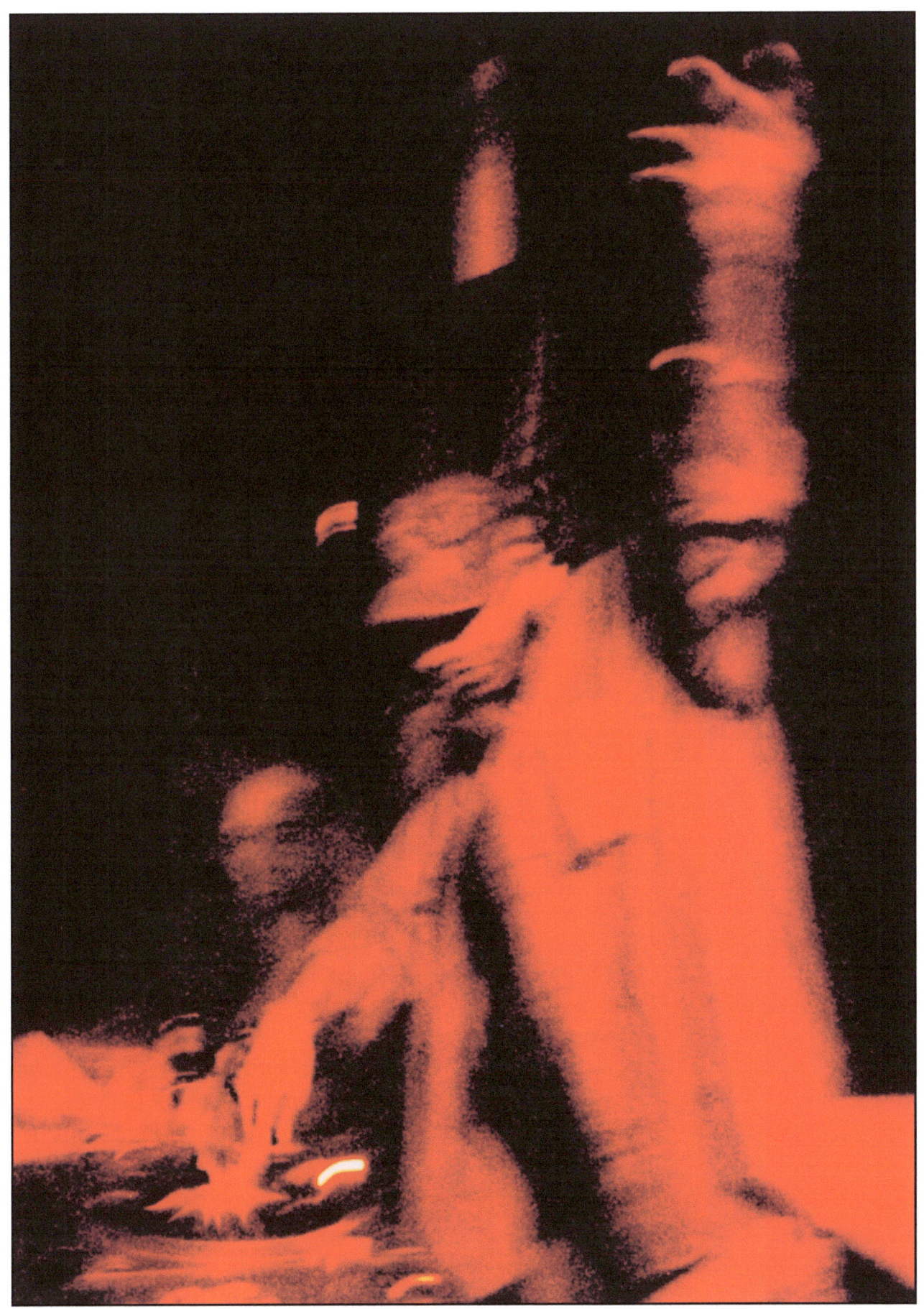

The Genius aka GZA of WuTang Clan

The Genius wanted to "out-gold"
all the other rappers. Rather
than wear a dozen gold
necklaces, I built him
a room of gold. He is wearing
my father's Damascus silk
bathrobe with little black men
hunting cheetahs

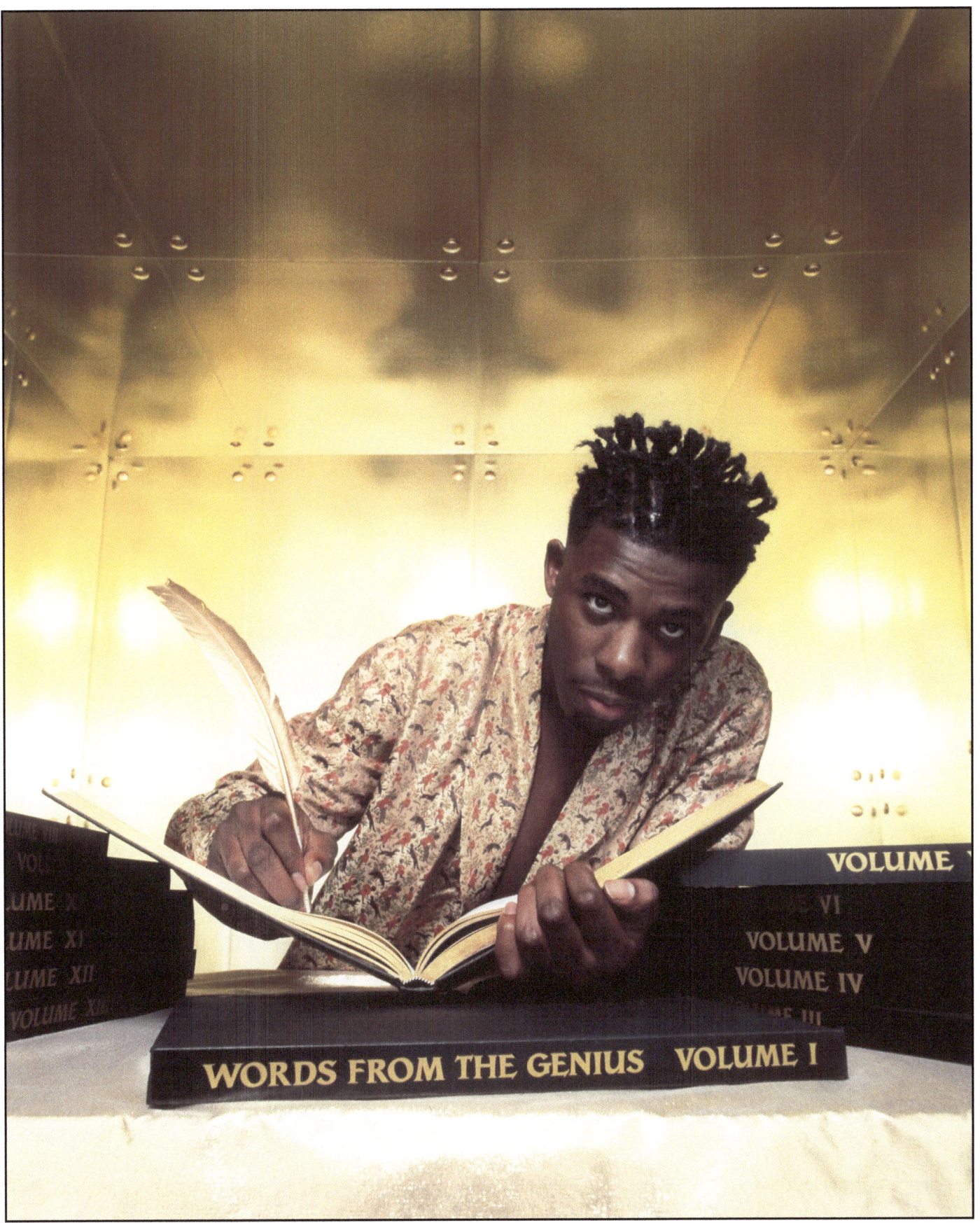

Kool G Rap
and DJ Polo

Wanted to rob a bank with
guns, but guns were
verboten by the label.
This Rube Goldberg attempt to
assassinate two undercover
police caused quite a stir, but
became the main graphic on
billboards on Flatbush Avenue
and 125th Street.

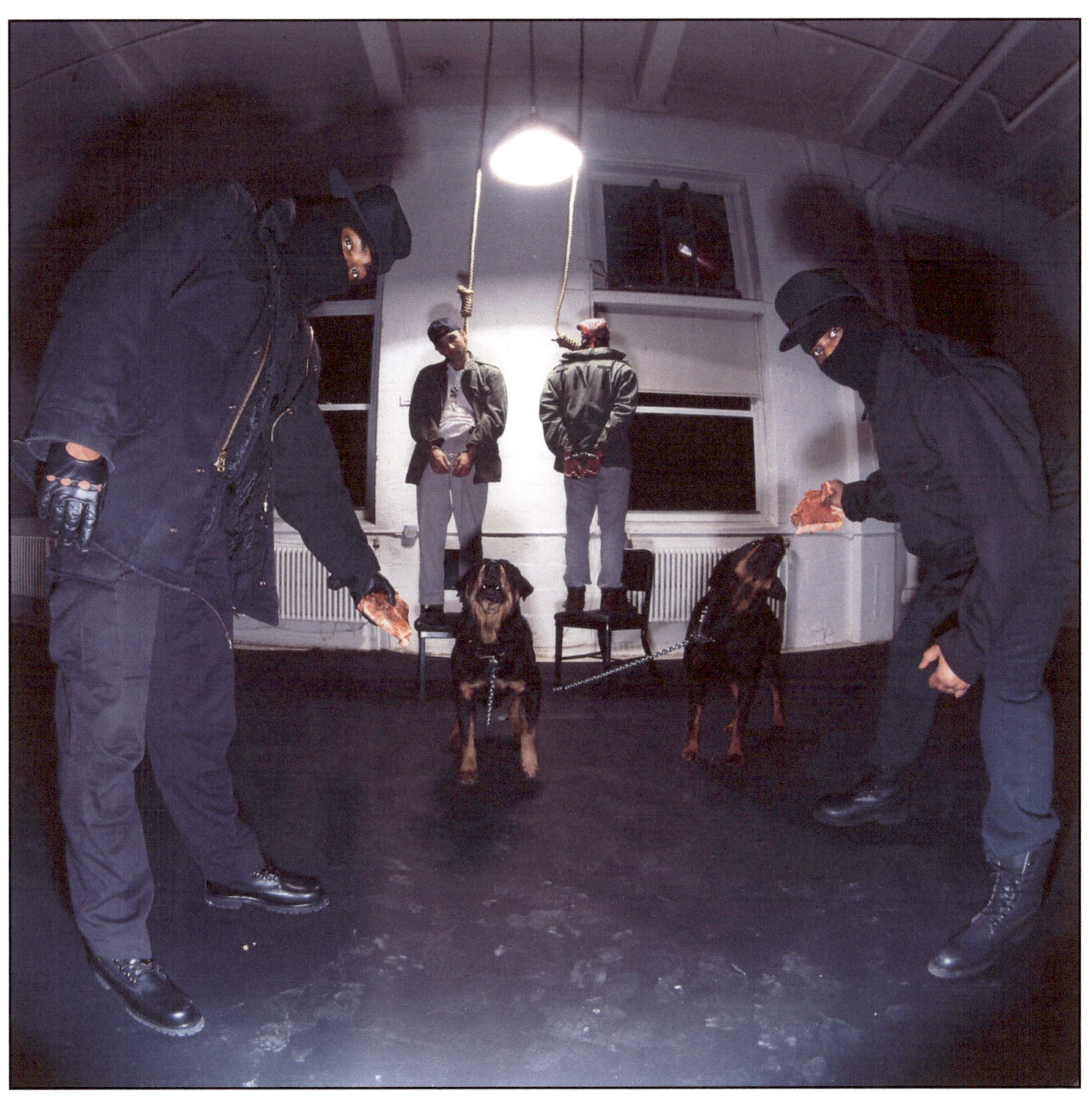

Huss and Hoden

German musicians who didn't
want to show their faces.
Good for them.

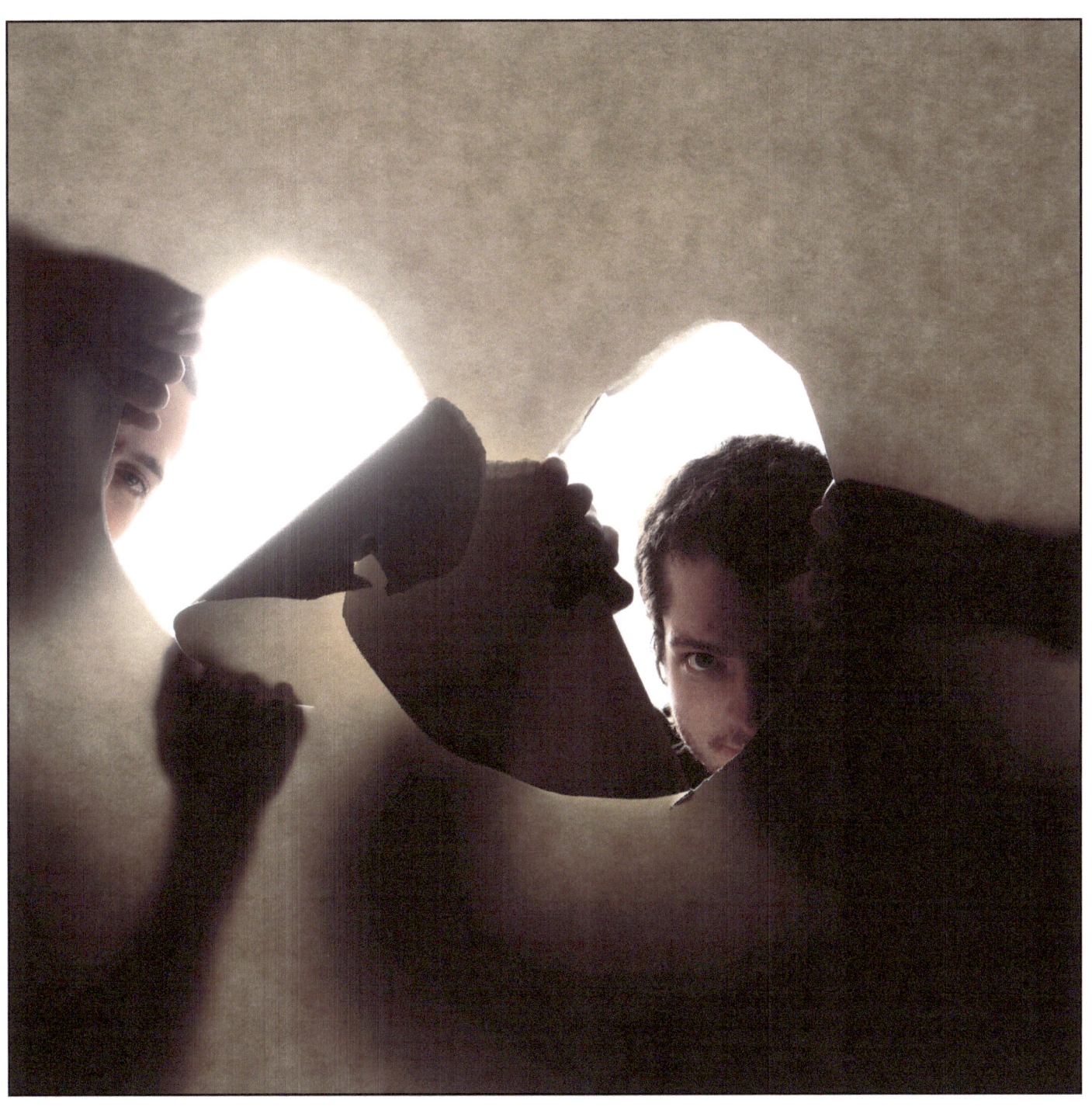

Isis

She was a member of XCLAN,
the black nationalist clan
from Brooklyn led by
Lumumba Carson, who is
standing in the background.
I did a lot of work with
Lumumba that is detailed
in The Big Book...

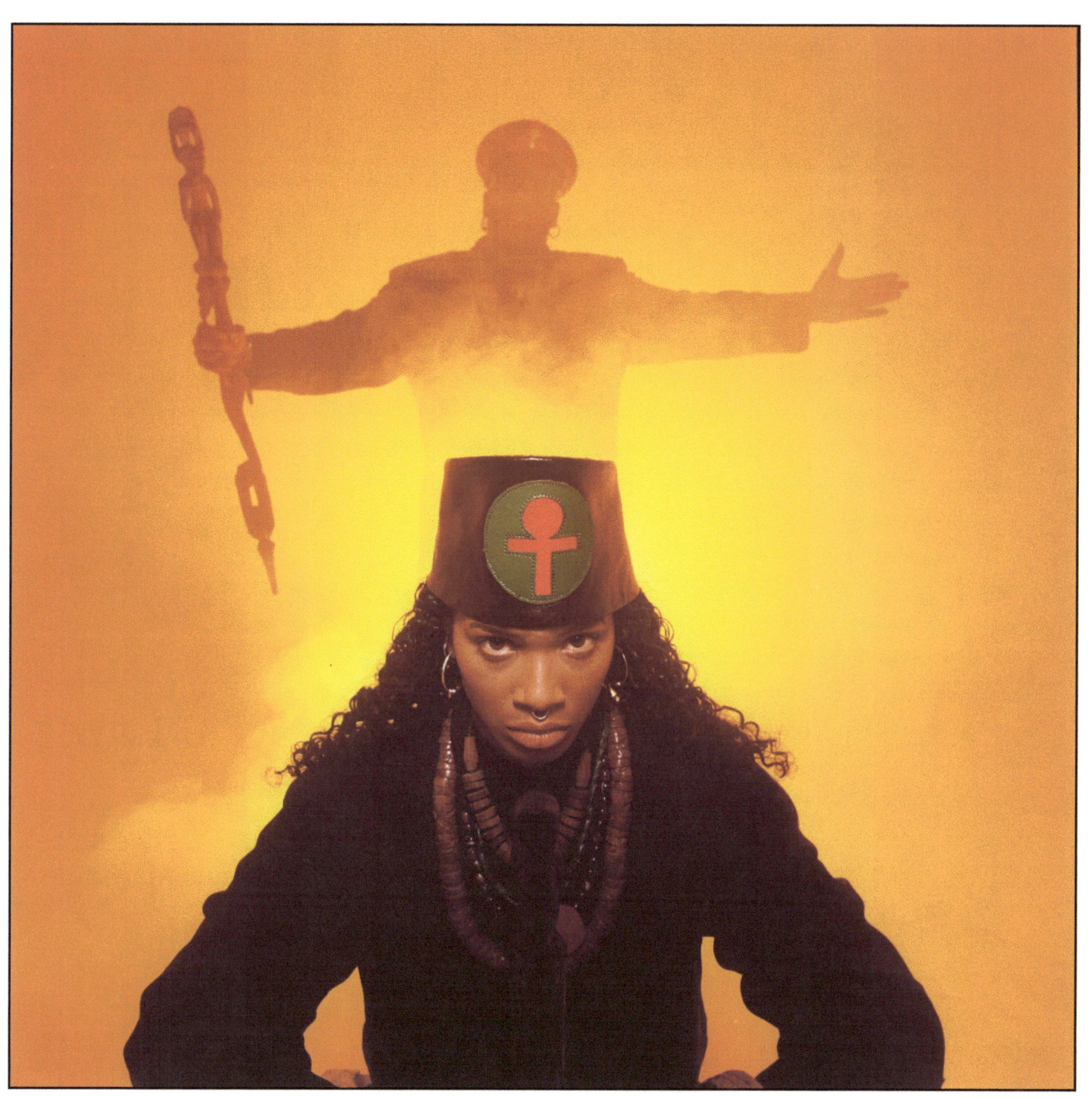

J Rawls

I shot him in a shoe store
for Juice magazine.

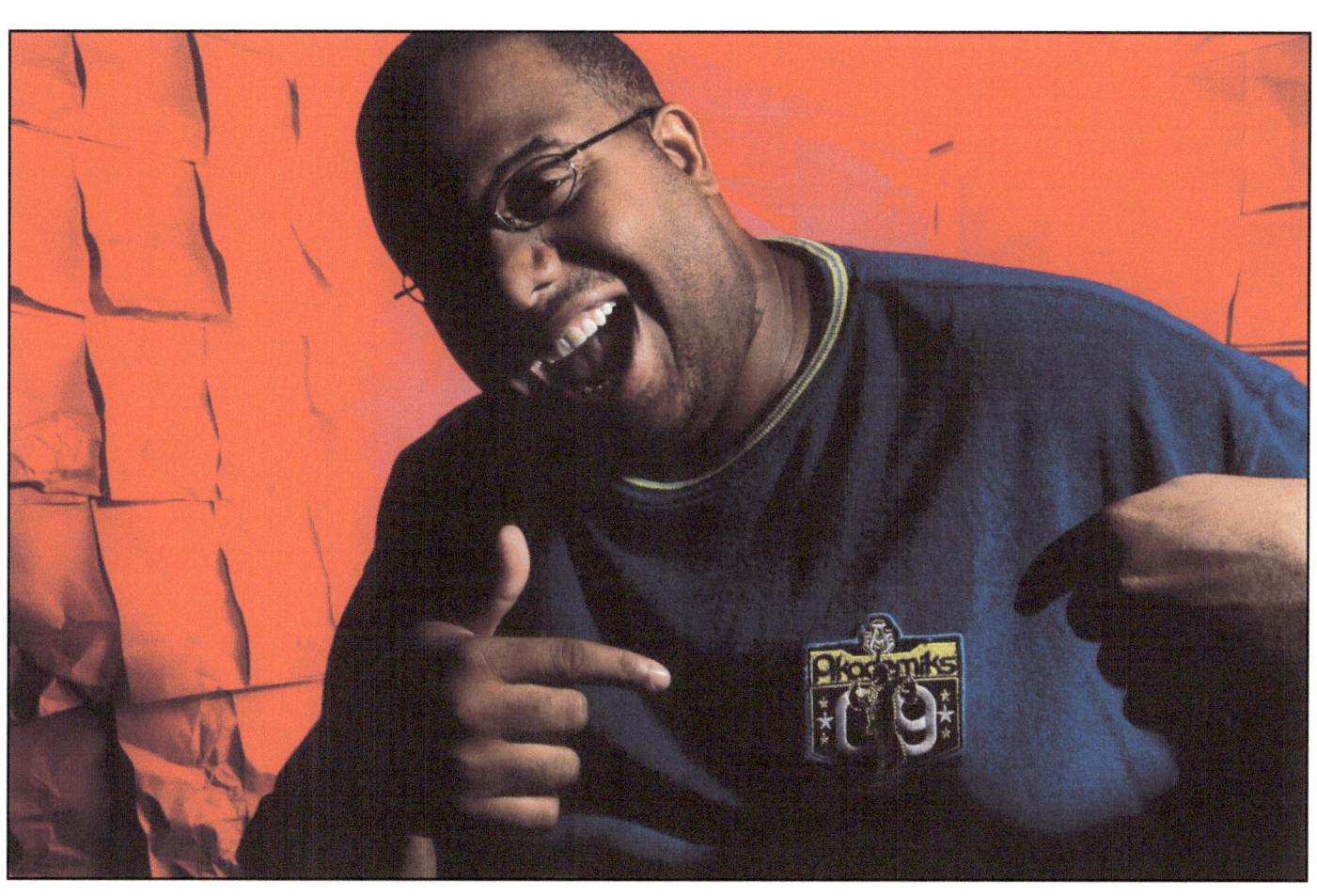

The Original Juice Crew Allstars

Here are most of the artists on the Cold Chillin' label. Polo and Shanté are missing. Hardly anybody can name ALL of the cats in this shot.

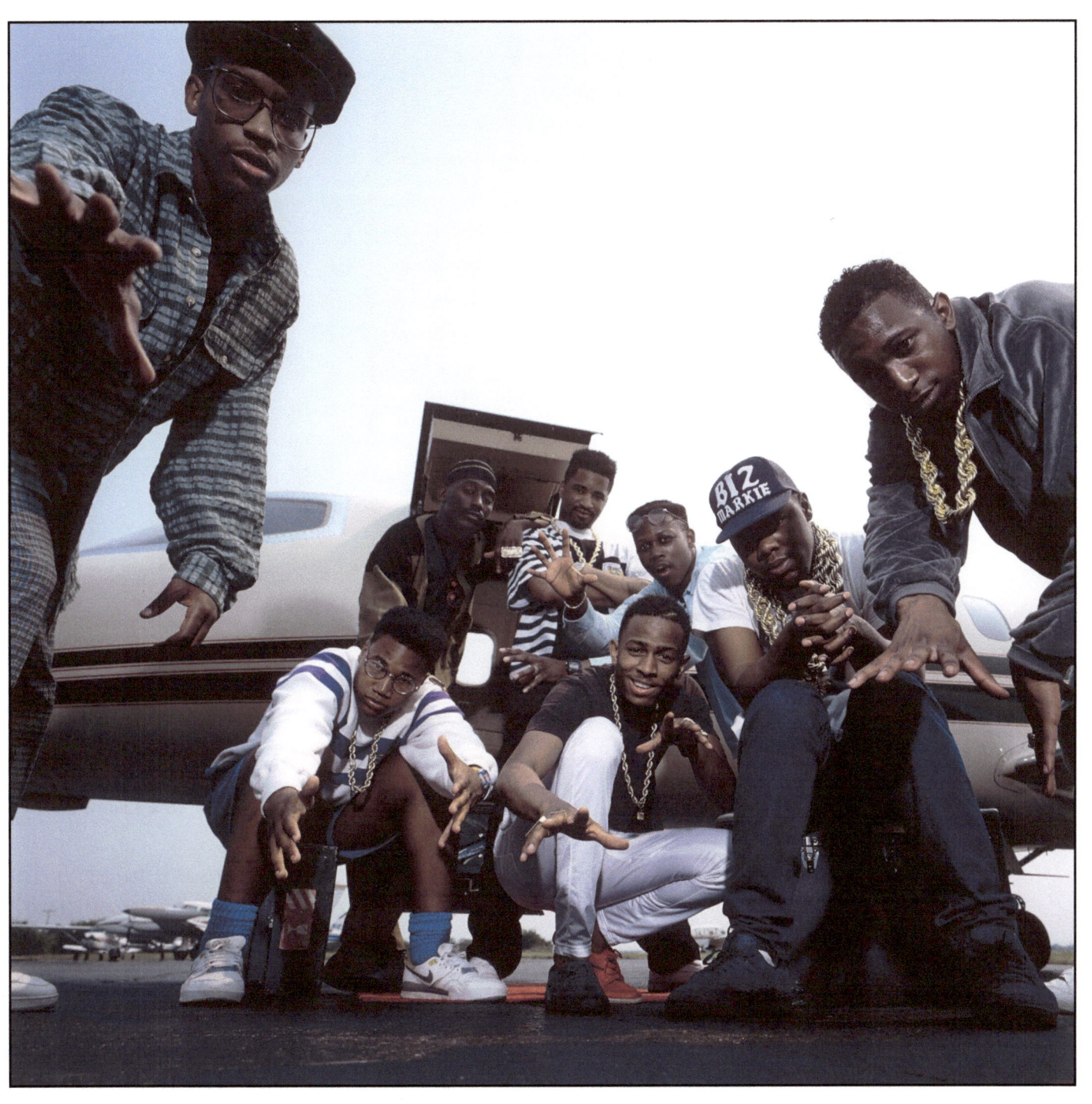

The Original
Juice Crew Allstars

About 30 years later. This
photo was taken backstage
at a gig in Den Haag,
The Netherlands. My concept
was to only show one shot of
each group, but these guys
bought me a house...

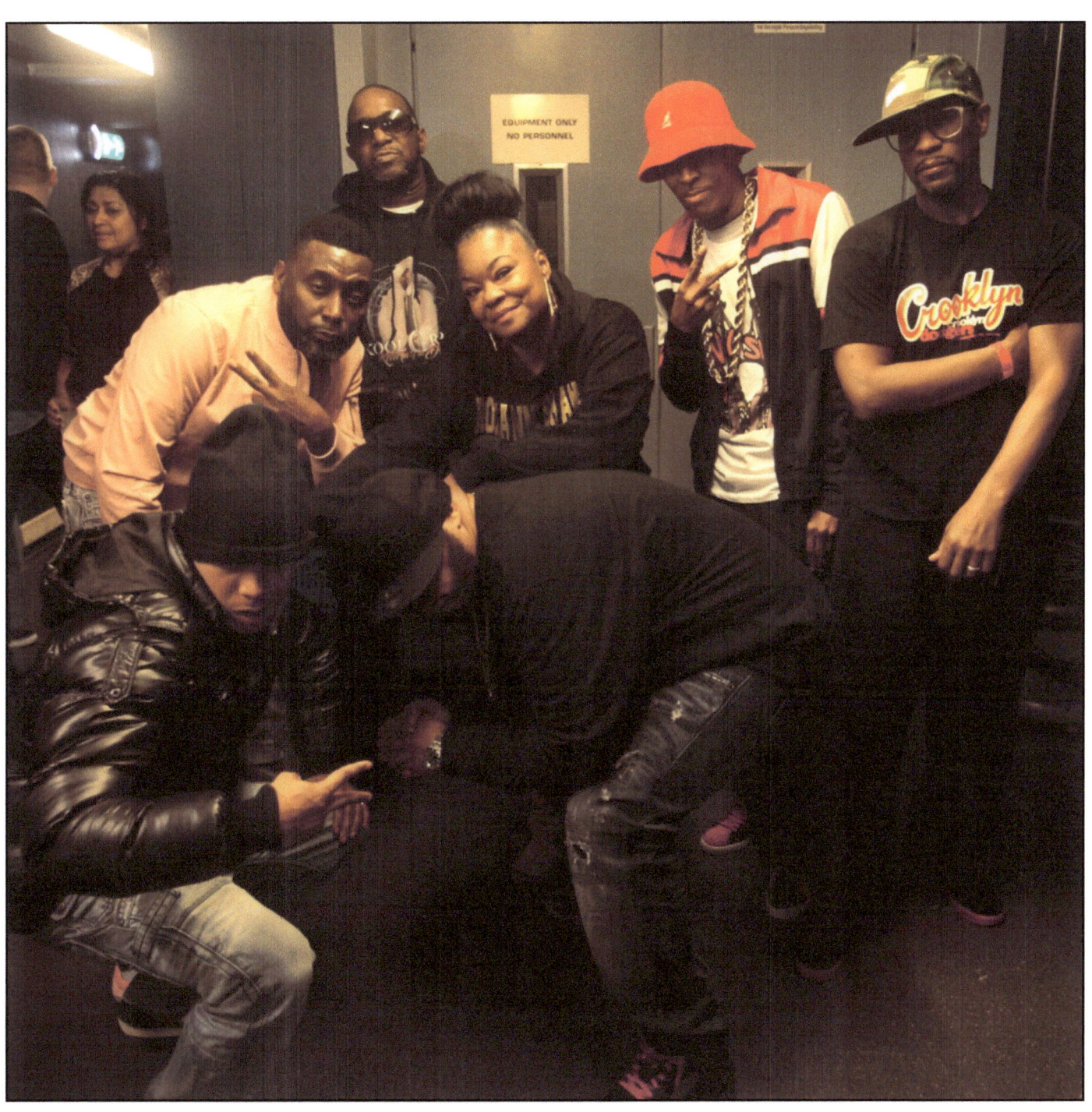

Big Daddy Kane

I did almost all his covers over
a 20 year period. There were
many and then there were
the singles.
The man is an amazing talent.
This is one of my favorite shots.
A real colored man...

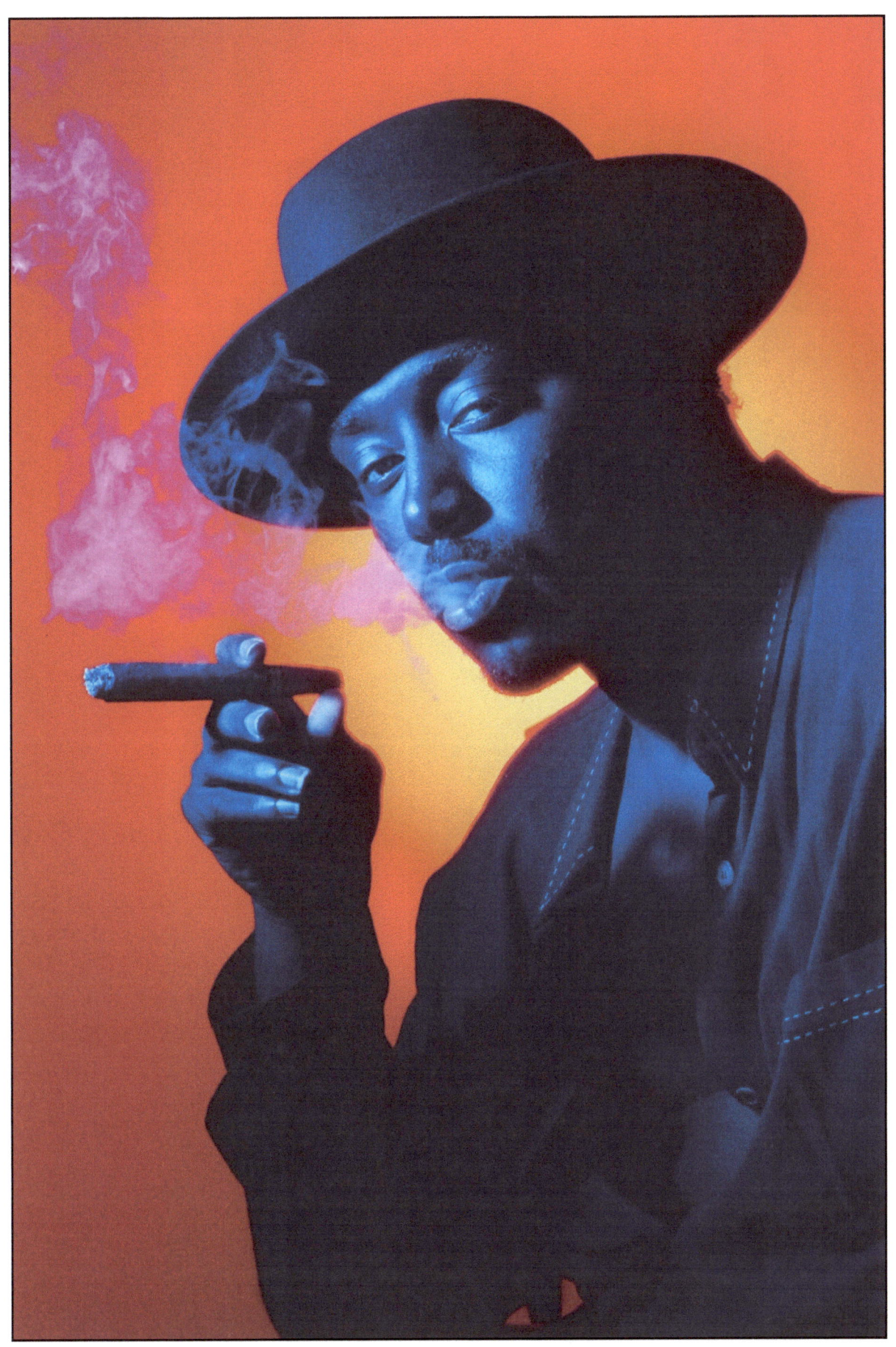

Kanye West

I shot this photo in the same
Cologne studio hallway where
I shot Bubba Sparxxx.
I was just shooting for my
portfolio, no assignment, but
when I told Kanye I had
worked with Biz and RunDMC,
he was all smiles...

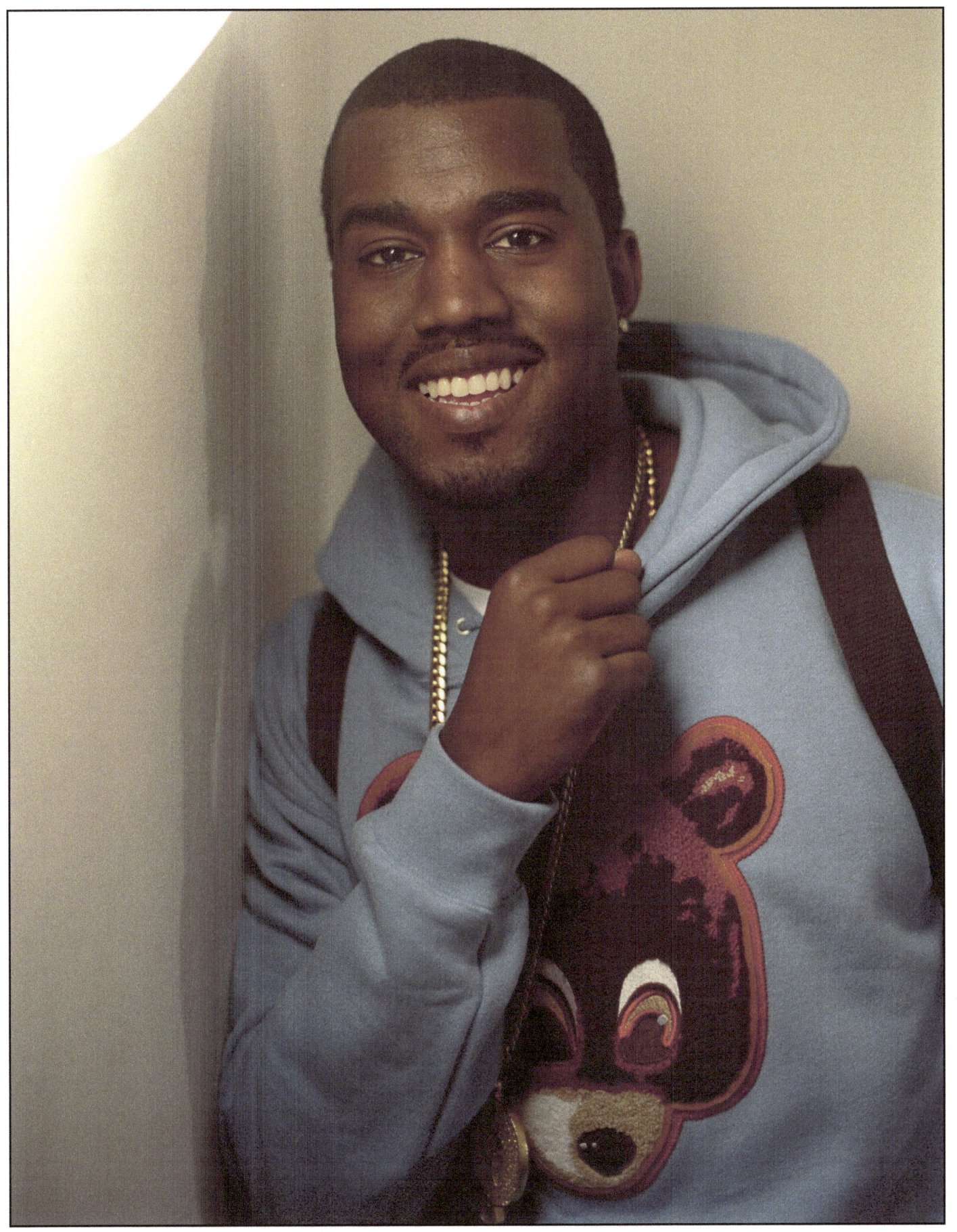

151

King Sun

Shot for his Cold Chillin' album,
but he then bootlegged his own
album after I gave him a print
of the cover art.
Yes...there is a Gun Hill subway
station in the Bronx and King
is rollin' a blunt unaware of
the policeman approaching
from behind.

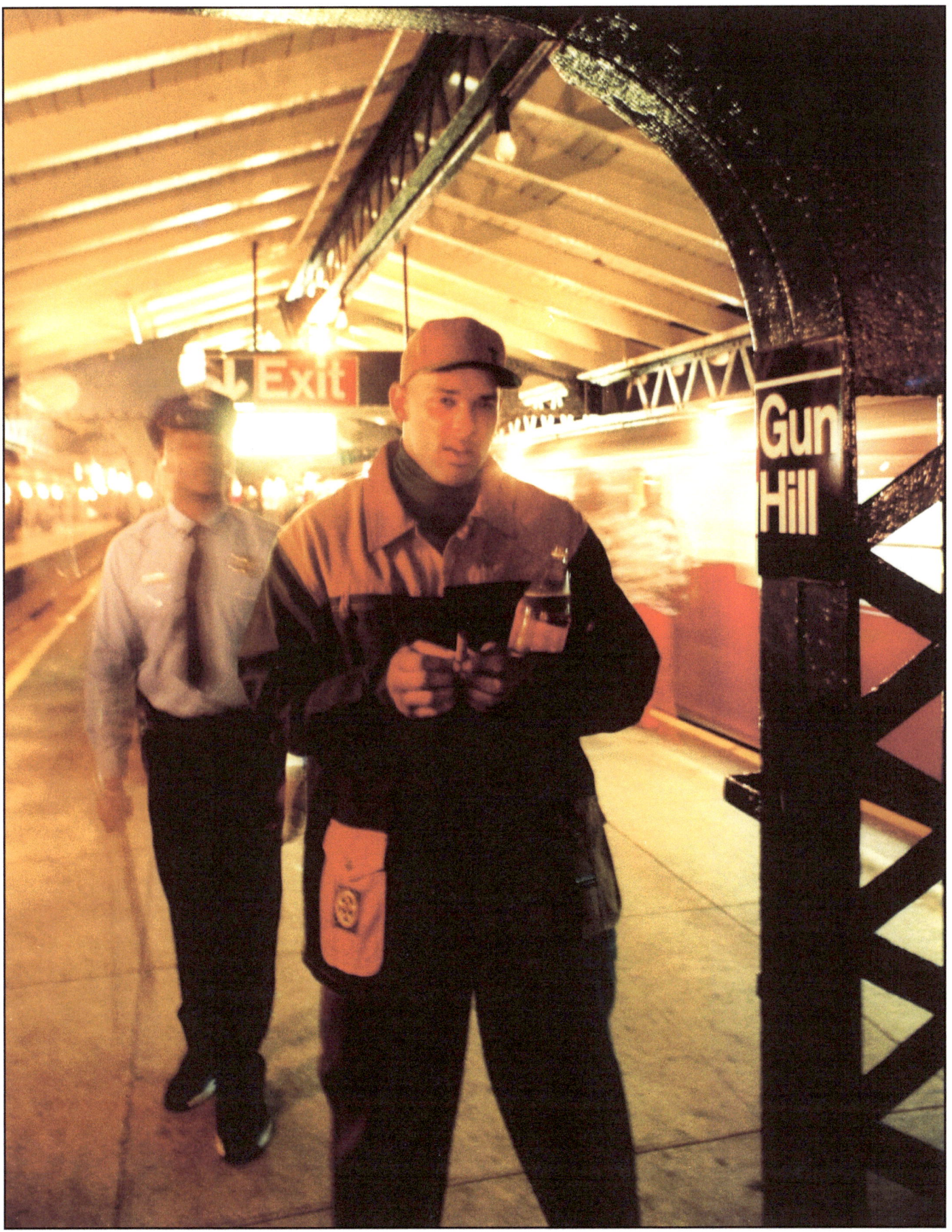

KooKoo
da Baggabonz

Kooks is from Brooklyn, but got an album sponsored and produced by a Swiss skiwear firm, hence the goggles. KooKoo wants to take over the world. The album is called "The Grustler", a combination of the words, grifter and hustler...

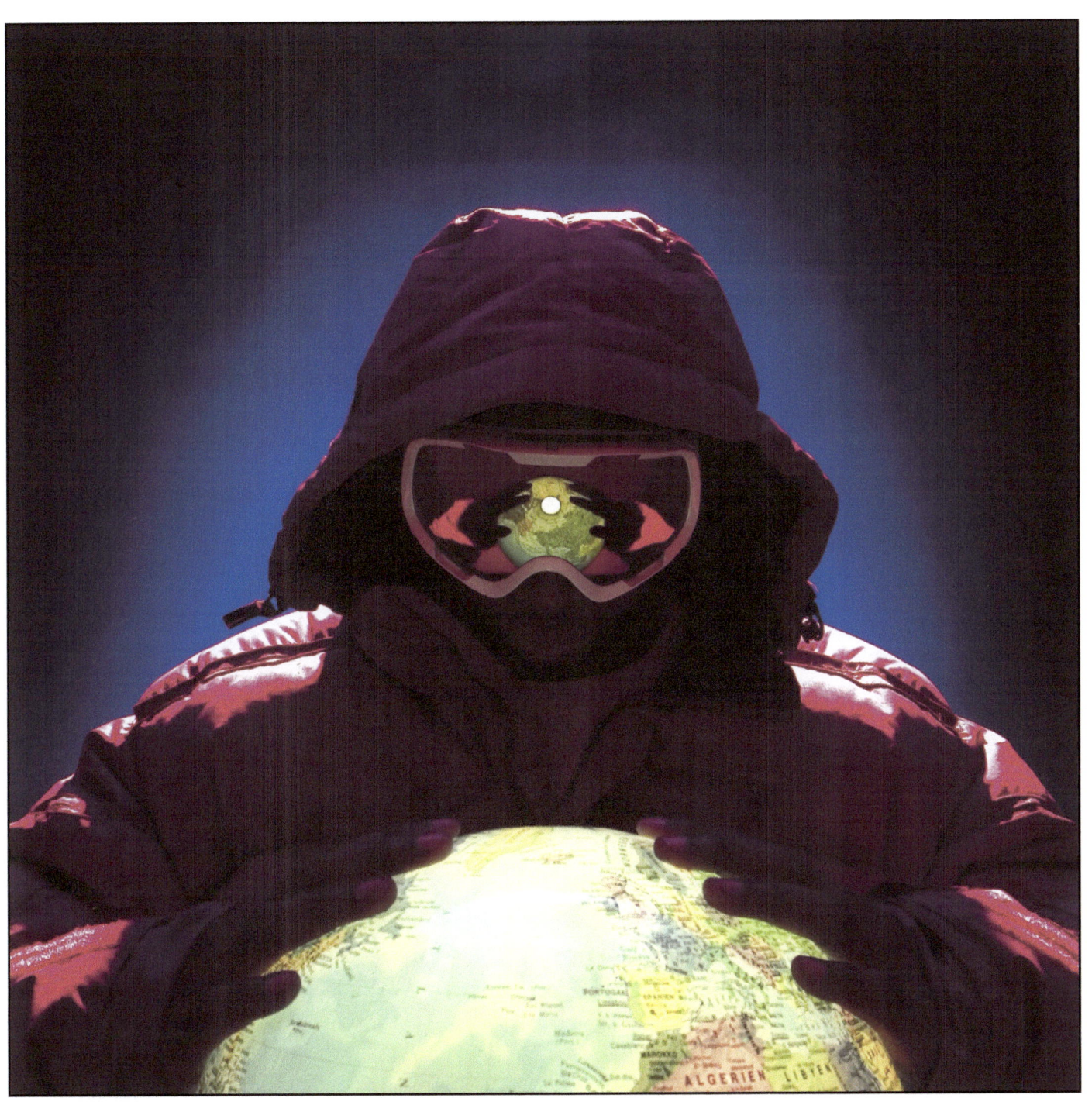

Lumumba Carson
aka Professor X

Lumumba was the leader of
the group XCLAN. Group? It was
more like a tribe. I don't know
how many followers Lumumba
had, but I can remember once
I photographed more than
40 people, one by one.
After a few bumps in the
beginning of our relationship,
we got on like gangbusters.

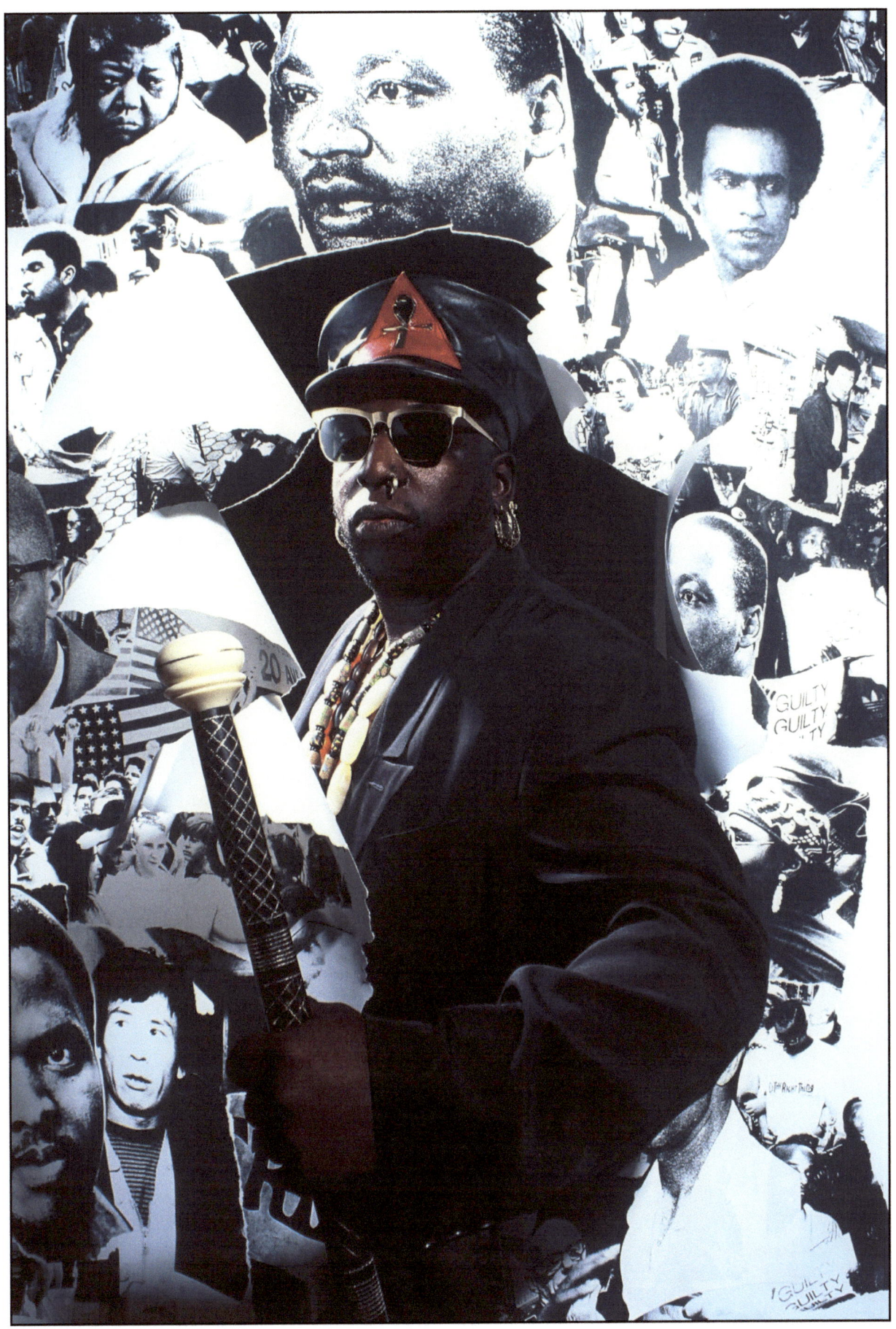

Ludacris

Another one of those shot
at the Cologne TV studio
for my portfolio.
Another guy who is not sure
about his age or his IQ.

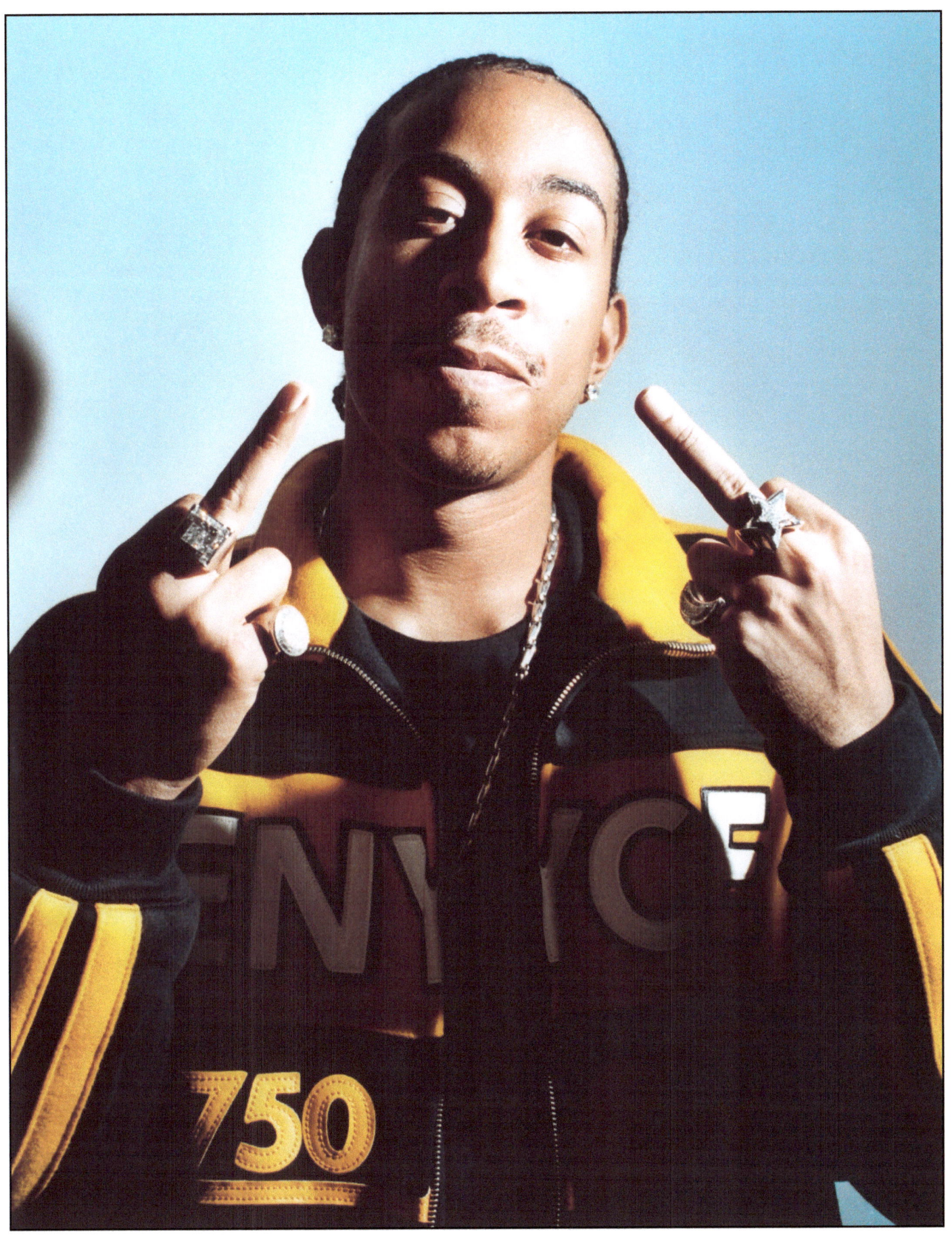

Ma Barker

I shot Ma in Atlantic City
for Juice. She was/is
Kool G. Rap's gunmoll.
She was nice anyway...

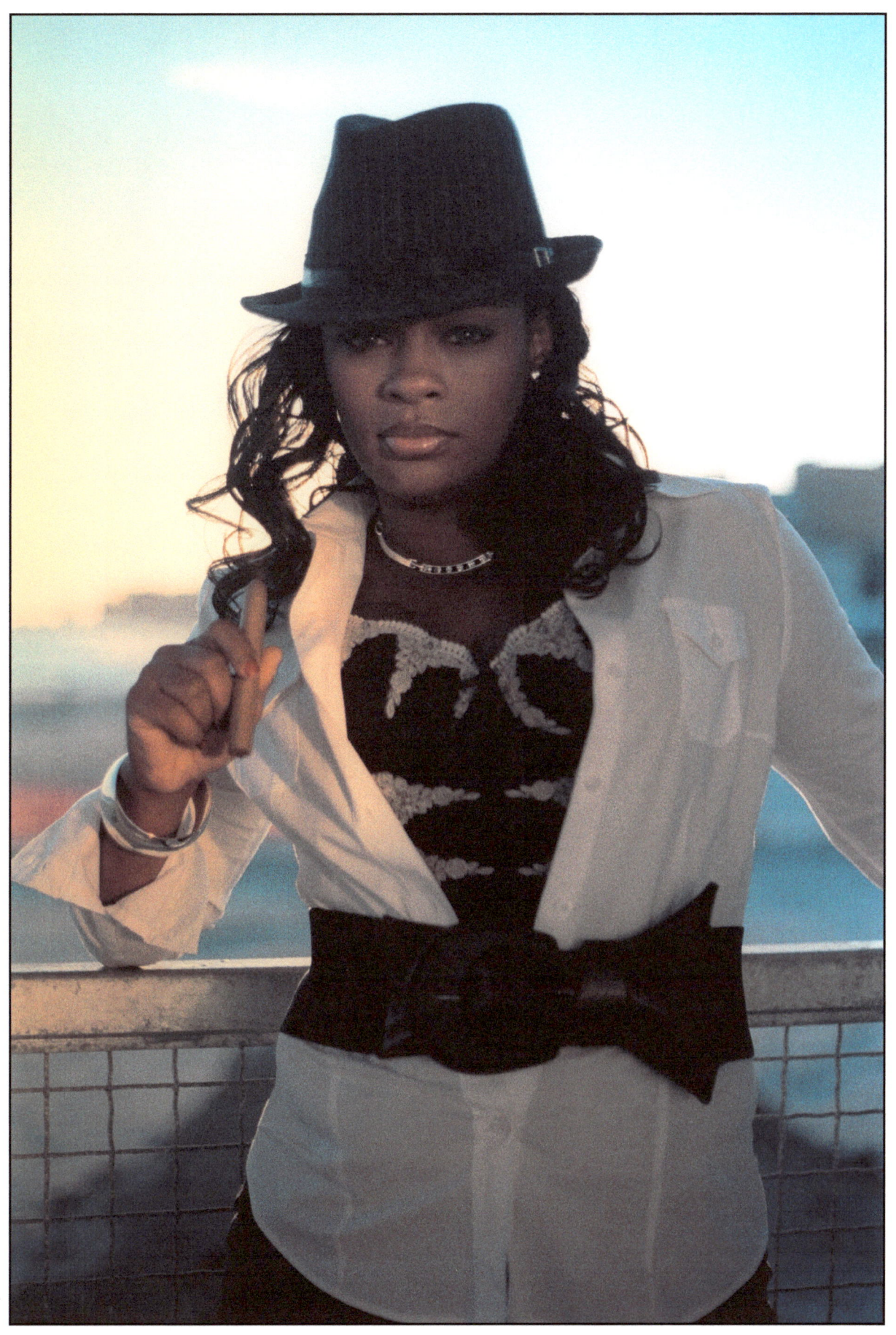

Malik

Malik is an Afghani refugee
living in Germany. He is a
rapper with a gangster attitude.
He is no terrorist. I think he had
a beef with record companies.
He is holding a Japanese rice
cutter, one that I had for the
shoot I did with Mobb Deep back
in the day...

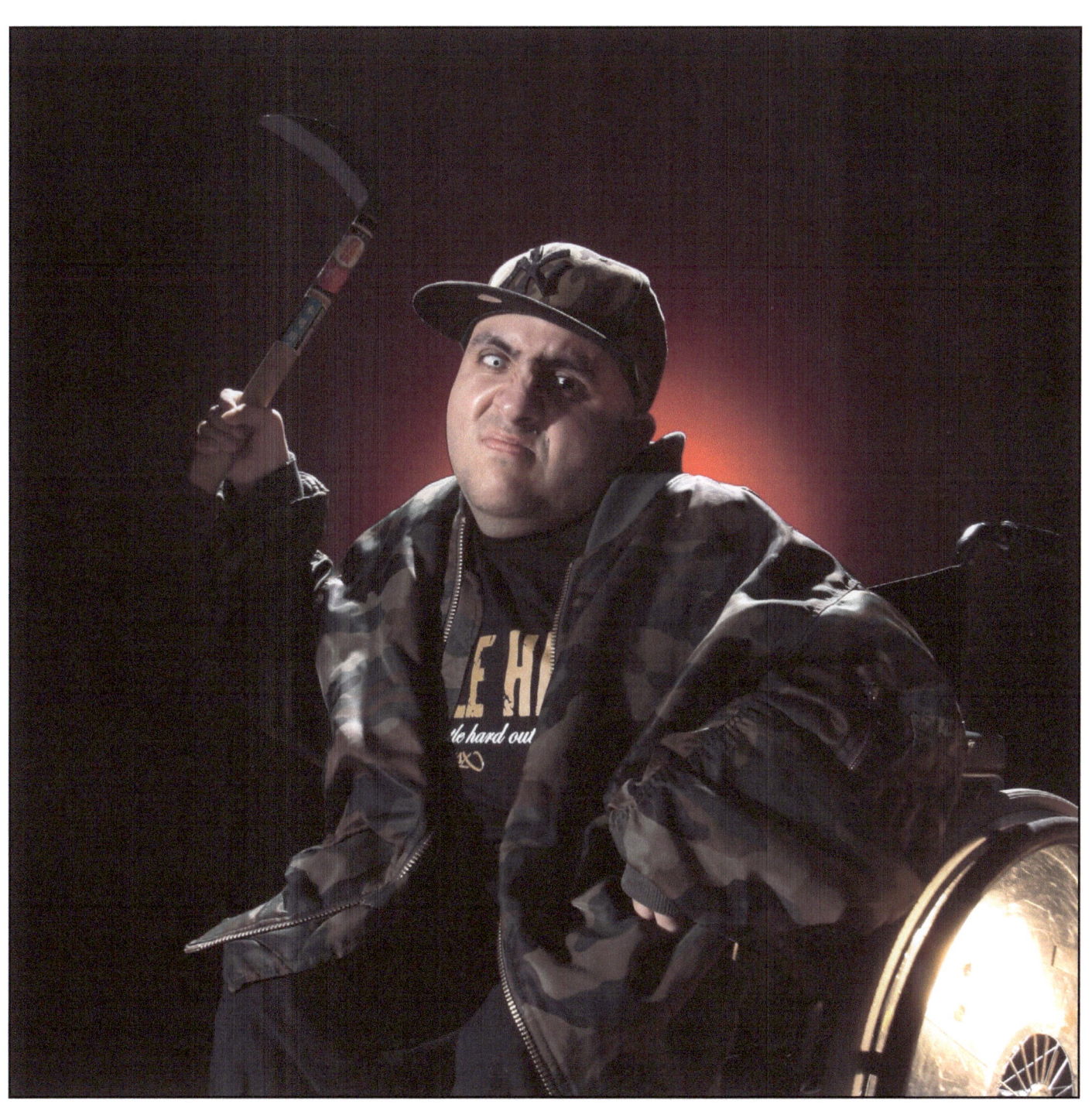

Marley Marl

The Hip-Hop producer.
He wanted to be "In Control"
and wanted a Learjet's cockpit
with lots of dials. Later we
learned that a Gulfstream jet
would have suited him better.

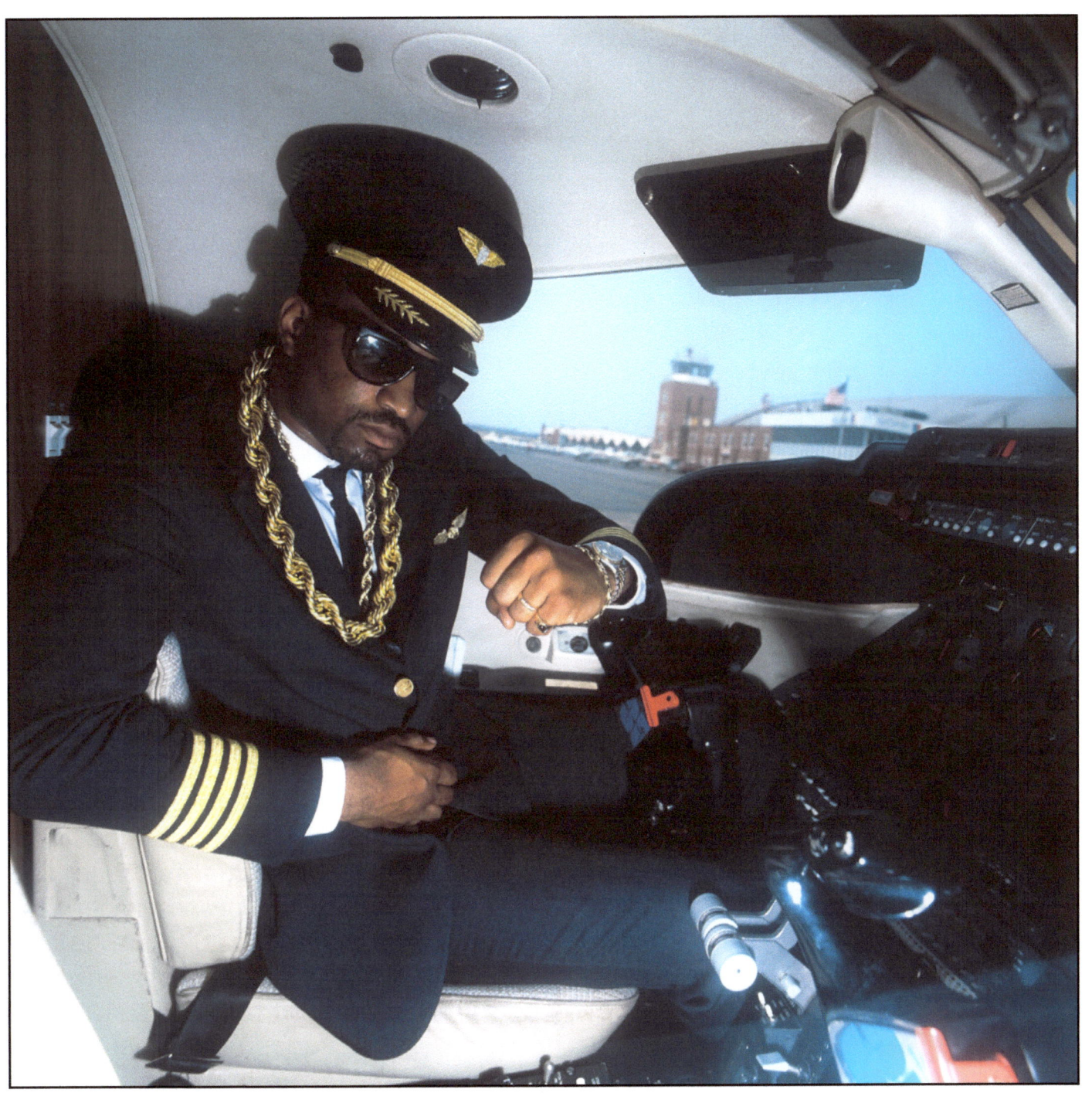

Masta Ace

This wonderful image was made
during a shooting for Ace's
album "Slaughtahouse. Ace
had an elaborate concept for
this shoot and when he saw
the final results, I think he
scared himself. I shot Ace
dozens of times for his
albums and singles.
The full story is in The Big Book...

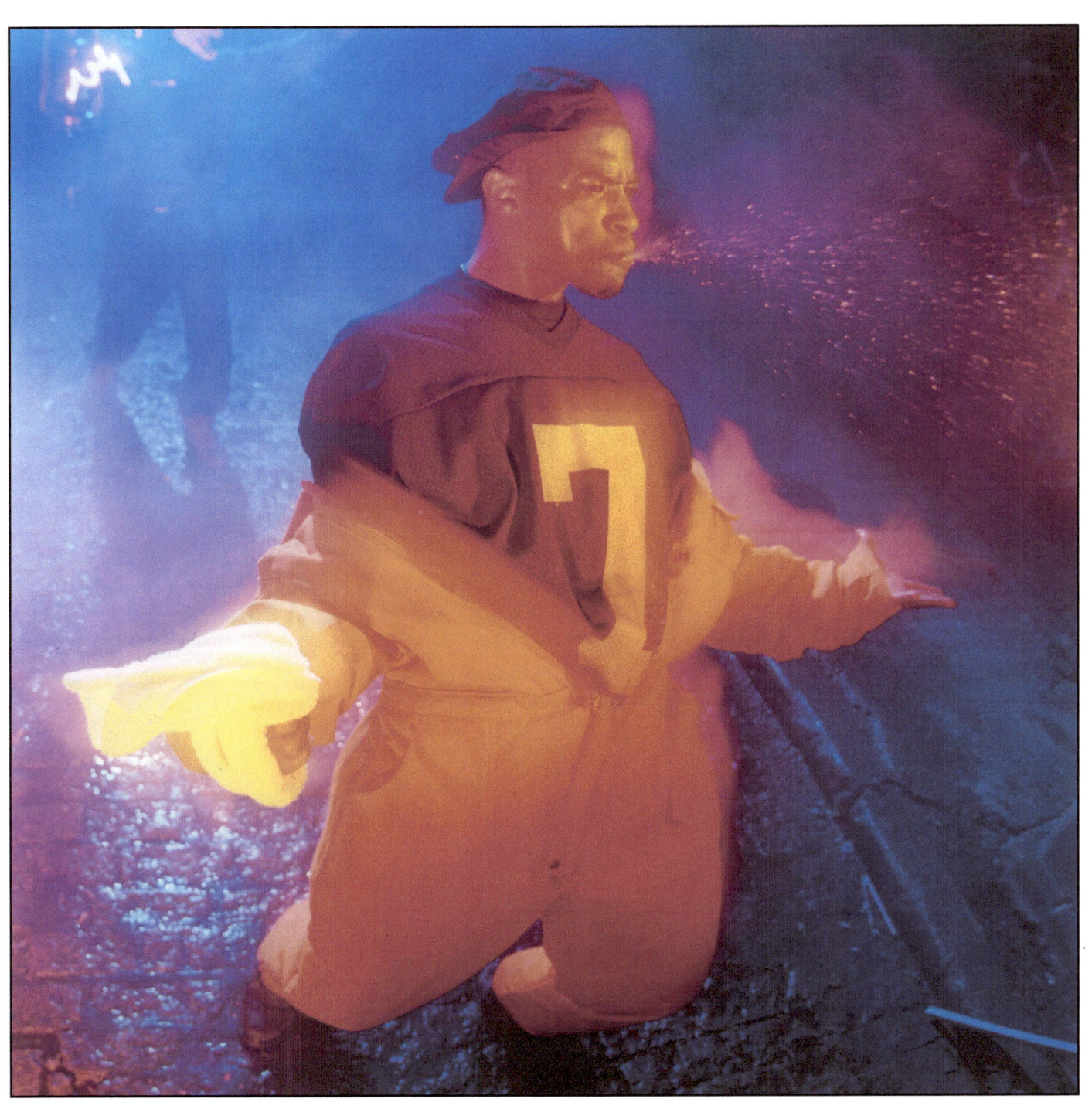

Mobb Deep

Prodigy and Havoc.
Real badboys from
Queensbridge. Fourteen years
old, smoking blunts and
drinkin' 40s...
I would have spanked them but
they had those rice cutters...

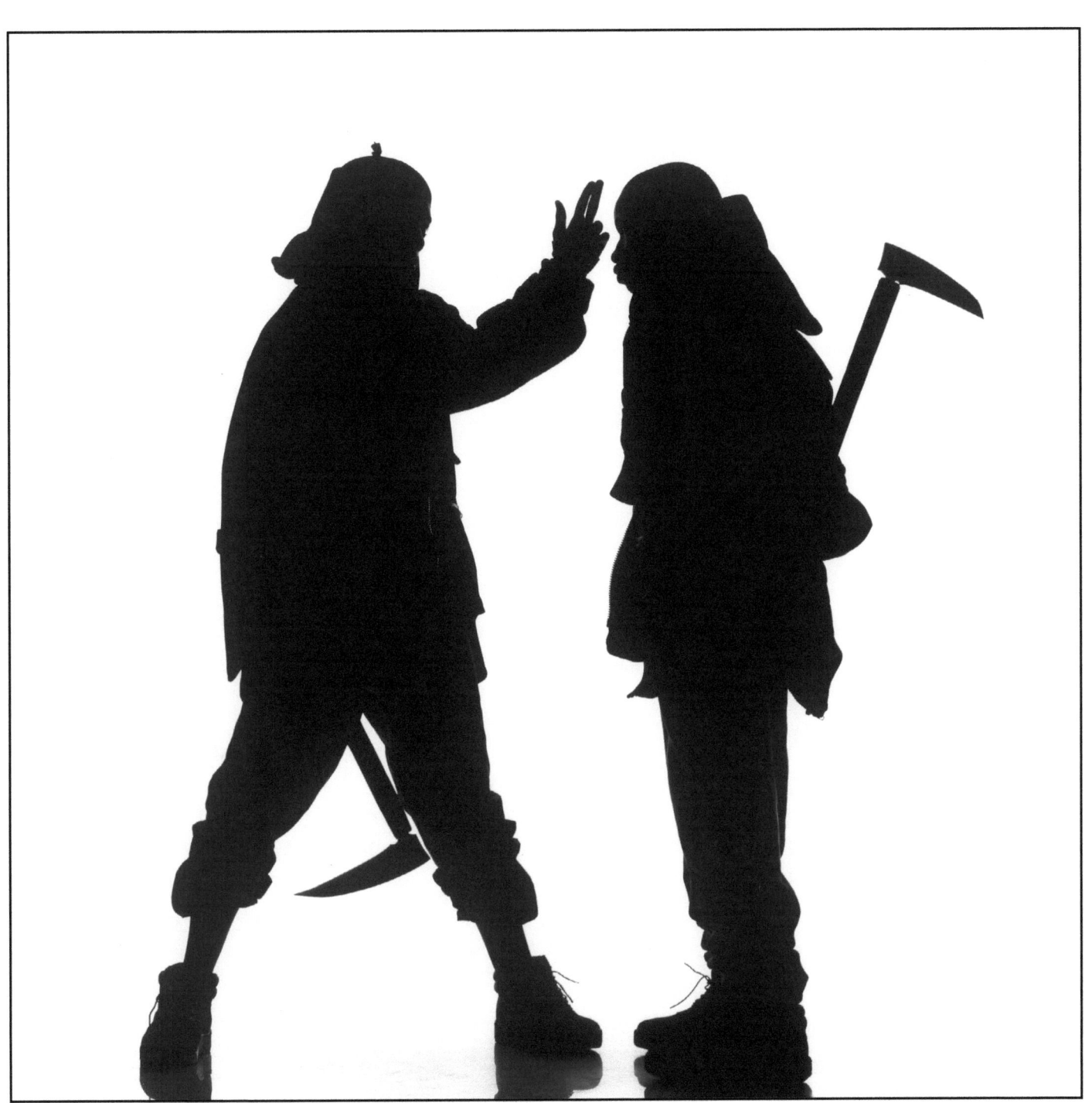

Mr. Magic

Never did know his real name.
He was a NYC DJ who was
a major influence in
breaking Hip-Hop.

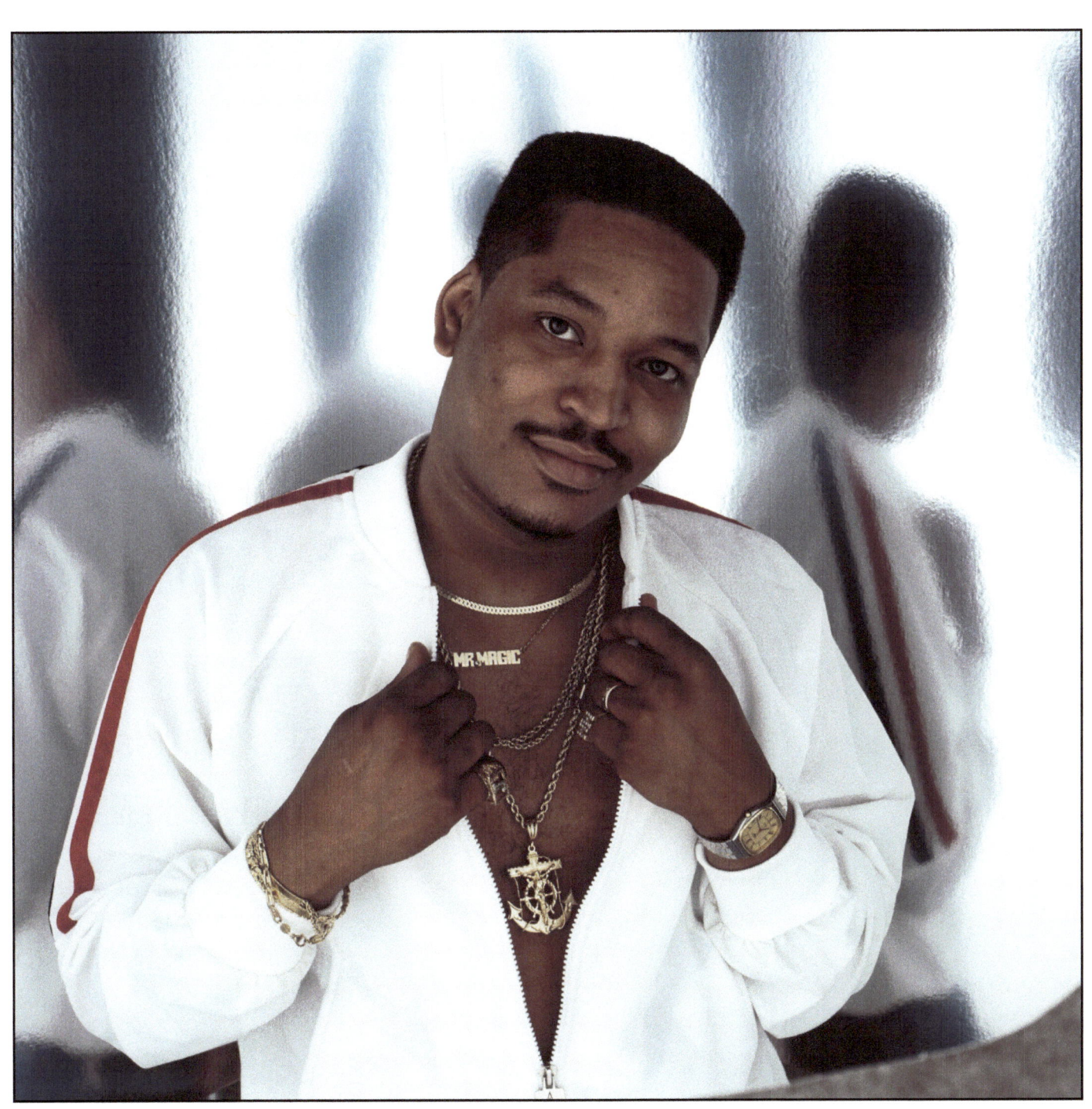

The NYC Breakers

One of the earliest professional
breakdancing teams. Here in
my 3rd Street studio, I shot
them again in Boston

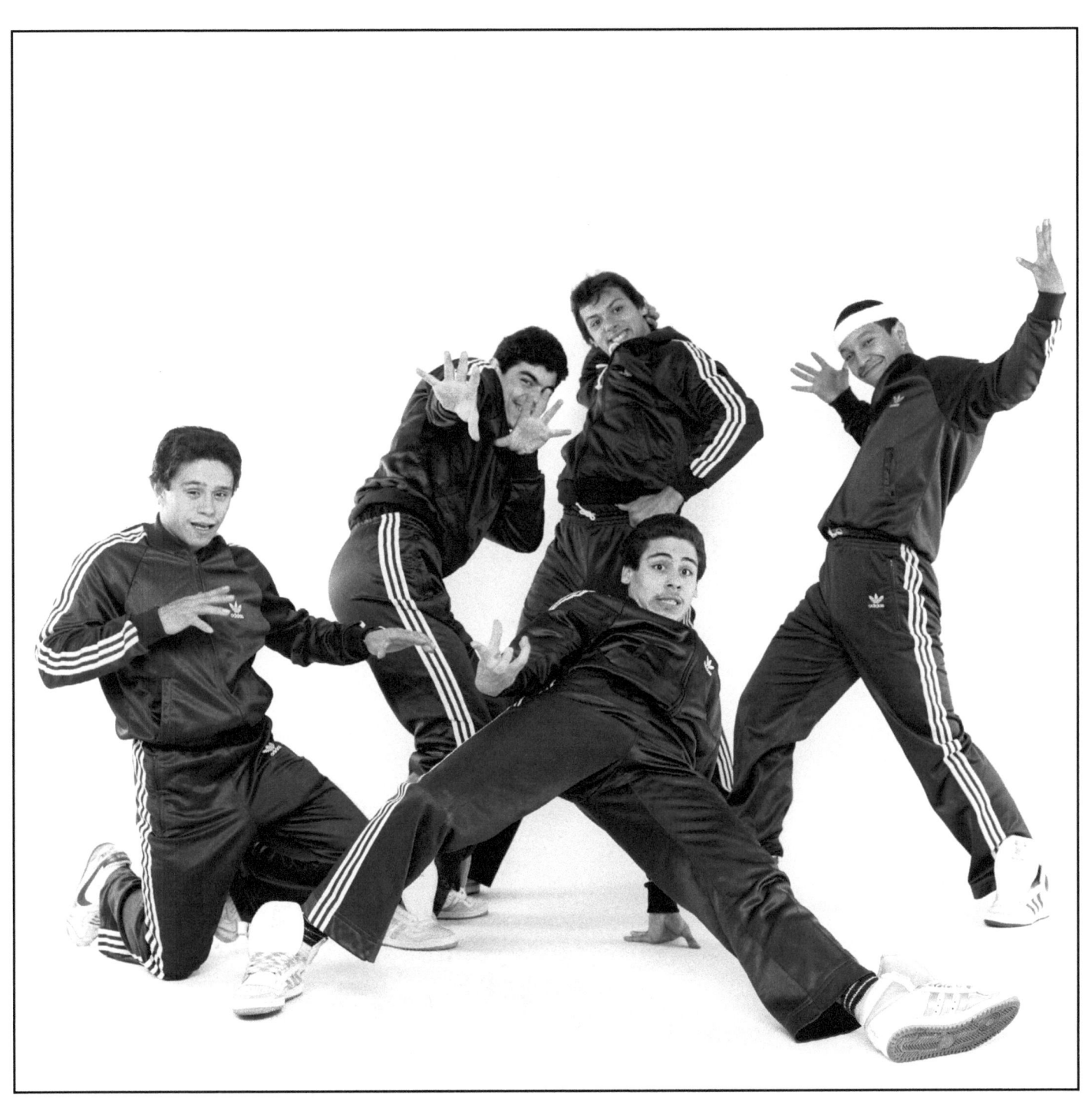

Unknown

Breakdancers

I like this shot falsely rotated to
give a wacky perspective...
Like my life...

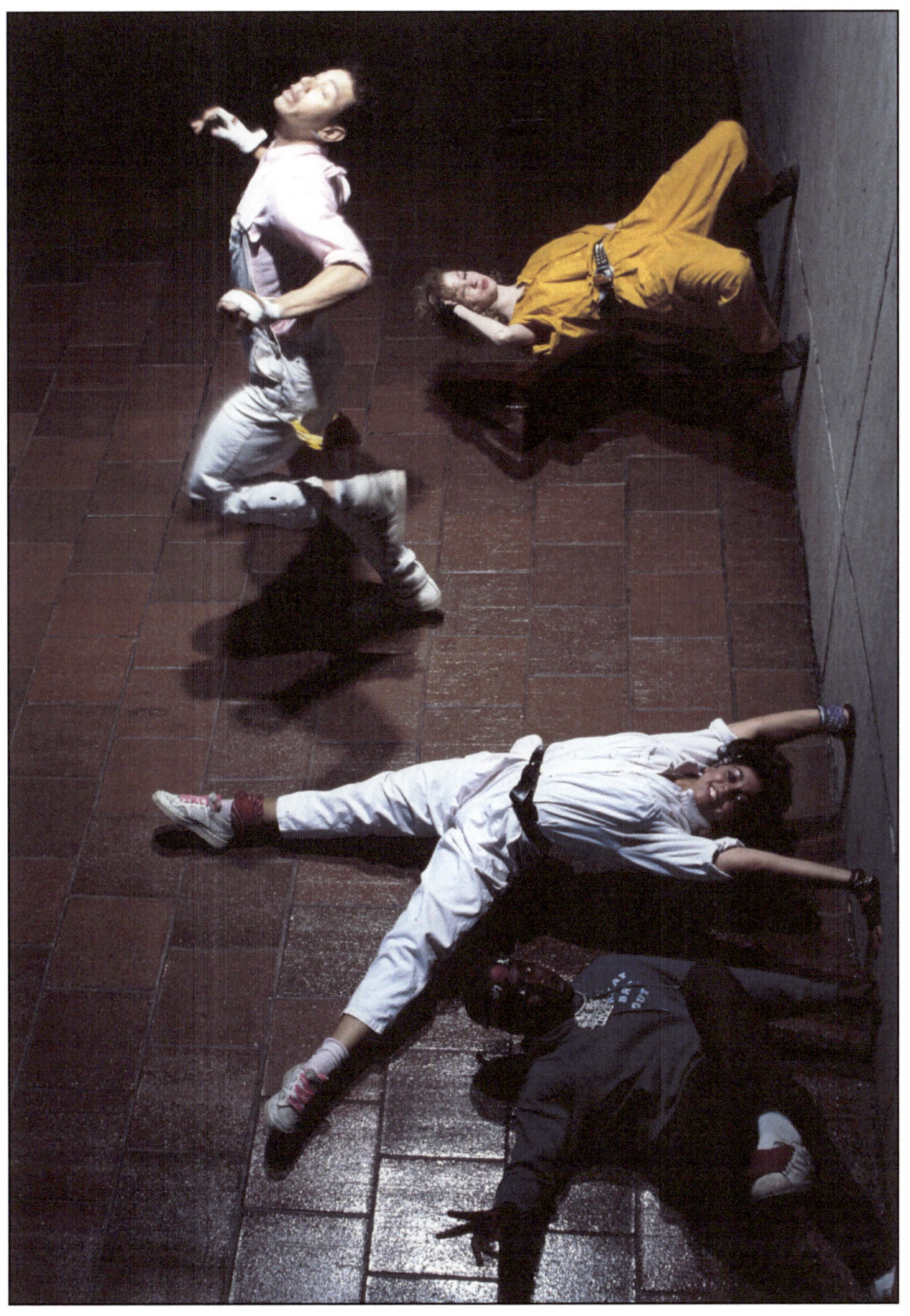

Ofei

A Ghananese living in London. Ofei is a brilliant musician still struggling to be discovered. We did this shot in a recording studio with no budget. Couldn't even afford a roll of background paper, so we taped several strips of one meter wide paper together. Cost about 2 pounds...

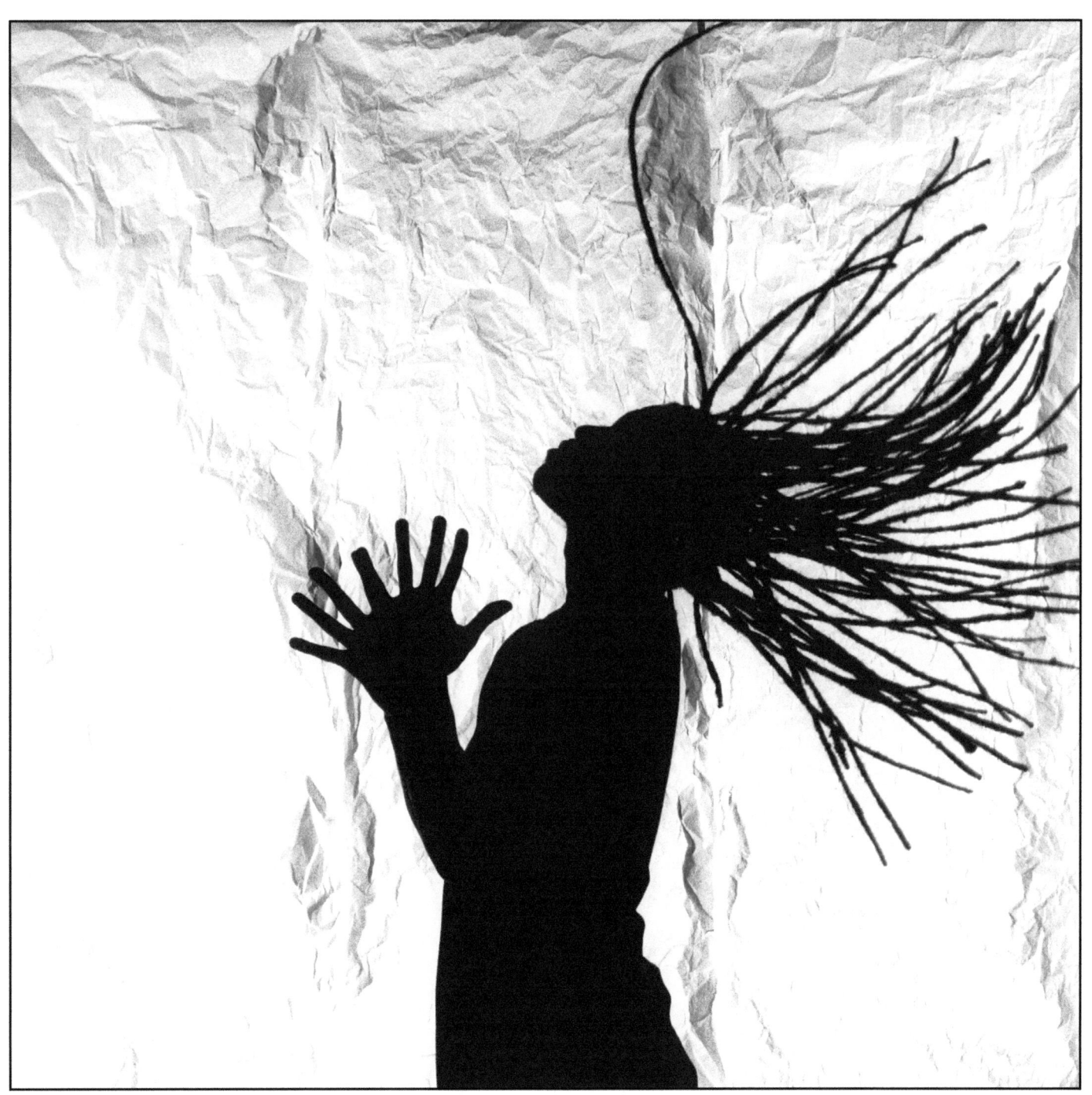

Pete Philly
and Perquisite

A Dutch Hip-Hop duo.
What I can do with 3 euros
worth of red typing paper.
Low budgets can make one
more creative?

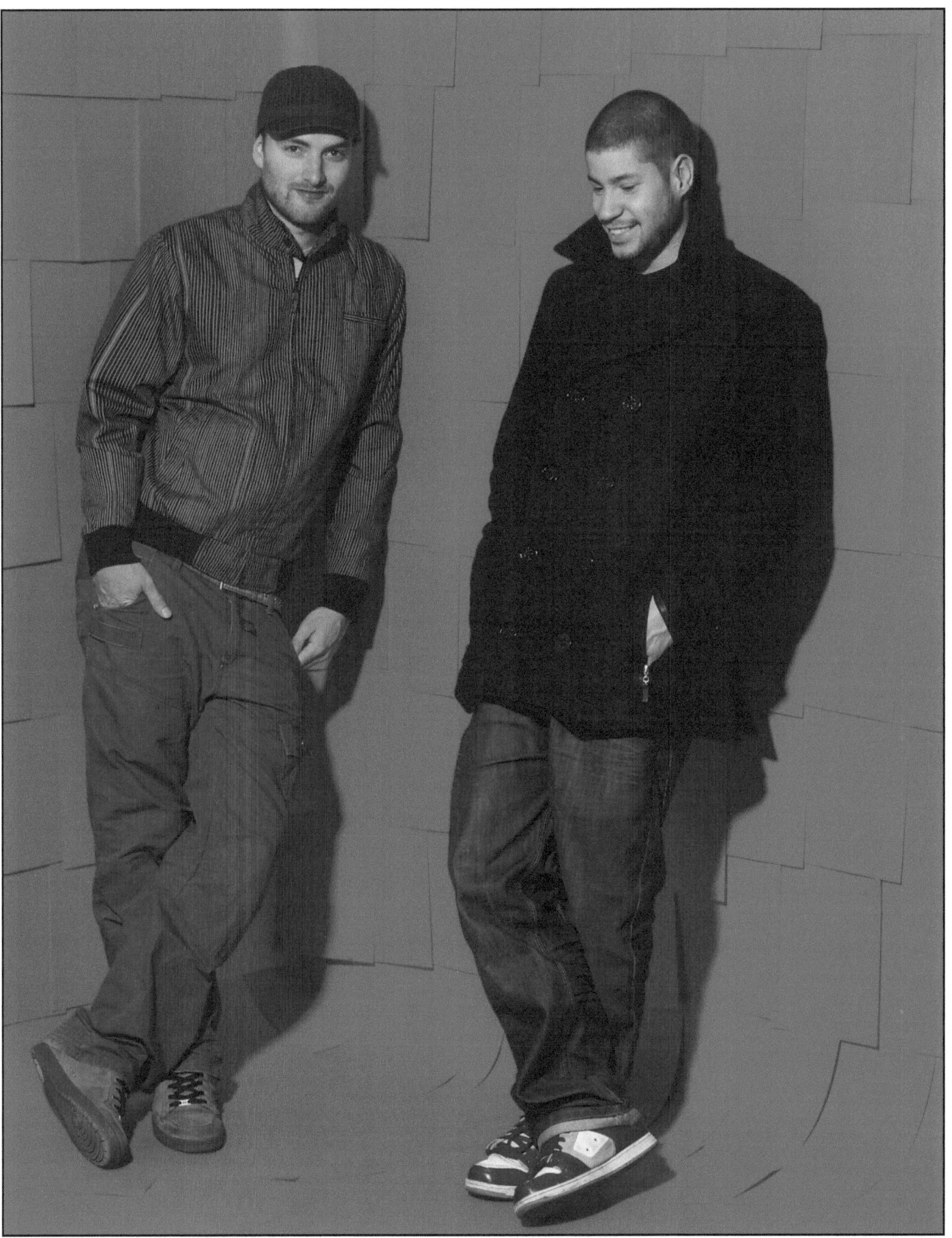

Prinz Pi

Shot for the German Hip-Hop
magazine "Juice".
Evidently, he was originally
called "Prinz Porno". Don't
think I want to go there...

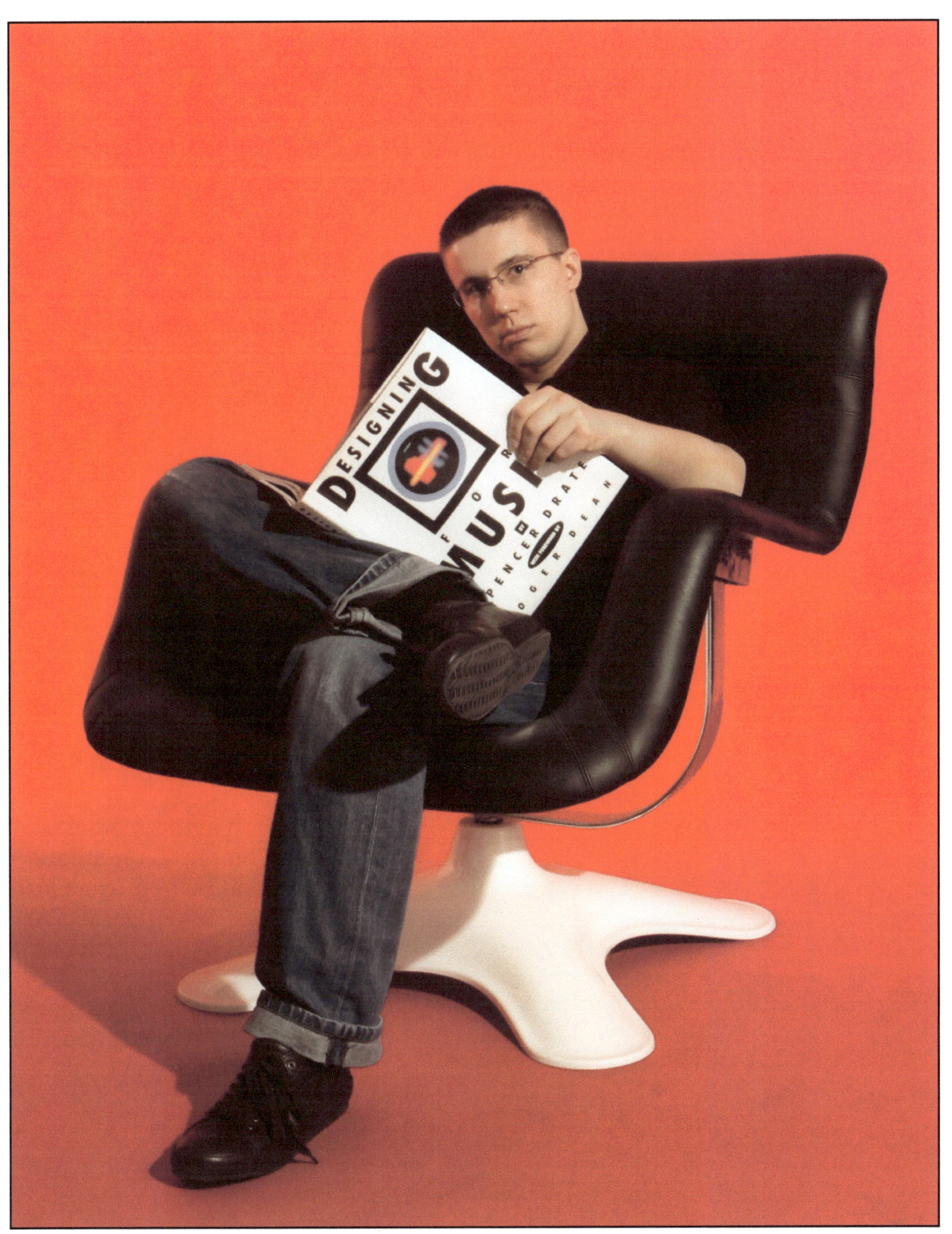

Pyranja

A Hip-Hop artist from East Germany. The photo technique I learned when I was an apprentice to Eric Boman, the famous fashion photographer, mixing strong tungsten light with strobe and a slow shutter speed. Pyranja hated this photo...

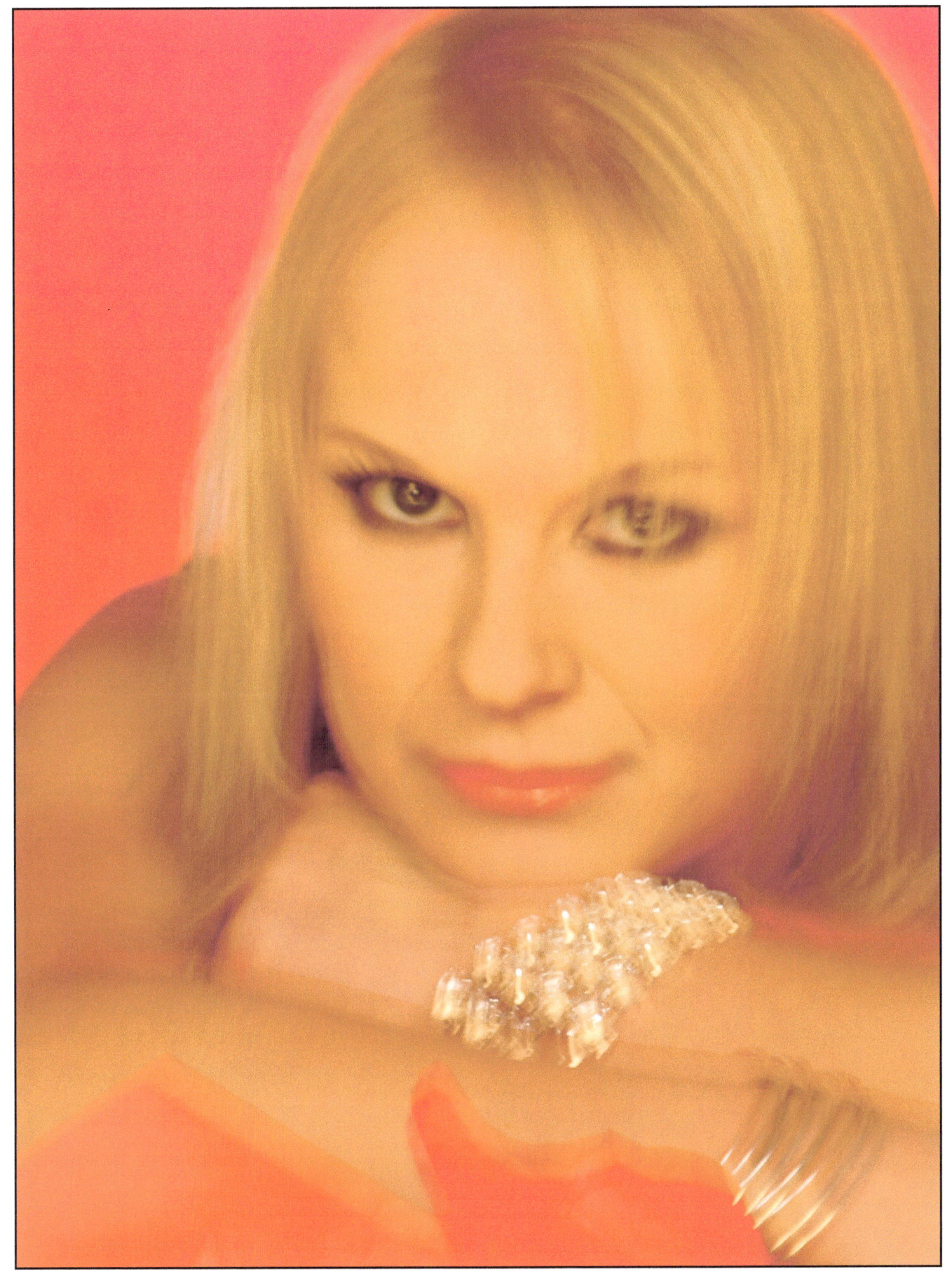

MadLib or Quasimoto

I wasn't sure who he was when
I shot him in a Cologne
hotel room for Juice.
He seemed to have
produced everybody
and then disappeared...

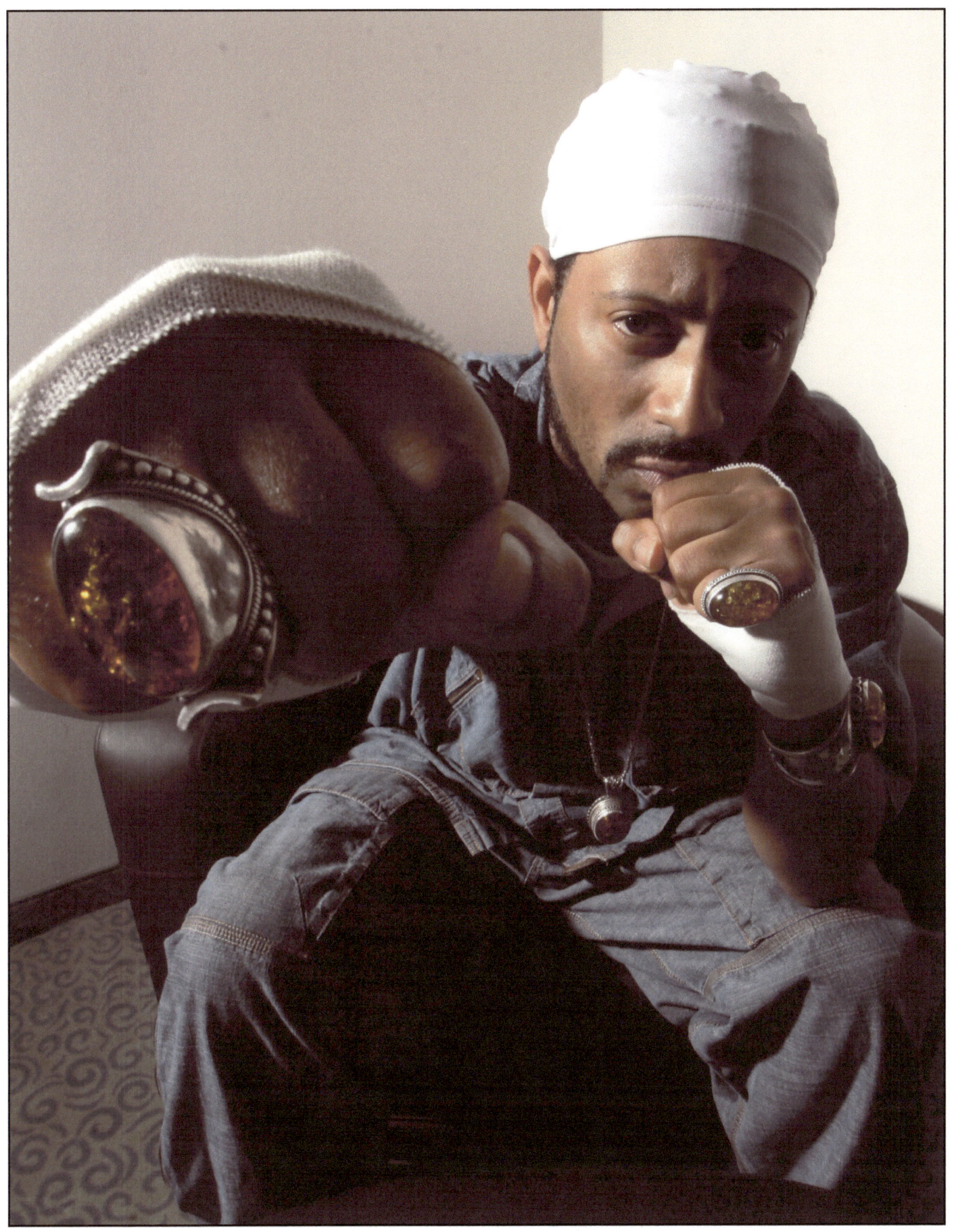

185

Rammellzee

Wearing boy-watcher
sunglasses, carrying
a self-made weapon of vacuum
cleaner and camera parts,
Rammellzee was a real mad
genius. More to the story of our
relationship in The Big Book

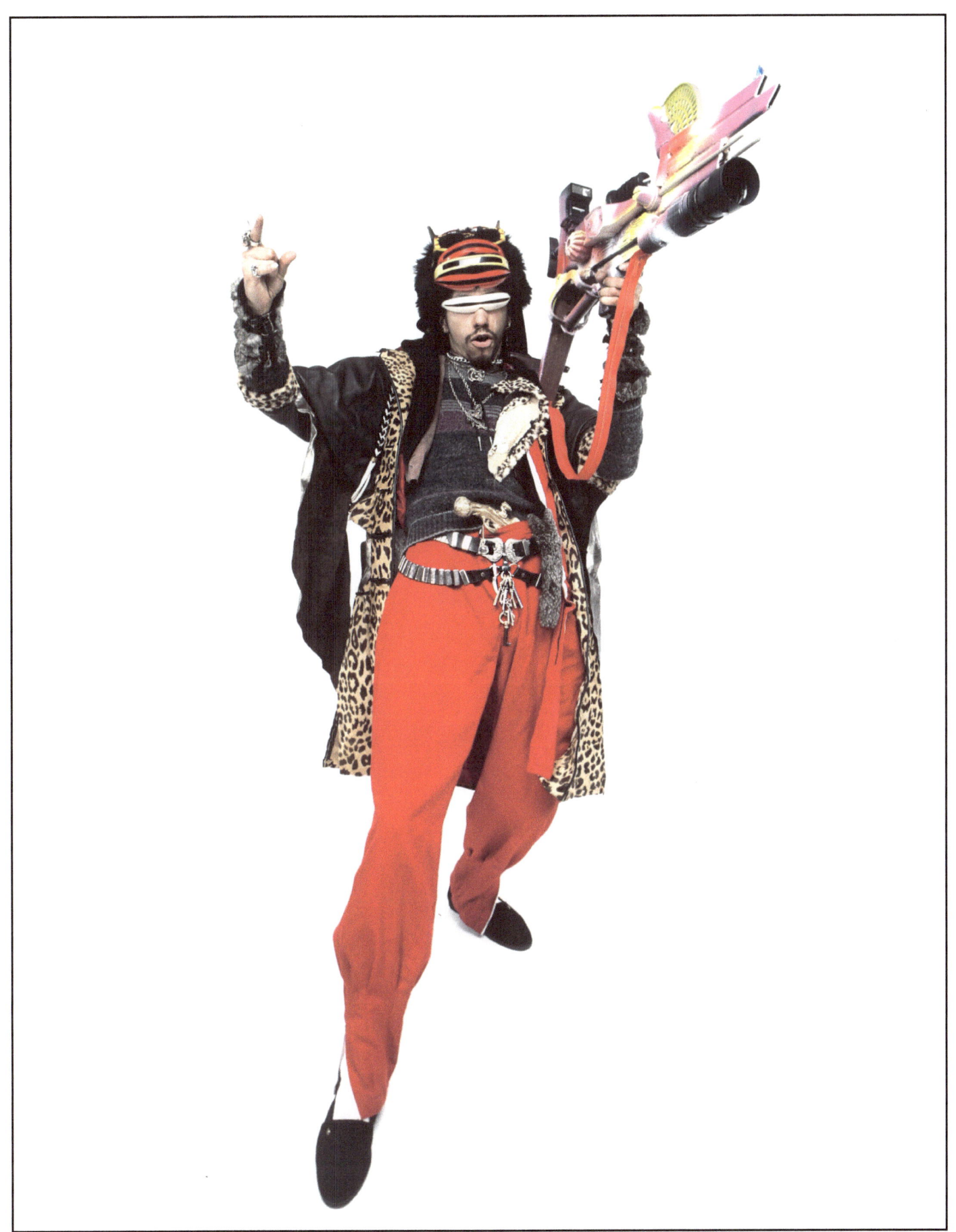

Roger Rekless

A German-Ugandan living in
Munich. He is a Hip-Hop DJ,
producer, rapper and guitarist.
I love the silver texture on the
wall of the music hall where
I shot him for Juice.

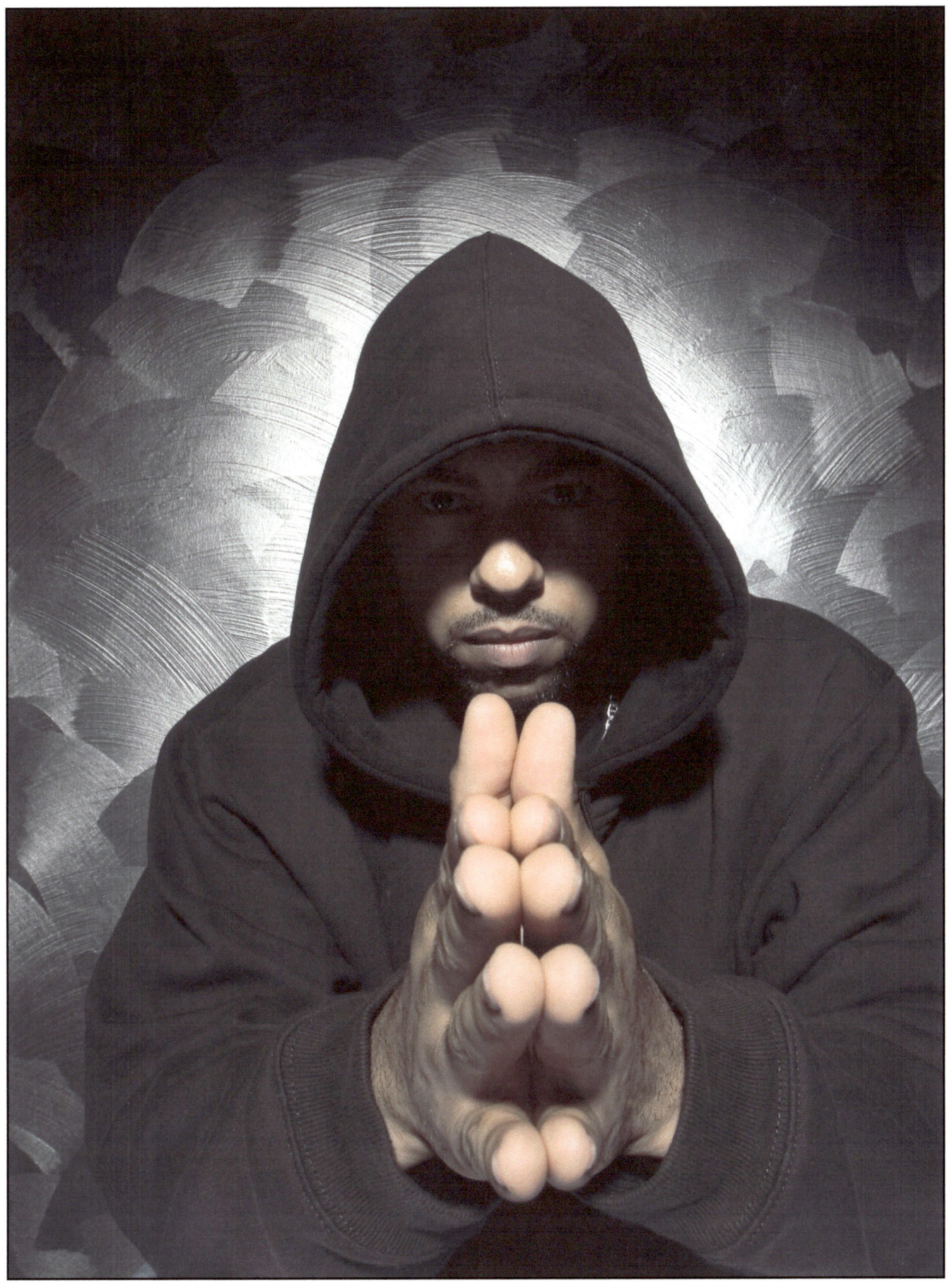

RJD2

A Hip-Hop producer and artist.
I shot him in a Cologne hotel for
Juice. I got him to smear ashes
on his face and put a pack of
Camels in his sleeve to
emulate a car mechanic.
Hence the auto work light.
Then the magical thing
happened...a double exposure.
Some of my best shots
are accidents.

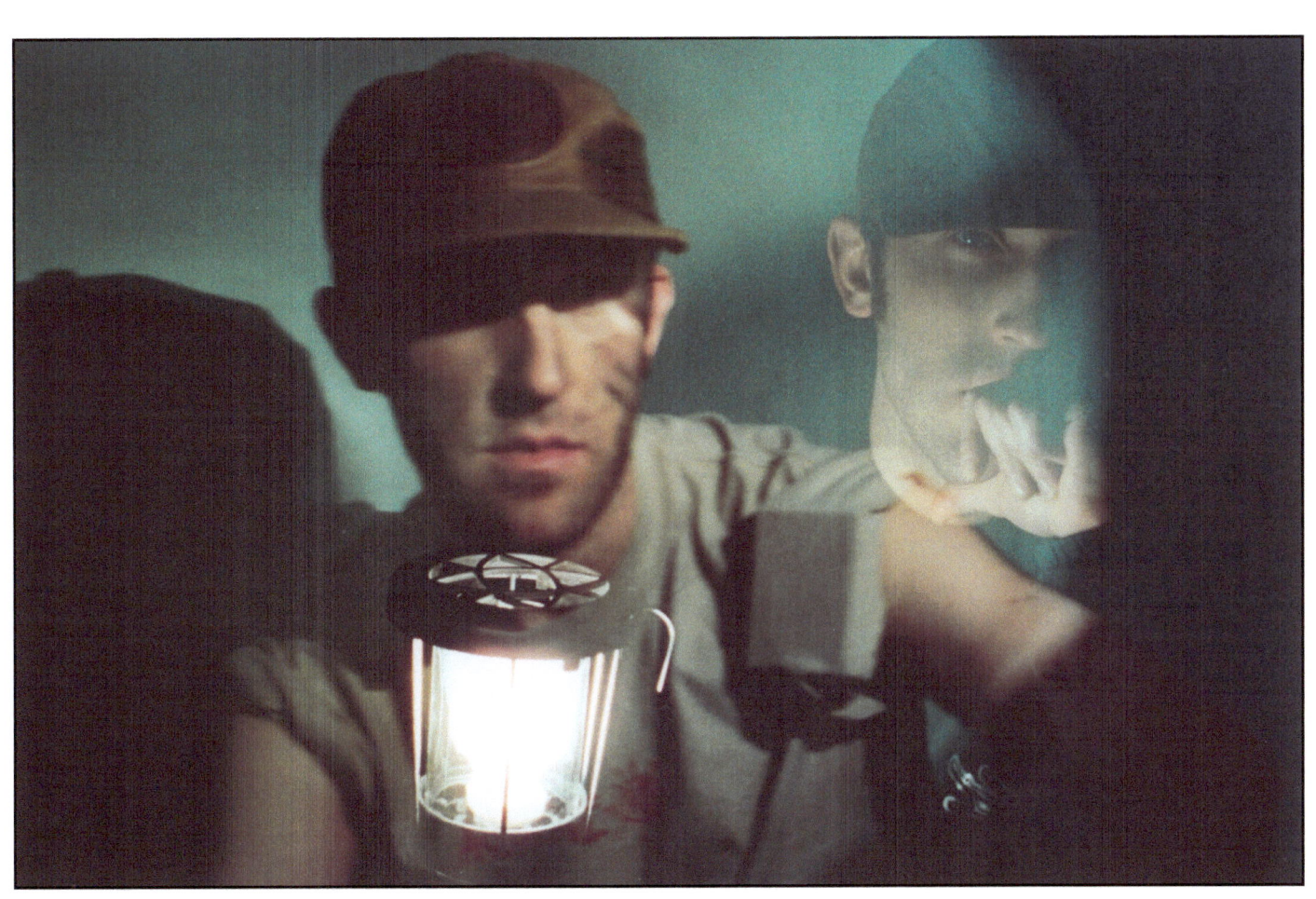

Roxanne Shanté

It was hard to pick my favorite
shot of Roxanne. We worked
together since she was
a teenager and had her first
release, "Have a Nice Day!".
Here she is making
the boys dance...
Sorry the flames from the
sawed-off shotguns don't look
more realistic.
Can't have everthing...

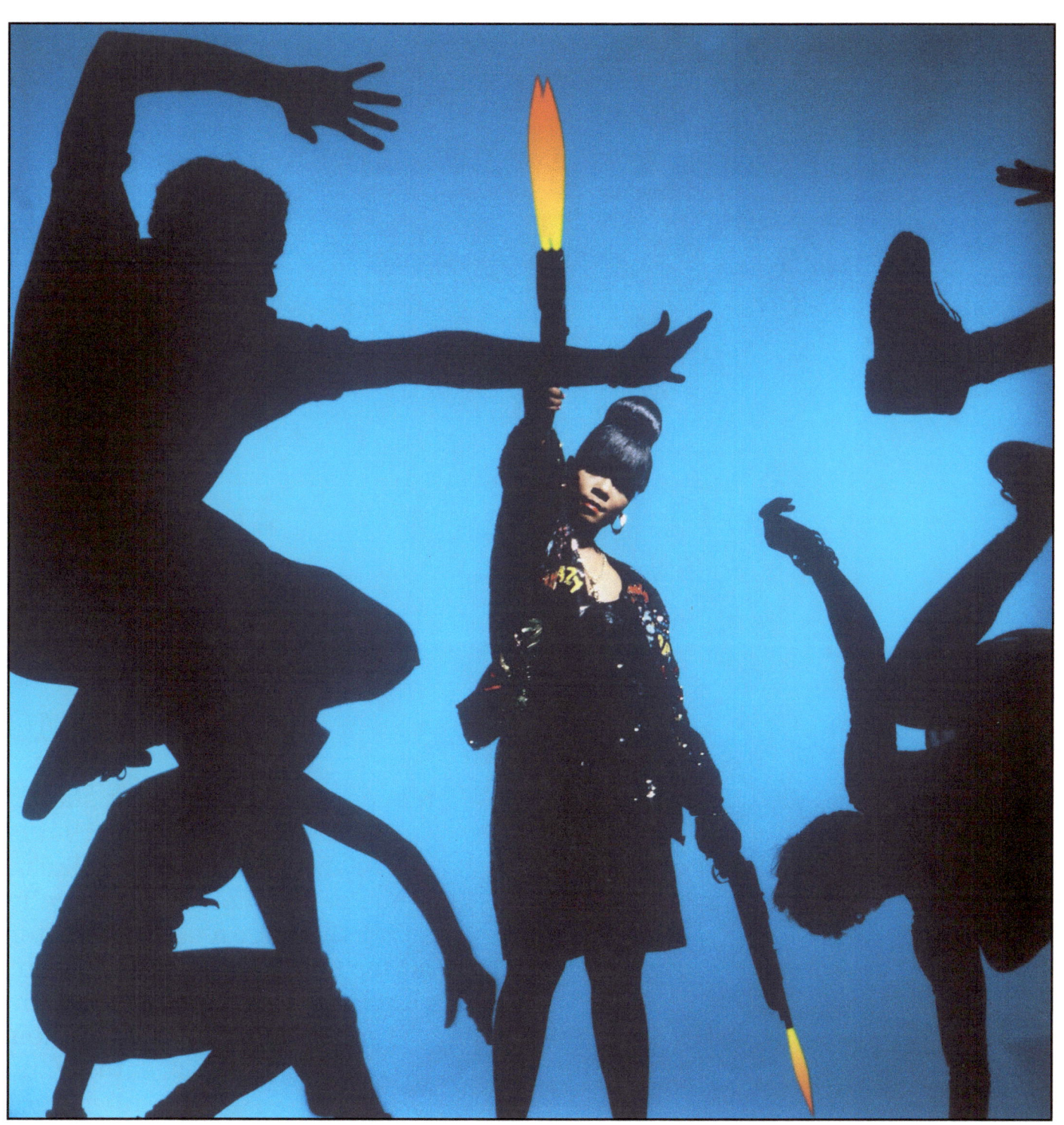

RunDMC

Maybe this isn't my best shot of
RunDMC, but it is one that is
rarely seen. I really like to
make silhouettes. I originally
shot them for a subway poster
ad for Penthouse magazine, but
another shot from this session
became the cover of their
greatest hits.
The full story...

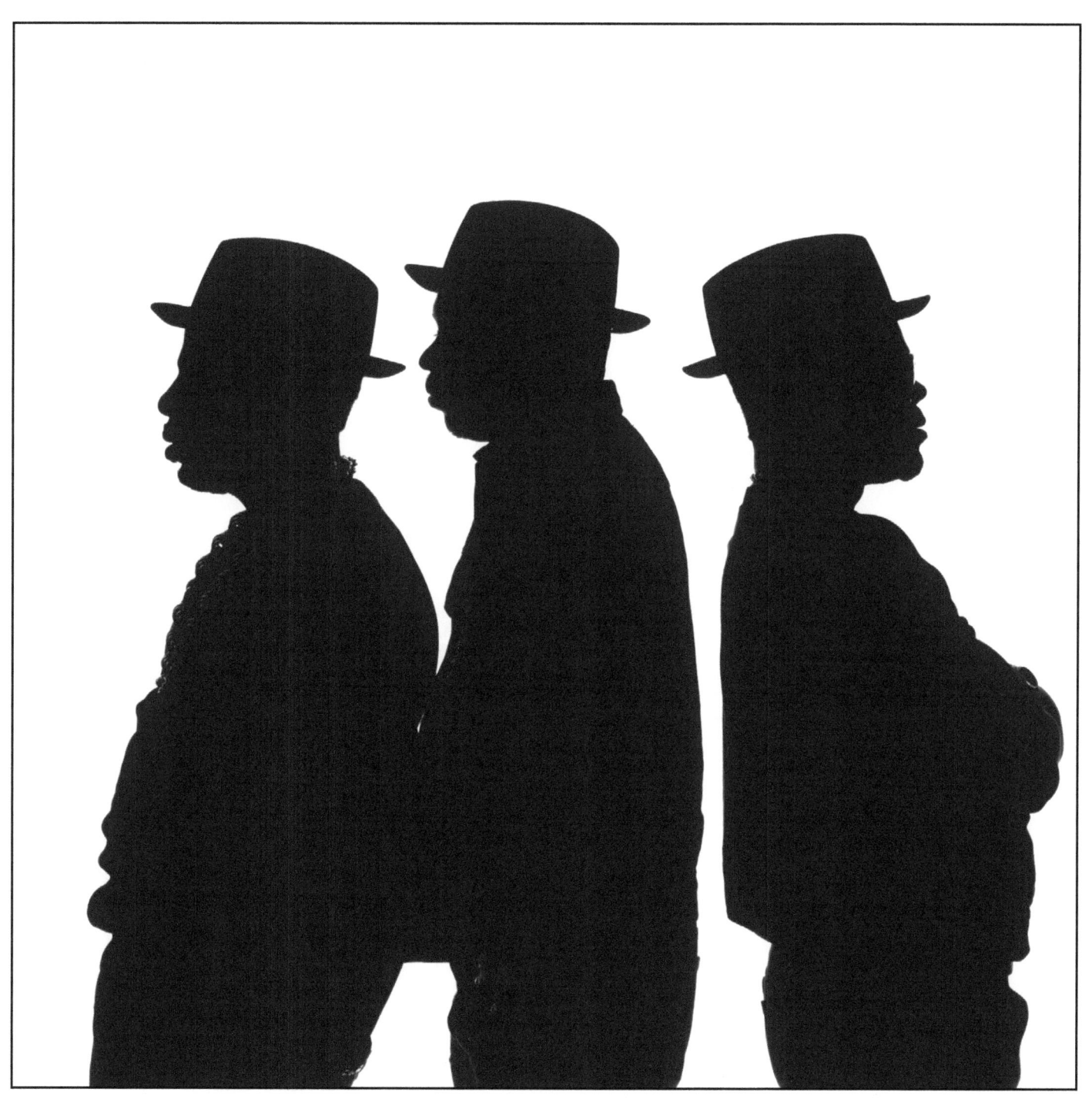

Sage Francis

Shot for Juice on
a rooftop in Amsterdam.
He didn't like this shot,
but it's my book...

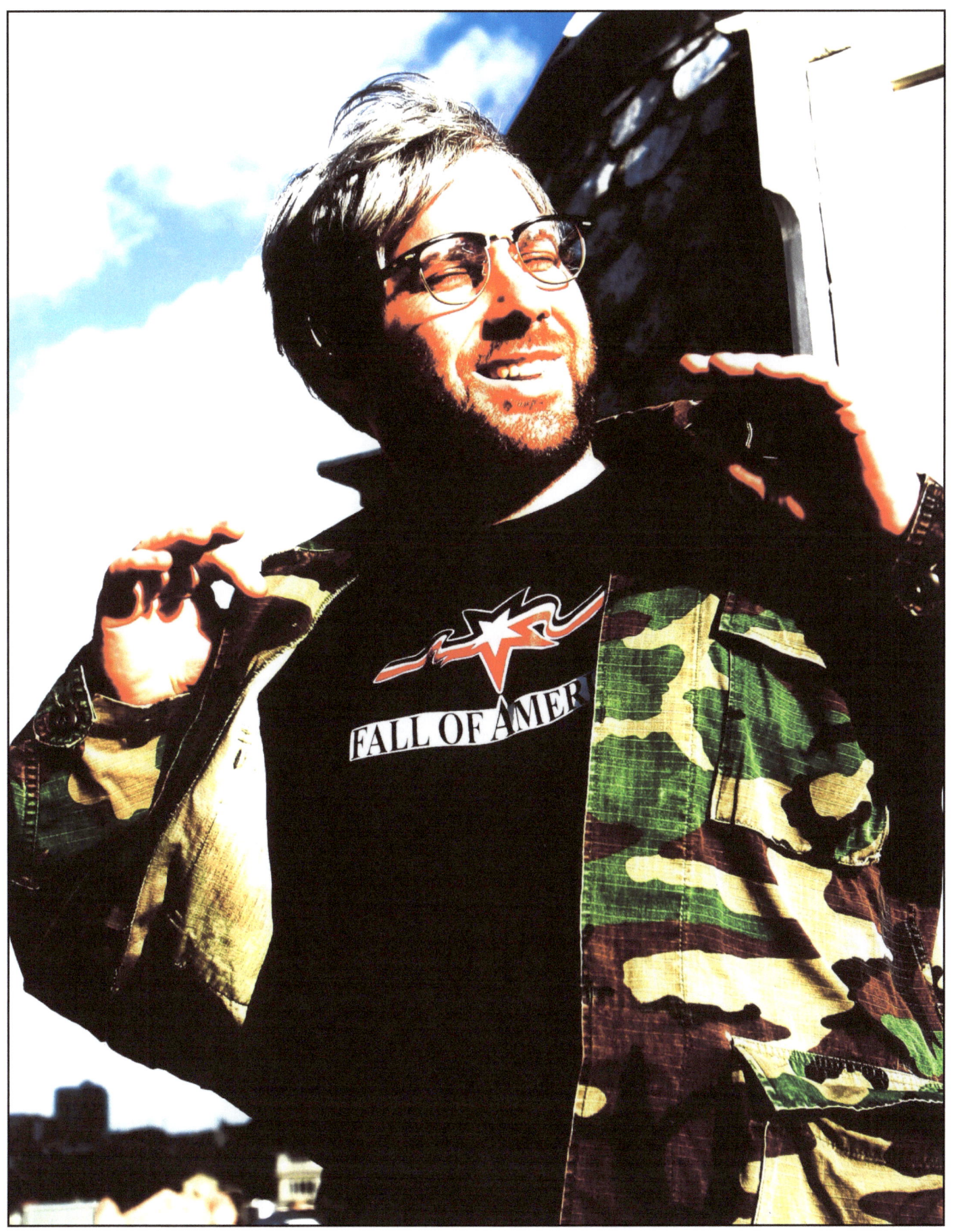

Scoob Lover

One of Big Daddy Kane's
dancers, this was the cover
shot for Scoob's single,
"Champagne on the Block".

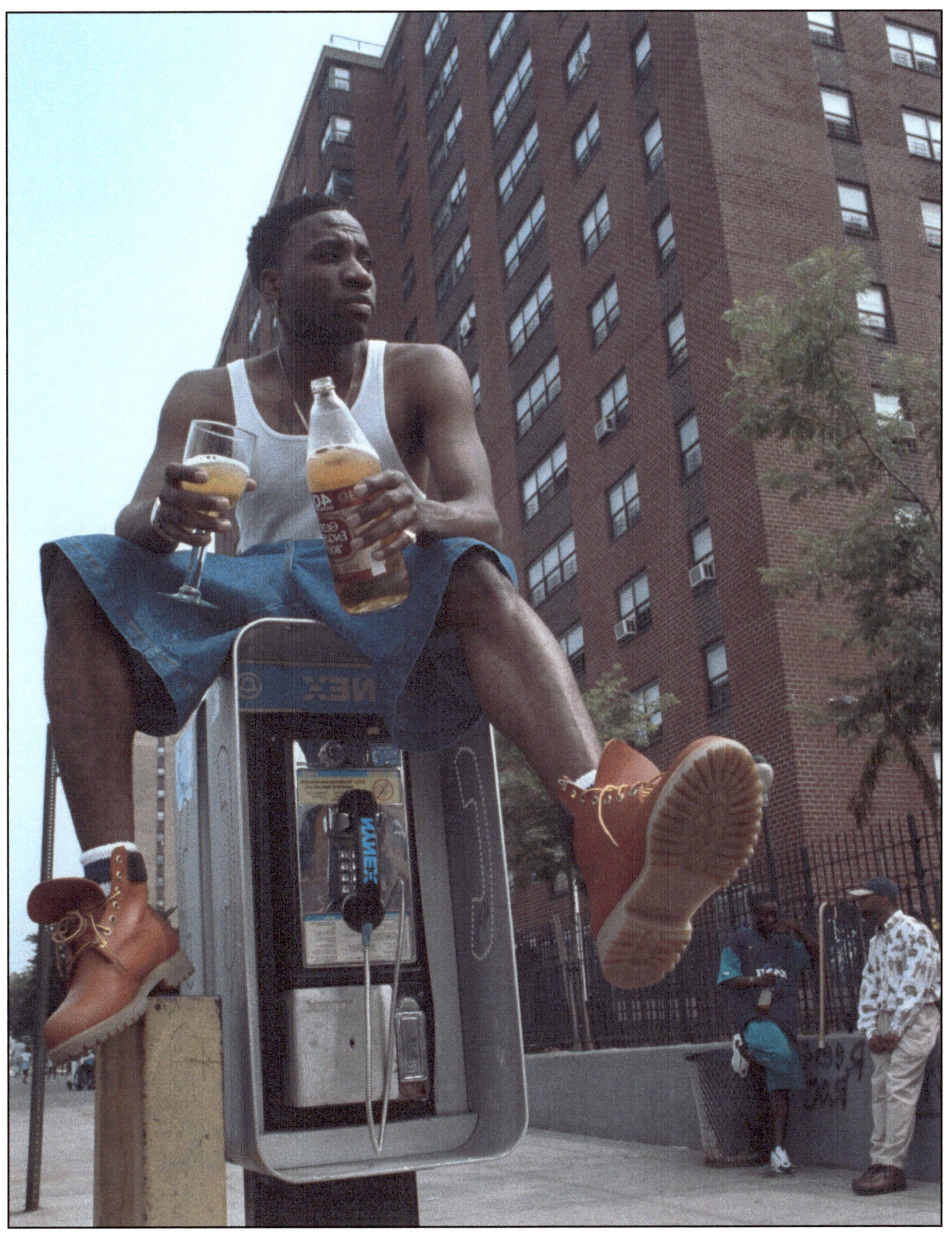

S Diddy or SD

A Cologne rap artist
I shot for Juice.
No further information
is available at this time.

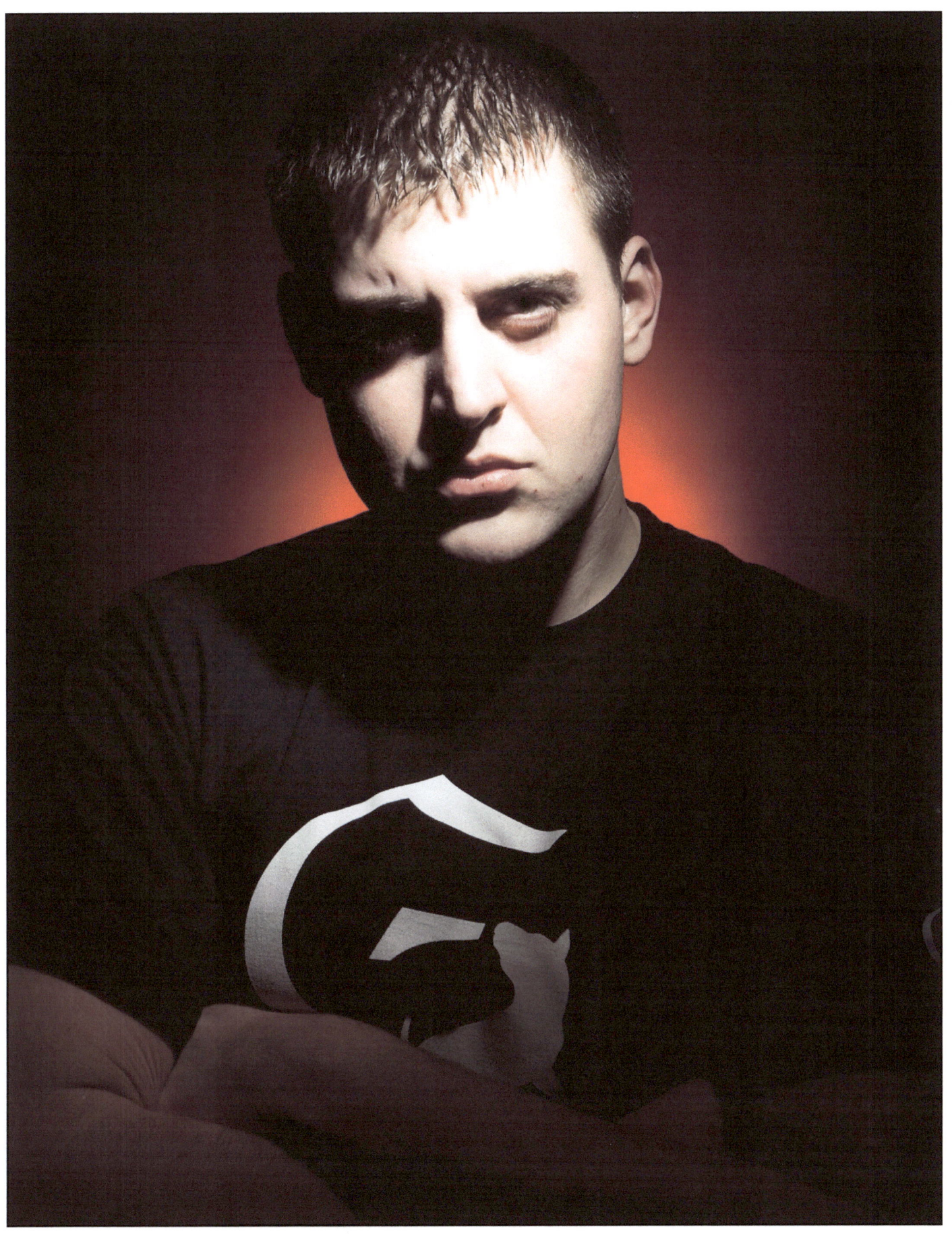

MC Shan

This was a shot for
Shan's first single
"Jane, Stop that Crazy Thing".
A pregnant woman
smoking a crackpipe.
This was shot in the
stairwell outside
Marley Marl's Queensbridge
apartment/recording studio.

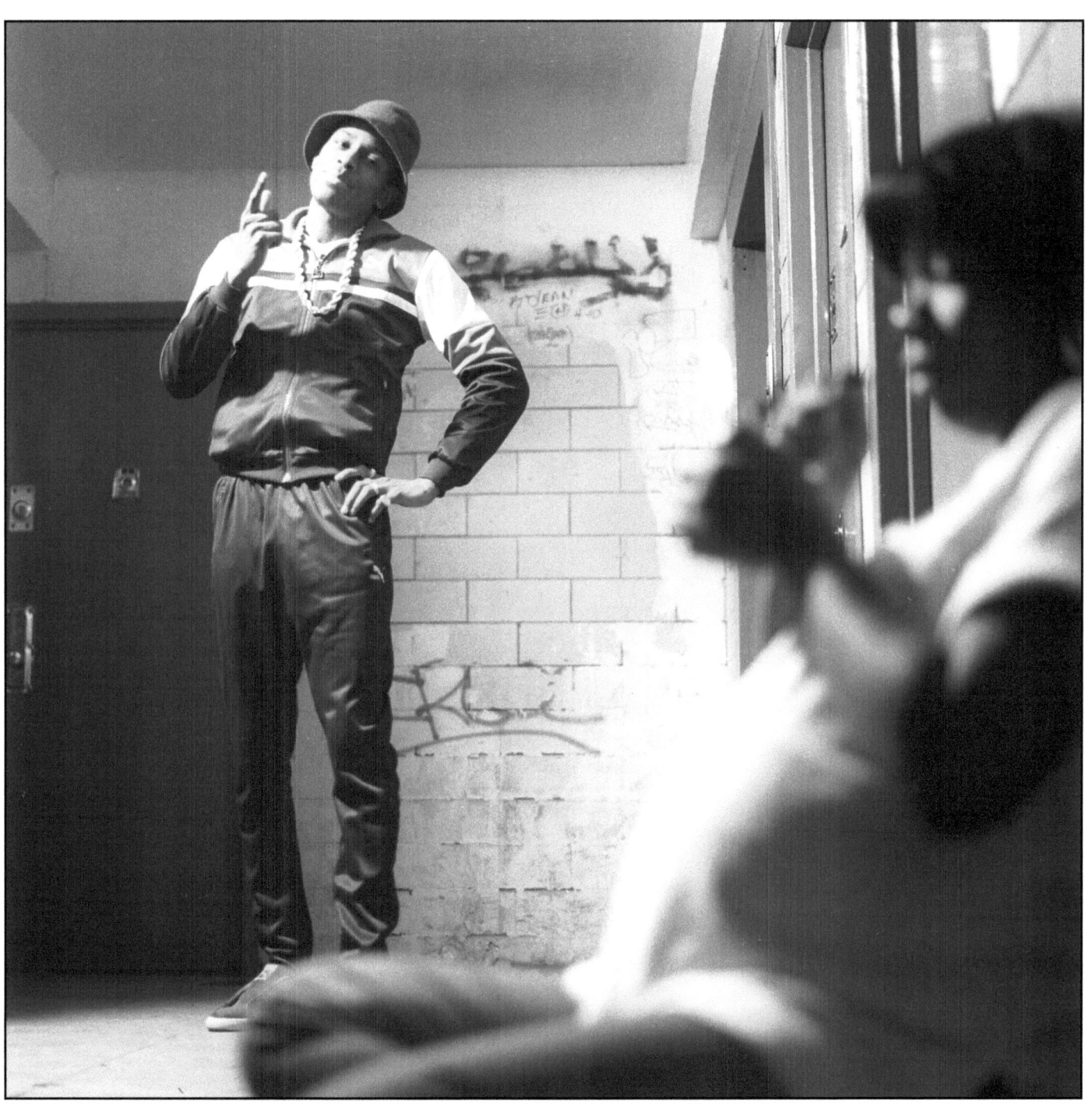

Shelly Thunder

She wanted to be the first
woman in the world. Since she
had a "new" leather outfit, she
had to have a new spear.
So I made her one...

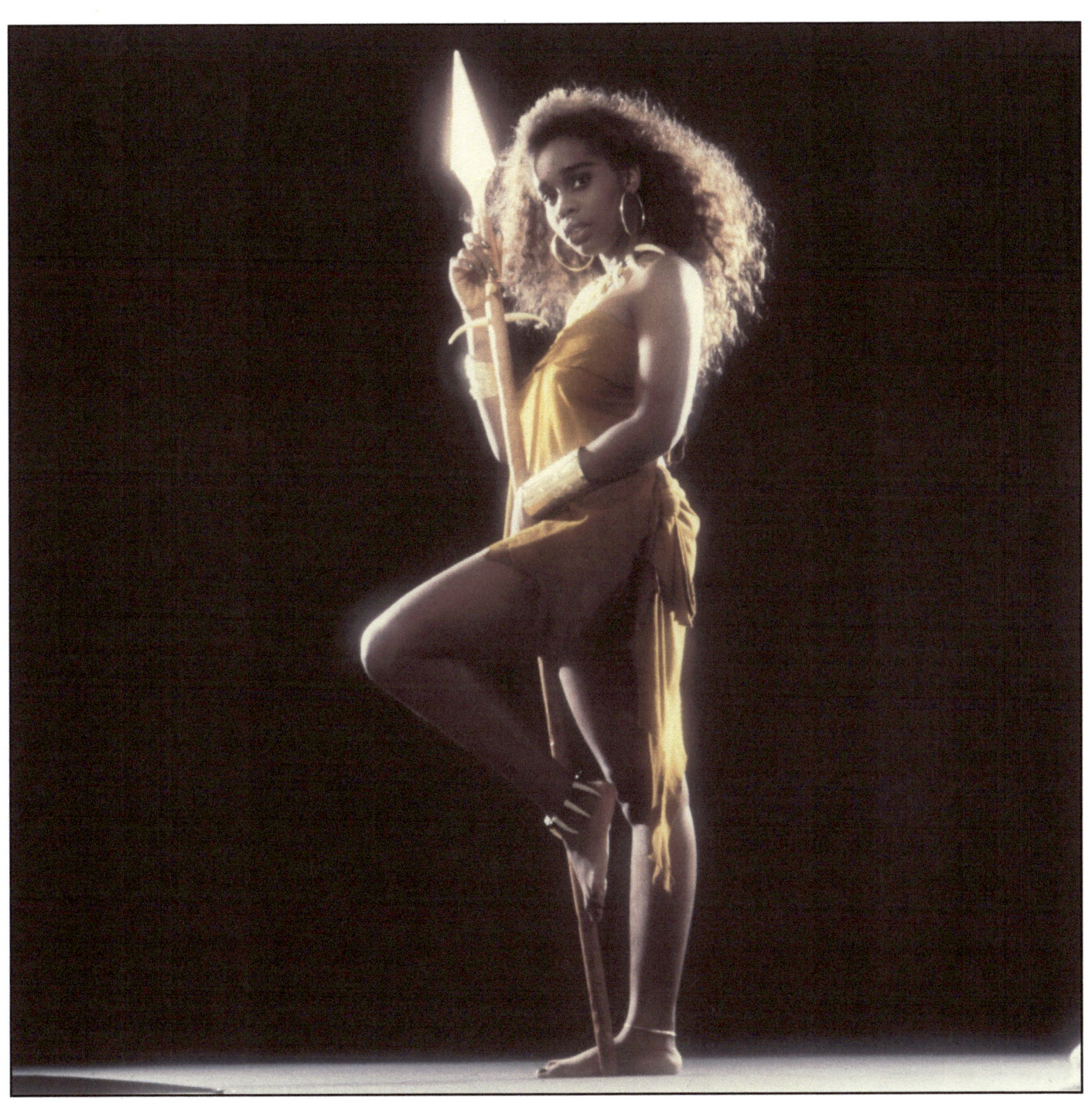

Sido

A German Hip-Hop artist
I shot in concert for Juice.
The deal was when he took off
his mask I had to stop shooting.
Well, he did and I did, but all
the other photographers
kept shooting.
I decided that Sido looked
better with his mask on.

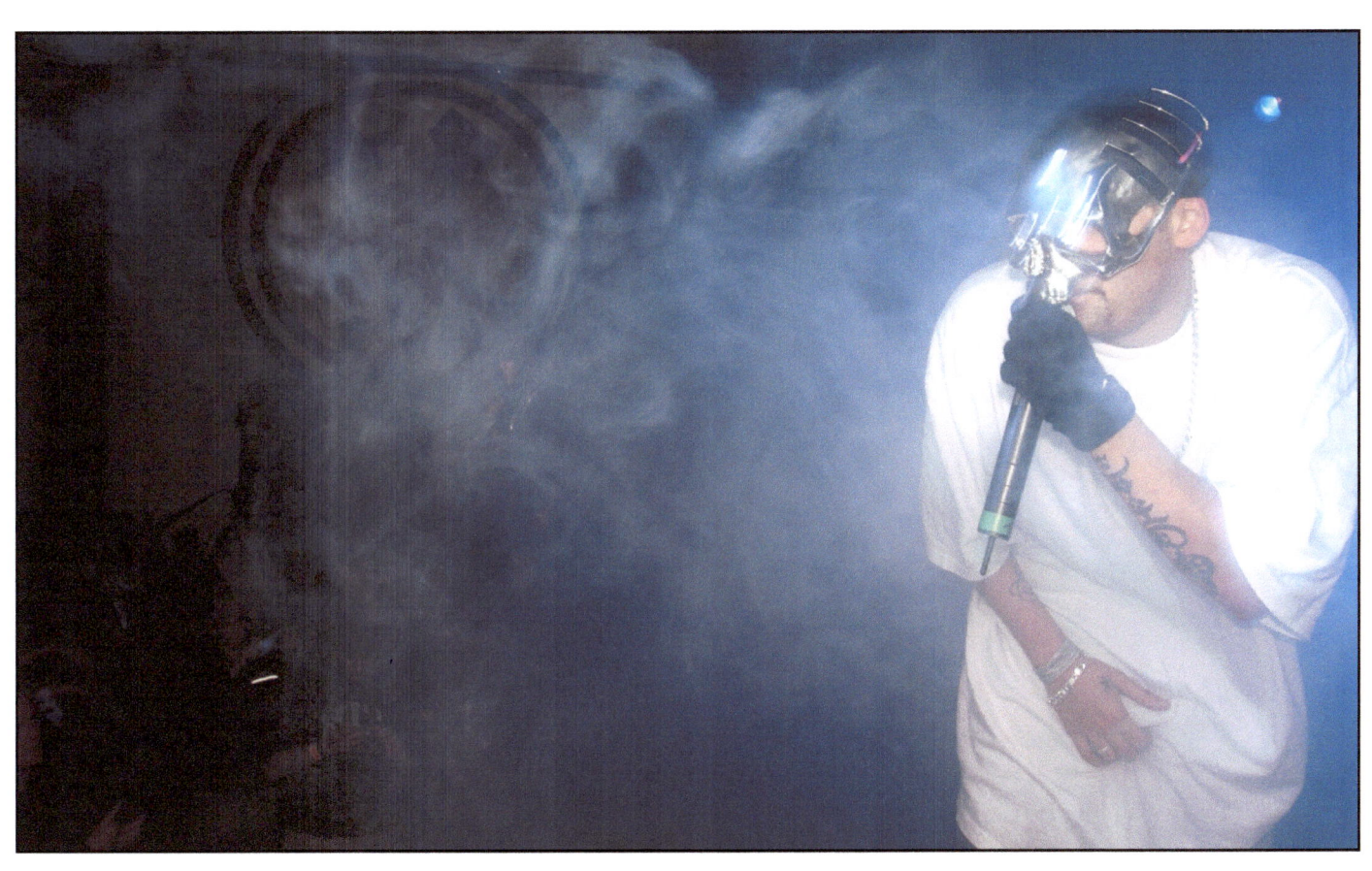

XCLAN

Featuring Lumumba Carson,
Brother J and Suger Shaft,
don't recall the names of the
other gentlemen in this photo.
XCLAN and The Blackwatch
Movement are still running,
but their output has fallen off.

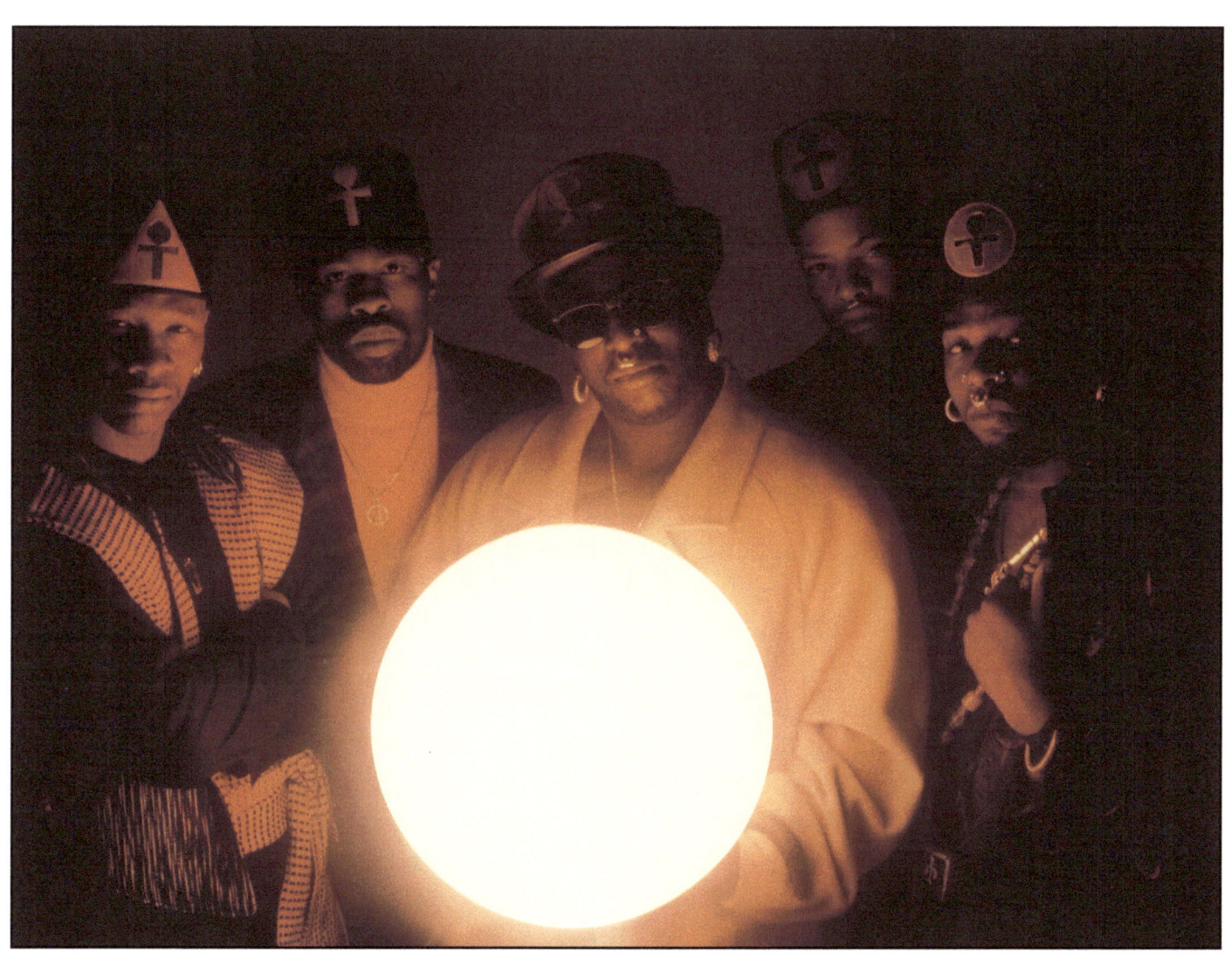

When I started to design this monograph, I pondered what photos to show in what order. I decided to show only one image from each band or artist. The title of the book, "My Best Shot" was obvious and in most cases the selection was easy, but in others, I used different criteria. The RunDMC shot here has never been printed and I think the silhouettes of the three gentlemen is as powerful as any other shot I made of them.

I never searched for a unique style to call my own. Rather, I got my inspiration from communicating with the artists, listening to their music and their ideas. I would often execute their idea, modify it to the agreement of both of us or make it possible to pull off. Half the time, I would just offer concepts and when one concept was rejected, another would come to mind and eventually, both parties were in agreement.

I never lost sight of the fact that I was working for the artist, he had to like his cover. He had to live with it for the rest of his life. If I wasn't particularly overjoyed about the direction of the shoot, I didn't have to put it in my portfolio.

The thought of organizing the book with a specific running order also boggled my mind, so I simply chose the photos in the alphabetical order that they appear in my archives. Most of the images are my favorite shots of the particular artist. In some cases, where I had too large a selection to choose from, I went with an image that I like a lot, but has never seen the light of day.

As an art director I am supposed to have the idea, as a photographer I am supposed to execute the idea and as the graphic designer, I am supposed to put the photo together with type. When the cover photo was selected and approved by the artist, I would take the predominate color from the photo and make the type relate to that color. My goal was always to give the photo full appreciation at the same time the graphics are giving information.

Back in the daze of vinyl, people would enter a record shop and there would be dozens of albums displayed. The covers with the

most interesting images and the most colorful type would be the first ones noticed. The other albums in the shop would be stored in bins where one would go to the section of the artist that one was interested in and then flip the albums forward.
All one would see was the artist name in the top of the cover, in fact Warner Bros. Records had a rule for 12" LPs and singles that the artist's name HAD to be in the top 1/3 of the front cover.

So I would try to produce photos and covers that would POP. From my own record buying experience, if the cover looked interesting, I would pick it up, turn it over for more information and since I was holding it, the chances that I was going to buy it were greatly increased.

In this book, I simply tried to make the photos as big as possible on the right-hand pages with a caption on the left-hand page. I chose the simplest type font, American Typewriter, simple and easy to read. Nothing fancy and nothing to detract from the photos. I have been a contributing photographer to many photo books and sometimes the designer gets a little...a lot...too much...heavy handed. I was in one book of Hip-Hop photography where the text pages were chock-a-block with tiny text and then...the designer over-layed the same text in different colors. I guess he didn't want anyone to read the text. Personally, I found that over-design immensely annoying and detracting from the photography. Which what the book was supposed to be about.

I was interviewed once and the author was describing design philosophies. One famous British designer, said he NEVER listened to the artist's music.
He just designed for himself?
That does no justice to the artist who is paying his wages.

A couple of tips to young photographers:

First, keep your day job. Since the release of the British movie "Blow Up" the world has been flooded with photographers. The situation has gotten worse with the advent of digital cameras and smart phones. Today, a chimpanzee will take a great photo given enough time and a good subject.

Try to shoot bands live, show them your shots and try to get them to pose for you, anywhere, backstage, any interesting location outdoors, in a studio if you have access to one.
Try to make the background have some relationship to the style of music of the artist.

Unless the artist is your best friend, try to work quickly and don't let the technical side of the production slow you down. Most musicians have a low tolerance for photoshoots, so the quicker the better. My cover for the Ramones "Halfway to Sanity" was shot in 15 minutes and the band drove away.

Shoot on the beat. Most musicians do interesting things on the beat. That's where the action is. If you are shooting digitally, get your exposure close to what you want and then shoot. Don't look at every image after you press the shutter, you are going to miss a lot of great moments that way and you can always adjust the levels and contrast in post-production. In fact, I always try to keep my digital images a bit on the dark side as I can always brighten the photos, but if the photo is too bright, one can't add details back into the over-exposed highlights.

If you shoot in a studio and use a colored background paper, it is great to light the paper separately and use gels on the background lights that are the same color. This will make the background color really pop.

When I was shooting analog all the time, I used high speed films that were grainy in structure. I like this effect and it isn't possible with digital photography. Push up the ISO on a digital camera and all you get is noise. When shooting older musicians, grainy film structure will often hide their facial wrinkles, making them look younger.

I would like to thank:

Lane Pederson - for taking a great
interest in my training and subse-
quent career. Many of my shots
were made in his studio. He is
a very generous man.

Eric Boman - who taught me how
important composition is and how
clients will always return for
a great lunch.

Johnny Ramone - for coming back
year after year. He hated photo
shoots and I made them as fast
and painless as possible.

Glenn O'Brien - RIP - for his support
throughout my career. Often lead-
ing me a bit astray, but his inten-
tions were always good. He also
wrote forewords and commen-
taries for several of my books.
I miss you, Glenn.

Gerd Saller - for his constant
patience, his eagle-eye for my
mistakes and toleration of my
old habits. My books wouldn't
look half as good without his help.

Notes:

214

www.ingramcontent.com/pod-product-compliance
Lightning Source LLC
Chambersburg PA
CBHW050711180526
45159CB00003B/1002